Journal of the Alamire Foundation
■

Journal of the Alamire Foundation

∎

Volume 5 - Number 2, Autumn 2013

∎

General editors:
David Burn
Katelijne Schiltz

Journal of the Alamire Foundation

Volume 5 - Number 2, Autumn 2013

BREPOLS

The *Journal of the Alamire Foundation* is published twice a year (spring and autumn)

- **General editors:**
  David Burn
  Katelijne Schiltz
- **Editorial board:**
  Barbara Haggh
  Christian Thomas Leitmeir
  Pedro Memelsdorff
  Klaus Pietschmann
  Dorit Tanay
  Giovanni Zanovello
- **Advisory board:**
  Bonnie J. Blackburn
  M. Jennifer Bloxam
  Anna Maria Busse-Berger
  Fabrice Fitch
  Sean Gallagher
  David Hiley
  Andrew Kirkman
  Karl Kügle
  John Milsom
  Emilio Ros-Fabregas
  Rudolf Rasch
  Thomas Schmidt-Beste
  Eugeen Schreurs
  Reinhard Strohm
  Philippe Vendrix
  Rob Wegman

- **Coordinator:**
  Stratton Bull
- **Music examples:**
  Vincent Besson
- **Music font:**
  Theodor Dumitrescu (CMME)

- **Subscriptions:**
  Brepols Publishers
  Begijnhof 67
  B-2300 Turnhout (Belgium)
  Tel.: +32 14448020
  Fax: +32 14428919
  periodicals@brepols.net

- **Submissions:**
  Journal of the Alamire Foundation
  c/o Prof. Dr. David Burn
  KU Leuven – Onderzoekseenheid Musicologie
  Mgr. Ladeuzeplein 21, bus 5591
  B-3000 Leuven (Belgium)
  jaf@alamirefoundation.be

  Submissions to the Journal can be sent at any time to the address listed above. For further information, including the Journal's style-sheet, see: http://www.alamirefoundation.org/en/publications/journal-alamire-foundation.

The Alamire Foundation was founded in 1991 as a collaborative venture between the Musicology Research Unit of the University of Leuven and Musica, Impulse Centre for Music. The organization is named after Petrus Alamire, one of the most important sixteenth-century music calligraphers. The Foundation aims to create an international platform for promoting research on music in or connected to the Low Countries from the earliest documents to the end of the Ancien Regime. The Foundation hopes especially to promote dialogue between the worlds of scholarship and performance. For more information, see: http://www.alamirefoundation.org/.

© 2013 Brepols Publishers NV

All rights reserved. No part of this publication may be reproduced, stored in a retrieval system or transmitted, in any form or by any means, electronic, mechanical, photocopying, recording, or otherwise, without the prior permission of the publisher.

ISBN: 978-2-503-54680-3
ISSN: 2032-5371
D/2013/0095/225

Table of Contents

Theme
Medieval Chant Traditions in the Low Countries and Surrounding Regions
Guest Editor: Pieter Mannaerts

Introduction	*Pieter Mannaerts*	141
The Evolution of Neumes into Square Notation in Chant Manuscripts	*Kate Helsen*	143
The Rhenish Heritage of the Preetz Antiphoner	*Alison Altstatt*	175
The Relationship between the Festal Office and the New Sequence: Evidence from Medieval Picardy	*Lori Kruckenberg*	201

Free Papers

Das „Gaudeamus omnes"-Zitat in Lassos Motette *Nunc gaudere licet* und sein Kontext – Aspekte der geistlichen Parodie bei Orlando di Lasso	*Bernhold Schmid*	237

Research and Performance Practice Forum

Re-constructing Jesuit Theatre for the Modern Stage: *Daphnis, Pastorale*, an Eighteenth-Century Jesuit College Music-Drama	*Elizabeth Dyer*	263

Contributors to this Issue   299

Theme

■

Medieval Chant Traditions in the Low Countries and Surrounding Regions

Guest Editor: Pieter Mannaerts

Introduction

Pieter Mannaerts

Given their position at the crossroads of cultural and sociopolitical influences in Europe, the importance of the Low Countries in medieval society is undisputed. The region's many abbeys, convents, collegiate churches, beguinages, and many other religious communities contributed to medieval culture in many ways. However, one of the least studied aspects of this contribution is the production of chant manuscripts and the composition and transmission of chant.

The papers presented in this chant theme section relate directly or indirectly to the Low Countries. They focus principally on notation and chant composition from the ninth to the fifteenth centuries. At the same time, they show that approaching the chant repertory of the Low Countries via neighbouring regions (the Rhineland, northern France) contributes valuably to an integrated view on chant as a European (post-) medieval musical phenomenon. Furthermore, they demonstrate the need for sound methodologies for the analysis of chant and its dissemination, and for a clearer and finer differentiaton between 'early' and 'later' chant.

In 'The Rhenish Heritage of the Preetz Antiphoner: Origins and Reform', Alison Altstatt connects the idiosyncratic notation of the fifteenth-century Preetz Antiphoner (from the diocese of Lübeck), as well as the office of St. Blaise that the antiphoner contains, with an origin in the Rhineland. Altstatt's close reading of texts and music reveals that the St. Blaise *historia* can be dated to between c. 850-1050. In addition, Altstatt discusses the problem of 'transitional' notations, in both chronological and geographical terms.

Lori Kruckenberg's article, 'The Relationship Between the Festal Office and the New Sequence: Evidence from Medieval Picardy', examines sequences from c. 1100 with contexts and transmission histories that point to an origin in the area of modern-day northeast France and southwest Belgium. The sequence *Celeste organum* is given an in-depth study. Of particular importance in Kruckenberg's contribution is her demonstration that mass and office chant cannot always be studied separately, because sequences possessed an unexpected degree of 'mobility' between the two.

Kate Helsen's 'The Evolution of Neumes into Square Notation in Chant Manuscripts' relates to a topic that has received renewed interest in chant scholarship in recent years.[1] Her comparison of neumes from a large sample of datable manuscripts reveals the important role played by northern France in the development of square notation. Helsen concludes that the transition from neumes to square notes begins in this region at the beginning of the twelfth century then spreads elsewhere, with the transition being completed in all areas studied by the end of the thirteenth.

Altstatt's and Kruckenberg's papers were first presented at the conference *Music for the Office and Its Sources in the Low Countries, 1050-1550*, at the Elzenveld Centre in Antwerp, 21-23 August 2010.

---

[1] See Michel Huglo, 'The Earliest Developments in Square Notation: Twelfth-Century Aquitaine', and Olivier Cullin, 'Notation in Carthusian Liturgical Books: Preliminary Remarks', in *The Calligraphy of Medieval Music*, ed. John Haines, Musica Medii Aevi 1 (Turnhout, 2011), 163-71 and 175-94.

The conference was dedicated to the memory of Ike de Loos (Universiteit Utrecht), one of the pioneering scholars in the field. Ike had accepted the invitation to be a member of the programme committee, but died prematurely at the age of fifty-five, before the conference itself took place. In recent decades, she had contributed enormously to the study of chant of the Low Countries. She published articles on responsories, *historiae*, and notation, and facilitated access to local chant sources by providing hundreds of manuscript references on her website.[2] In addition to her work on chant in the Low Countries, De Loos also contributed to the study and edition of the Middle Dutch song repertory, including the so-called Gruuthuse Manuscript.[3]

The conference was made possible by funding from the Research Foundation - Flanders. The conference received organizational support from the Alamire Foundation and the University of Leuven, and was hosted by AMUZ and the Flanders Festival Antwerp. It was further supported by the International Musicological Society Study Group 'Cantus Planus'; indeed, the conference was the first 'external' conference supported by Cantus Planus. The help of the former chairs of the Study Group, Barbara Haggh (University of Maryland) and Roman Hankeln (University of Trondheim), is gratefully acknowledged.

---

[2] A recent anthology of her work is Ike de Loos, *Patronen ontrafeld. Studies over gregoriaanse gezangen en Middelnederlandse liederen*, Middeleeuwse studies en bronnen 139, ed. José van Aelst, Karl Kügle, Dieuwke van der Poel, and Els Rose (Hilversum, 2012).

[3] Herman Brinkman and Ike de Loos (eds.), *Het Gruuthuse-handschrift. Hs. Den Haag, Koninklijke Bibliotheek, 79 K 10*, Middeleeuwse Verzamelhandschriften uit de Nederlanden 4 (Hilversum 2013).

The Evolution of Neumes into Square Notation in Chant Manuscripts

Kate Helsen

One of the defining characteristics of chant in the Middle Ages is its notation. From the ninth century onward, neumes were written above chant texts as memory aids for singers already familiar with the melodies to be sung. Throughout the eleventh and twelfth centuries, notation continued to evolve at different rates and in different ways across European chant centres, culminating ultimately in various kinds of square notation on a musical staff in the early thirteenth century.[1] The major distinction between early neumes and square notation is that the latter contains sufficient musical information for a performance by a singer who had not previously memorized the melody. Musicologists studying early medieval neumes and later medieval square notation face a conceptual dichotomy: musical notation as a memory aid, and musical notation as instructions for performing a previously-unknown melody. The fascinating interplay between notation's function and what it represents continues to be a focal point in the study of all music. The focus of the present study is the transition period between early neume forms and notations made of individual note-heads placed on a staff, usually called 'square' notation.

As is well known, the earliest staffless neumes, found in manuscripts from as early as the ninth century, were not intended to be read and performed at sight, since these glyphs do not represent absolute pitches or musical intervals but rather melodic gestures. Prior to the twelfth century, various neume traditions had appeared, defined mostly by geographical region. These traditions distributed pitches more accurately along a vertical axis which, in some cases, was made visible through the introduction of the musical staff. As singers came to depend on these accurate graphic representations of melody to help them reconstruct chants, they did not have to rely on their memories alone to ensure a good performance, although the relationship of memory to performance continued to be an important and complex one even after musical literacy had become a standard requirement for trained singers.[2] Over the course of the Middle Ages, notation continued to change in order to more accurately reflect pitch and rhythm, while increasingly abandoning the rhetorical and gestural elements of early neumes.

Traditionally, the study of medieval chant notations has focused on either the early, staffless neumes found in manuscripts from the ninth century onward or that of the square notation found throughout most of Europe by the end of the thirteenth

---

[1] Not all areas of Europe adopted square notation at the same time or at the same rate, and in some regions it was never fully standardized, such as in central and eastern Europe, where Gothic notation held sway. This is discussed in greater detail below.
[2] For a more complete discussion of memory's role, primarily in the memorization of organum and Notre Dame polyphony, see Anna Maria Busse Berger, *Medieval Music and the Art of Memory* (Berkeley, 2005). A set of thorough studies on the interaction between memory and the earliest notation is found in Leo Treitler, *With Voice and Pen* (Oxford, 2003). Other relevant studies include Kenneth Levy, 'On Gregorian Orality', in *Journal of the American Musicological Society* 43 (1990), 185-227; 'Essay 1' in Theodore Karp, *Aspects of Orality and Formularity in Gregorian Chant* (Evanston, IL., 1998); Mary Carruthers, *The Book of Memory: A Study of Memory in Medieval Culture* (Cambridge, 1990).

century.[3] Some early neume types, such as St. Gall notation or northern, 'Messine', French neumes have been extensively studied for over a century. Square notation, however, has not had the same long history of scholarly attention. John Haines has suggested that 'the development of early square musical script has yet to be described in even the most basic graphic terms', due to a 'prejudice against late medieval music calligraphy.'[4] Indeed, the explorations to date of square notation have been limited mostly to critical editions of thirteenth-century music treatises,[5] a situation that may be compared with the large number of excellent studies of earlier neume notation by the Solesmes scholars as well as Peter Wagner, Oskar Fleischer, Michel Huglo, Solange Corbin, Wulf Arlt, Kenneth Levy, David Hiley, and others.[6] More recently, investigations into late medieval saints' offices and related research projects have brought square notation research to the fore once again.[7] Yet the thirteenth-century transition between these two forms of notation has remained relatively unstudied. The purpose of the present study is to focus on this transition period. In addition, some reasons for such a fundamental and consequential change will be suggested.

The Manuscripts

The first stage of research began with collecting data about musical manuscripts themselves.[8] I focused only on those manuscripts that were listed with a precise date, or at the most, were given a very narrow chronological window, in manuscript catalogues. Since it is difficult to determine precise dating in most cases, my resulting database contains only approximately 300 manuscripts datable to within a quarter of a century, beginning in the ninth century and ending in the first half of the sixteenth century.[9] This number includes any entry in any printed or online catalogue that lists musical manuscripts, and it was not necessary for such a catalogue to include an image of the

---

[3] By the thirteenth century, mensural notation was also developing. This was applied predominantly to polyphonic music, a subject that transcends the scope of this study.
[4] John Haines, 'From Point to Square: Graphic Change in Medieval Music Script', in *Textual Cultures* 3 (2008), 35.
[5] *Johannes de Garlandia: De mensurabili musica. Kritische Edition mit Kommentar und Interpretation der Notationslehre*, ed. Erich Reimer, 2 vols., Beihefte zum Archiv für Musikwissenschaft 10-11 (Wiesbaden, 1972); Martin Gerbert (ed.), *Scriptores ecclesiastici de musica sacra potissimum*, 3 vols. (St. Blaise, 1784; repr. Hildesheim, 1963); Hans Müller, *Eine Abhandlung über Mensuralmusik in der Karlsruher Handschrift* (Leipzig, 1886); *Franconis de Colonia: Ars cantus mensurabilis*, ed. Gilbert Reaney and André Gilles, Corpus scriptorum de musica 18 (Rome, 1974), 23-82; *Der Musiktraktat des Anonymus 4*, ed. Fritz Reckow, 2 vols., Beihefte zum Archiv für Musikwissenschaft 4-5 (Wiesbaden, 1967).
[6] André Mocquereau, 'Neumes-accents liquescents ou sémi-vocaux', in *Paléographie Musicale* 2 (1891); Eugène Cardine, 'Neumes et rythme. Les coupures neumatiques', in *Études grégoriennes* 3 (1960), 145-54; Eugène Cardine, 'Preuves paléographiques du principe des "coupures" dans les neumes', in *Études grégoriennes* 4 (1961), 43-54; Eugène Cardine, 'Sémiologie grégorienne', in *Études grégoriennes* 11 (1970); Peter Wagner, *Einführung in die gregorianischen Melodien*, vol. 3: *Neumenkunde. Paläographie des liturgischen Gesangs* (Leipzig, 1912); Oskar Fleischer, *Die germanischen Neumen als Schlüssel zum altchristlichen und gregorianischen Gesang* (Frankfurt am Main, 1923); Michel Huglo, 'Les Noms des neumes et leur origine', in *Études grégoriennes* 1 (1954), 53-67; Solange Corbin, *Die Neumen, Palaeographie der Musik* 1/3 (Cologne, 1977); Wulf Arlt, 'Anschaulichkeit und analytischer Charakter. Kriterien der Beschreibung und Analyse früher Neumenschriften' in *Musicologie médiévale: Notations et séquences, Table ronde du CNRS à l'IRHT d'Orléans-La Source, 10-12 Septembre 1982*, ed. Michel Huglo (Paris and Geneva, 1987), 29-55; Kenneth Levy, 'On the Origin of Neumes', in *Early Music History* 7 (1987), 59-90; David Hiley, *Western Plainchant: A Handbook* (Oxford, 1993).
[7] One such project is the University of Toronto's *Nota Quadrata* project, <http://www.notaquadrata.ca>.
[8] See Appendix and the list of manuscripts therein.
[9] This database is available online at: <https://sites.google.com/site/katehelsen/academics/research-projects>.

source (either facsimile or digital) in order for me to include it in the database.[10] The reader interested primarily in my sources for this database is referred to the Appendix where these catalogues are discussed in more detail.

One third of the some 300 manuscripts with precise dates included images, either in facsimile or digital reproduction online. Those sources with notation were then arranged chronologically and geographically, so that specific notations could be contextualized over the centuries. This takes a broad approach not usually favoured among semiologists and musicologists who have tended to specialize in a single area of scribal tradition. Many of the transitional and late notational forms (particularly the German and central European notations of the thirteenth century) are especially enigmatic and have typically been considered under the broad category 'German Gothic' or 'eastern European'. By comparing datable sources in the timeframe in which neumes were evolving into square notation, the broad, overall impression is that the most important factor in the change is actually *continuity*: it is possible to isolate the defining features of a given neume and observe how they determine the appearance of the particular type of square note toward which it evolves. For this study, three different geographical regions, shown in Figure 1 with the numbers 1, 2, and 3 on the map of Western Europe, provide the sources from which a graphic model of notational transformation from 900 to 1500 has been developed.

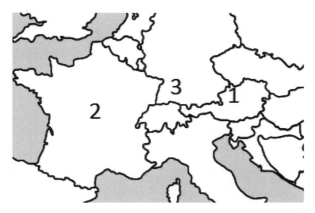

Figure 1. Notational regions of Western Europe in this study

A Case-Study of Three Neume Shapes

The full set of neume signs is large. For example, the Solesmes studies of St. Gall notation contain a chart displaying twenty-five of the core notational forms. Modifications to these forms for liquescents, accentual, or rhythmic stress make this number closer to one hundred. In addition, there are many graphically distinct forms of early neumes

---

[10] While this number may seem low to those who work with manuscript catalogues frequently, it was my strict requirement that only manuscripts which were given a secure date be included in this study. Of course, many fine and well-known catalogues, such as those in *Paléographie Musicale* and the Michel Huglo's 1999 publication of the two-volume Processional series in RISM contain useful information about manuscripts which are, in most cases, not possible to date any more precisely than to half a century.

which are usually given a name which reflects where they are supposed to have originated, such as Aquitanian or Beneventan. Despite these differences, however, some of the same neume signs with the same basic shapes are found consistently across Europe beginning in the ninth century, making it possible for scholars to create comparative neume tables like those found in any chant textbook.

Most neume charts contain approximately fifteen different basic signs that can be combined to represent longer melismatic passages or modified by stress accents.[11] In his article 'From Point to Square: Graphic Change in Medieval Music Script', Haines narrows his field of examination to three signs: the *punctum*, the *pes*, and the *climacus*.[12] He chooses the *punctum* for its 'primacy in the notational gamut', the *pes* for its simplicity and ubiquity in representing two pitches with one continuous line, and the *climacus* for its inclusion of rhomboid shapes in its square notation form. He then traces the evolution of these three signs throughout the twelfth and thirteenth centuries, using mainly French sources. Using this as a model for further exploration, the present study focuses on three more neume signs: the *virga*, the *clivis*, and the liquescent neume (in any form presented in the images available to me.) For each of these neume forms, I created three parallel charts comparing notations from geographical regions and across time, beginning at 900 (see 'Comparison' section, below.) Of course, one must be aware that by limiting this study to only three neumes, it cannot claim to give a full account of the development of early notation into square notation, especially when considering the more complex neume shapes. But by adding three more neumes to Haines' initial exploration, the graphic repertory of neume signs exposed to this sort of scrutiny has doubled, and it is hoped that these studies may serve as examples for subsequent research.[13]

The *virga*, shown in three of its most typical forms in Figure 2, has typically been considered one of the 'two basic neumes', as Treitler explains in his article 'The Early History of Music Writing in the West'.[14]

Figure 2. The three most typical forms of the early *virga*

The *virga* has been traditionally considered an 'accent neume', defined by Parrish as a neume 'characterized by the predominant use of...strokes representing [a] note.'[15] The *virga* probably signifies a 'high pitch' in the earliest notations in accordance with its role in rhetorical accentuation.[16] The *virga* is also found in combination with other

---

[11] For a representative standard neume chart, see Hiley, *Western Plainchant*, 342-43.
[12] Haines, 'From Point to Square', 30.
[13] It has also been possible to increase significantly the number of securely datable medieval musical manuscripts from Haines' pool of sources included on the *Nota Quadrata* website.
[14] Leo Treitler, 'The Early History of Music Writing in the West', in *Journal of the American Musicological Society* 35 (1982), 237-79 at 249.
[15] Carl Parrish, *The Notation of Medieval Music*. (New York, 1959), 10. This theory first appears in Edmond de Coussemaker's *Histoire de l'harmonie au moyen age* (Paris, 1852), ch. II, 'Origine des neumes'. The *punctum* is the other 'basic accent neume'.
[16] Cardine, 'Sémiologie grégorienne', 6.

neumes where it symbolizes the top note of an ascending group of pitches, or, as shown in Figure 3, the top pitch of a group of descending pitches known as the *climacus*.

Figure 3. A *virga* with two descending *'puncta'*

Virgae are often slightly slanted to the right, reflecting the same skewed arrangement of neumes representing ascending pitches. Even unheightened neumes reflect this direction, giving the overall appearance of the neumes a 'directionality' in two-dimensional space.[17] In the comparison table for *virgae* that follows (Table 1), one can observe that the *virga*'s horizontal tip becomes more pronounced and that the vertical (sometimes slanted) shaft of the *virga* becomes progressively thinner. The result of this evolution is that the *virga* shape resembles a note-head on a stem, representing a single pitch.

The *clivis* represents two pitches in a single sign, the second pitch lower than the first. The three main forms are shown in Figure 4.

Figure 4. The three most typical forms of the early *clivis*

Once again, directionality is a major factor in the interpretation of this neume. It represents two discrete pitches by way of one continuous, curved line: the first higher, after the line has reached its apex, and the second lower, after the descent on the right side, as indicated by the small circles in Figure 5.

Figure 5. Symbolized pitches, as relative heights, circled on the *clivis*

Reading the neume from left to right, the early *clivis* is a clear indication that directionality is present even in unheightened notation. The evolution of the *clivis*, as shown in Table 2, renders the top and right-bottom of the sign thicker and the connecting line between the two, thinner, revealing the two-note ligature of descent we recognize in square notation.

The third and final graphic feature of notation considered here is liquescence. This is not a separate neume, but rather a *modification* of a neume to indicate something

---

[17] Treitler, 'The Early History', 250.

about the vocal articulation of the text. Liquescence is usually found in connection with sonant consonants, but may also be found at diphthongs or surd consonant combinations. Solesmes scholars have asserted that liquescent neumes facilitate the phonetic aspects of the chant, but they do acknowledge the ambiguity which has always plagued the interpretation of this sign.[18] It has recently been suggested that the liquescent neumes, at least in the scriptoria of St. Gall, might have had an exegetical meaning as well, in that they are sometimes found over particular words in the chant text relevant to the theme of the feast day.[19]

In general, liquescence is added to a main neume character by adding a 'hook' to the part of the neume where the sonant consonant or diphthong appears. Figure 6 shows some of the standard forms of liquescence as found on a *virga*, a *clivis*, and a *punctum*, from the tenth to the early thirteenth centuries. The hook form is found at the top of the *virga*, or added to the end of the *clivis,* or used to extend the *punctum* into the shape of an exaggerated apostrophe.

Figure 6. Typical liquescent *virga, clivis,* and *punctum*

Figure 6 shows liquescents which have been added to *virgae* and *clives*. In some cases, it was necessary to include in the research pool liquescent versions of other signs as well, in order to get a sense of how liquescence is expressed in any given image of the manuscript.

As the liquescent neume forms evolved into the fourteenth and fifteenth centuries, the graphic norms of square notation caused these neumes to be rendered increasingly like *plicas*. *Plicas* are perhaps better known for their presence in thirteenth-century polyphonic music, denoting a small passing tone between main pitches and influencing rhythm, but the same sign is found in chant written at the same time, representing liquescence. As David Hiley notes, in the thirteenth century, 'notational forms usually referred to as the *plica* (a single note-head with descending or ascending tails on either side, sometimes a single tail ascending to the right) or ligatures with *plica* added (an additional ascending or descending tail is added at the end of the last note-head) are exactly those used to indicate liquescence in contemporary plainchant sources in square notation.'[20] By tracing the development of the liquescent neume into the shape of the *plica* in square notation, a graphic link between the two becomes clear. Figure 7 compares an early thirteenth-century *plica* (from Paris lat. 1112, c. 1225) with one drawn about a hundred years later (Paris lat. 1107, c. 1300).[21]

---

[18] Cardine, 'Sémiologie grégorienne', 133-38.
[19] Dirk van Betteray, *Quomodo cantabimus canticum Domini in terra aliena: Liqueszenzen als Schlüssel zur Textinterpretation* (Hildesheim, 2007).
[20] David Hiley, 'The Plica and Liquescence', in *Gordon Athol Anderson (1929-1981): In Memoriam von seinen Studenten, Freunden und Kollegen*, ed. Luther Dittmer, 2 vols., Musicological Studies 39 (1984), vol. 2, 379-91.
[21] I am grateful to David Hiley for his contribution of these images.

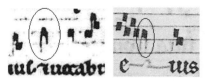

Figure 7. A century of *plica* evolution

Indeed, Hiley has shown that the *plica*'s function in the two- and three-voice conductus of the thirteenth century in Florence is often linked to text enunciation—like liquescence—as well as to passing tones and rhythms, typical of the *plica*. While this study does not include polyphonic sources, the evolution of the liquescent neume through the important centuries of transition illustrate that the *plica* owes at least its *graphic* conception to the liquescent.

The Comparison

Below are three comparative charts, one for each of the graphic subjects: the *virga*, the *clivis*, and the liquescent neume. Table 1 compares the *virga* as written in: Area 1 (the regions of what is now Austria, the Czech lands and some of eastern Germany); Area 2 (northern France); and Area 3 (southern Germany and Switzerland) from the year 900 to the year 1500, as found in manuscripts that could be securely dated to within a quarter-century. Table 2 contains a similar chart, focussing on the *clivis*. Table 3 shows liquescent neumes written in the same three areas. All three of these comparative charts show, at the most, one square centimetre of the source listed. These tables, organized according to geographical areas, represent but one out of many ways of displaying the evolving scribal traditions. Similar tables for particular monastic orders or participants in reforms would also yield interesting results, but these are not within the scope of the present project. Some sections of these charts remain tantalizingly empty, such as the gap between 900 and 1050 for Area 1, or in the first half of the fourteenth century in Area 3. Someday, I hope it will be possible to fill these gaps with notation from manuscripts which can be securely dated to these times for the regions in question. The lack of liquescents in manuscripts from the last half of the fifteenth century reflects the dwindling use of the *plica* as square notation becomes widely standardized. Where very large gaps in the tables threatened to compromise the graphic flow, images from manuscripts dated to within *half* a century have been inserted. There are thirteen such manuscripts involved in the comparison, and they are marked by square brackets.

Graphic transformation as a whole, from early neumes to square notation, has rarely been studied.[22] Haines was well aware of the dearth of studies concerning late-medieval notation in 2004 when he wrote that 'paleographic desiderata for square

---

[22] René Jean Hesbert's study of the musical manuscripts from Jumièges, France, does provide a prototype for research on graphic changes in notation in one geographical area (see René Jean Hesbert, *Les Manuscrits musicaux de Jumièges*, Monumenta Musicae Sacrae 2 [Macon, 1954]). However, out of some forty manuscripts he describes, and for which he includes representative images, only one can be dated securely (this is the Missal of Jumièges, held in the Bibliothèque municipale at Rouen as A. 10 [365] olim K.6, dated to 1497). The rest are listed according to century or, in a handful of cases, half-century. The present study attempts to build on his model by including only those manuscripts that can be dated securely to within thirty years, no matter where they come from.

notation include…a graphic history of its origins and earliest regional dialects.'[23] Preliminary descriptions of late-medieval notation are given in Andrew Hughes' contribution to the *Oxford Handbook of Paleography*.[24] The charts presented here are an attempt to improve our understanding of the overall view of the development of the notation of the virga, the clivis, and the liquescent.

Table 1. The *virga* from 900 to 1500

Time Period	Austrian, Czech lands, etc.	French	Swiss / southern Germanic
925			[Vienna 1609][a]
950		Schøyen 1275/19	
975			[Vienna 1888]
1000			Schøyen 1664
			St.Gallen 390/391
1025		Schøyen 658	Schøyen 98
1050		Schøyen 630	[Vienna 1845]
		Paris 1092	[Vienna 1043]
1075	[Vienna 573]	Bodleian 579	Munich 29316 (6
			Munich 29316 (11
1100	[Vienna 1826]	Madrid 289	

[a] Manuscripts given between square brackets have only been dated to within half a century.

[23] John Haines, 'Erasures in Thirteenth-Century Music', in *Music and Medieval Manuscripts: Paleography and Performance*, ed. John Haines and Randall Rosenfeld (Aldershot, 2004), 61.
[24] Andrew Hughes, 'Late Medieval Notations', in *Oxford Handbook of Paleography*, ed. Frank Coulson, in preparation.

Table 1. (continued)

Time Period	Austrian, Czech lands, etc.	French	Swiss / southern Germanic
1125	Schøyen 1574	Paris 12044	St. Gallen 375
1150			Schøyen 1670
1175	[Vienna 1355]		
1200	[Vienna ser. n. 2701 +2]		Munich 2542
			[Vienna 1890]
1225	Vienna 1799**	Cambrai 28	Vienna 1226
		Rouen 277	
		Worcester F 160	
1250	[Vienna 1768]	Cambrai 38	Munich 23083
	[Vienna 1827]	Vendôme 17E	Munich 2643
1275	Vienna 1774 (Late 13th-c. hand)	Paris 1105	
1300	Vienna 14208	Cambridge 298	
	Vienna 14208 (Gothic hand)		

Table 1. (continued)

Time Period	Austrian, Czech lands, etc.	French	Swiss / southern Germanic
1325	Vienna 1774 (primary hand) Vienna 1793 [Vienna 1813]	Cambrai 157	
1350			Munich 17003
1375	Vienna 12865 Vienna 1026 (secondary hand)	Cambrai 29	Munich 2542 (marginalia)
1400	Vienna 1462		
1425	Vienna ser. n. 4642		Vienna 1848
1450			Vienna 1824 Munich 4303 Munich 4305
1475	Vienna 3079		
1500	Vienna mus. hs. 19179		Munich 4306

Table 2. The *clivis* from 900 to 1500

Time Period	Austrian, Czech lands, etc.	French	Swiss / southern Germanic
925			[Vienna 1609][a]
950		Schøyen 1275/19	
975			[Vienna 1888]
1000			Schøyen 1664
			St.Gallen 390/391
1025		Schøyen 658	Schøyen 98
1050		Schøyen 630	[Vienna 1845]
		Paris 1092	[Vienna 1043]
1075	[Vienna 573]	Bodleian 579	Munich 29316 (6
			Munich 29316 (11
1100	[Vienna 1826]		
1125	Schøyen 1574	Paris 12044	St. Gallen 375
1150		Cambrai 27	Schøyen 1670

[a] Manuscripts given between square brackets have only been dated to within half a century.

Table 2. (continued)

Time Period	Austrian, Czech lands, etc.	French	Swiss / southern Germanic
1175	[Vienna 1355]		
1200	[Vienna ser. n. 2701 +2]	Cambrai 46	Munich 2542
			[Vienna 1890]
1225	Vienna 1799**	Cambrai 37	Vienna 1226
		Cambrai 28	
		Rouen 277	
		Worcester F 160	
1250	[Vienna 1768]	Cambrai 38	Munich 23083
	[Vienna 1827]	Vendôme 17E	Munich 2643
1275	Vienna 1774 (Late 13th c. hand)	Paris 1105	Munich 7907
1300	Vienna 14208	Cambridge 298	
	Vienna 14208 (Gothic hand)		

Table 2. (continued)

Time Period	Austrian, Czech lands, etc.	French	Swiss / southern Germanic
1325	Vienna 1774 (primary hand)	Cambrai 157	
	Vienna 1793		
	[Vienna 1813]		
1350			Munich 17003
1375	Vienna 12865	Cambrai 29	Munich 2542 (marginalia)
	Vienna 1026 (secondary hand)		
1400	Vienna 1462	Schøyen Ms. 1275/28	
1425	Vienna ser. n. 4642		Vienna 1848
1450			Vienna 1824
			Munich 4303
			Munich 4305
1475	Vienna 3079		
	Schøyen 087		
1500	Vienna mus. hs. 19179		Munich 4306

THE EVOLUTION OF NEUMES INTO SQUARE NOTATION IN CHANT MANUSCRIPTS ■ 155

Table 3. The liquescent from 900 to 1500

Time Period	Austrian, Czech lands, etc.	French	Swiss / southern Germanic
925			[Vienna 1609][a]
950		Schøyen 1275/19	
975			[Vienna 1888]
1000			Schøyen 1664
			St. Gallen 390/391
1025			Schøyen 98
1050		Schøyen 630	[Vienna 1845]
			[Vienna 1043]
1075	[Vienna 573]		Munich 29316 (6
			Munich 29316 (11
1100	[Vienna 1826]	Madrid 289	
1125	Schøyen 1574	Paris 12044	St. Gallen 375
1150		Cambrai 27	Schøyen 1670

[a] Manuscripts given between square brackets have only been dated to within half a century.

Table 3. (continued)

Time Period	Austrian, Czech lands, etc.	French	Swiss / southern Germanic
1175	[Vienna 1355]		
1200	[Vienna ser. n. 2701 +2]	Cambrai 46	Munich 2542
			[Vienna 1890]
1225	Vienna 1799**	Cambrai 28	Vienna 1226
		Rouen 277	
		Worcester F 160	
1250	[Vienna 1768]	Cambrai 38	Munich 23083
	[Vienna 1827]	Vendôme 17E	Munich 2643
1275		Paris 1105	Munich 7907
1300	Vienna 14208	Cambridge 298	
1325	Vienna 1793	Cambrai 157	
1350			
1375	Vienna 12865		
	Vienna 1026 (secondary hand)		

THE EVOLUTION OF NEUMES INTO SQUARE NOTATION IN CHANT MANUSCRIPTS ■ 157

Table 3. (continued)

Time Period	Austrian, Czech lands, etc.	French	Swiss / southern Germanic
1400	Vienna 1462		
1425	Vienna ser. n. 4642		Vienna 1848
1450			
1475			
1500			

The graphic evidence in the charts confirms that the shift from neumes to square notation took place in the twelfth and thirteenth centuries. Haines has shown how this change affected the *punctum*, the *pes,* and the *climacus*. The data concerning the *virga*, the *clivis*, and liquescent neumes from 900 to 1500, above, support his findings: neumes first became more angular in the early twelfth century, beginning in northern France. The southern German scribal tradition began to show more angular lines and pronounced note-heads in what is sometimes referred to as 'German Gothic' notation, or *Hufnagelschrift*, a little more than half a century later than the first changes in northern French notation.

Since northern French scribes seem to have led the change in graphic style—at least in comparison with the other scribal traditions compared here—it seems natural that they would also be the first to attain graphic stability at the beginning of the thirteenth century. There is no significant change in either the *virga* or the *clivis* after 1225 in northern French sources, and the liquescent's square incarnation achieves its '*plica*' shape by the end of the thirteenth century. In general, the Austrian and southern-German / Swiss areas tend to preserve the neume shapes for longer, and even, in some cases, to use the neume shapes alongside the new, more angular notation in the same manuscript.[25] Although it is impossible to draw final conclusions from the limited number of representative folios, it may be that the older style of *clivis* was used more often within a group of neumes to be sung on one syllable, whereas the angular *clivis* more often depicted a falling interval at the beginnings of a word or syllable. This observation is by no means offered as a rule *per se*; rather, it may only be concluded that the new angular style of notation made its way into the Austrian and German scriptoria slowly and gradually. In France, however, there appears to have been two rather abrupt changes in notational form: the first occurs at the turn of the twelfth century, where the *virga* changes in one generation from being depicted as a nearly vertical line to a note-head on a stem. The second change took place around 1225, when the connected 'z' shape of the *clivis* appears in several sources as two squares, connected by a thin line.

---

[25] Examples of this are found in Munich Clm 2542 and Vienna Cod. 1799** (both written in the first half of the thirteenth century), where one finds the old and the new form of the *clivis* in the same hand.

Table 3 shows that the changing shape of liquescent neumes follows the same general pattern as the *virga* and *clivis*. They appear more angular in northern French sources around the beginning of the twelfth century, and then in the other regions several generations later. Liquescent neumes are distinct from the *virga* and the *clivis* in that it is the shape of the neume itself which determines the method of its performance, and this characteristic persists even into the late thirteenth century. By the mid-fourteenth century, however, it appears that the general convention of using stems or 'tails' to denote liquescents had been widely accepted and so these notes began to look identical to their plicated counterparts in polyphonic contexts. However, in the fifteenth century, Area 1 still contains a hint of liquescent neumes in their rounded and hook-like predecessors.

The Process of Change

Establishing where and when the change from neumes to note-heads took place is relatively easily done, provided enough graphic evidence for the given scribal tradition remains. The tables above provide basic images of neumes to which other manuscripts might be compared. A more interesting question, and a more difficult one to answer, concerns *how* the transition from neumes to note-heads took place.

The graphic change from neumes to square notation can be correlated to the increasing size of manuscripts, and the space in them allotted to the notation. By and large, the earliest notations are found in small manuscripts which might have been personal books of reference or repositories of a musical tradition kept in a library for consultation. But during the time that notation began to standardize and represent pitch vertically, the dimensions of the manuscripts were also increasing. These new, larger books often include ornate decorations at initials or depictions of biblical or ecclesiastical scenes, and were probably used by singers in a worship service itself. By the thirteenth century, the widely spaced staff and large proportions given to each written pitch were standard in musical liturgical books. Consequently, the notational characters had increased in size as well, exposing every feature of every sign to higher scrutiny. For example, in the early days of a *clivis*, any sort of small, upside-down 'U' would have been understood as an indication for two pitches, the first of which is higher than the second. But as dimensions increased, each quill stroke would have been 'magnified', as it were, and the angles and quill-strokes standardized as a result.

The increase in size of the notation coincides with another graphic change which took place across Europe in the thirteenth century in the visual appearance of texts: *Gothic textualis* script.[26] This type of bookhand is characterized by the predominance of straight lines, sharp angles, a predilection for vertical lines, a deliberate distinction between thick and thin lines, uniformity in height, and a consistency of appearance for each letter in the alphabet. In the making of musical books with *Gothic textualis* script, quills with wider tips were used for rendering square note-heads more easily, and the necessity for ruled parchment increased so that the lay-out of each musical book could

---

[26] Albert Derolez, *The Palaeography of Gothic Manuscript Books: From the Twelfth to the Early Seventeenth Century* (Cambridge, 2003), 74.

progress smoothly. The appearance of musical notation would surely have been included in the new aesthetic, and consequently, the slanted *virga*, curvaceous *clivis*, and ornamental-looking liquescent neume would have been straightened, standardized, and rendered more angular.

In even broader terms, the Gothic aesthetic sweeping across European architecture at the time is also reflected in the preponderance of right angles and square shapes in what is now called square notation. Although it is impossible to prove any sort of causal relationship between Gothic ideals of beauty and the increasing angularity of musical notation at the time, it is more than likely that scribes would have gravitated towards straight lines and geometrically expressed angles to depict the same melodies which would have been rendered in a more fluid script just a century before. Perhaps the standardization of notation for use in early polyphony is another reason why books of chant adopted this notation as standard. Indeed, thirteenth-century medieval commentators on music saw the square note (or a '*perfect long*', in the terminology of 'Franconian' notation,) as 'the universal symbol for the measurable material world.'[27]

In square notation, there are two main features of each figure: the note-head (square or slightly rectangular) and the stem. Note-heads were made with the broad stroke of the quill, stems with the thin edge. Note-heads and stems are always perpendicular to each other, with the note-head placed along the horizontal axis (shown in most cases by staff lines) and the stem along the vertical axis. By contrast, early neumes are not made up of two different elements (the note-head and the stem), but instead, are lines and segments of lines which are generally slanted towards the right in a manner reminiscent of cursive handwriting. How, then, are neumes to be understood as the ancestors of square notation?

Two observations connect the neume *virga* and *clivis* to their square notation counterparts. First, the section of a neume line that is more horizontal than vertical (when seen on an imaginary grid) will usually correspond to the placement of the note-head in square notation. Second, the section of the neume line that is more vertical than horizontal usually corresponds to the stem in square notation (as imagined on that same grid.)

The square notation form of the *virga*, as it is found in the French and German late scribal traditions, provides the clearest illustration of these two correspondences. The square notation *virga* consists of a note-head at the top, and to the left of, a thin stem. If the note-head were thought of as corresponding to a horizontal line, and the stem to a vertical line angled slightly to the right (as in cursive handwriting), it is possible to see the neume version as residual within the square notation sign (Figure 8).

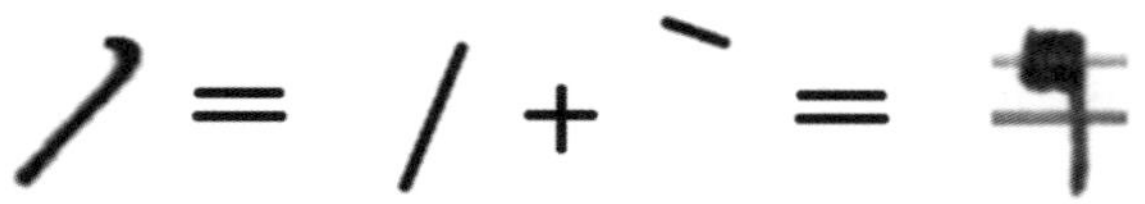

Figure 8. The *virga* in the northern French and Germanic tradition: neume to square

[27] Haines, 'From Point to Square', 44.

The placement of the small horizontal line at the top of the *virga* in the neumes (that is, on the *right* of the vertical slanted line and not the *left*) can then be seen to correspond to the later placement of the square note-head in the *virga*, as shown in Figure 9.

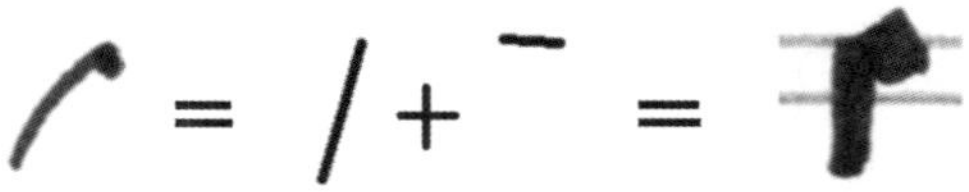

Figure 9. The *virga* in the Austrian / Czech tradition: neume to square

Similarly, when the neume version of the *clivis* is understood as four component parts, as shown in Figure 10, we can derive the square notation form: (1) the initial vertical angle; (2) the horizontal flattening of the line at the apex; (3) the near-vertical line connecting the apex to the bottom; and (4) the lower portion of the line as flattening out once more to the horizontal. Rendering these four parts into their square note equivalents gives: (1) an initial stem; (2) a note-head to the right of the stem; (3) another vertical stem on the right of the note-head; and (4) a final note-head at the bottom of the second stem. The *clivis* in Figure 10 is the form found in St. Gallen 375, in Table 2.

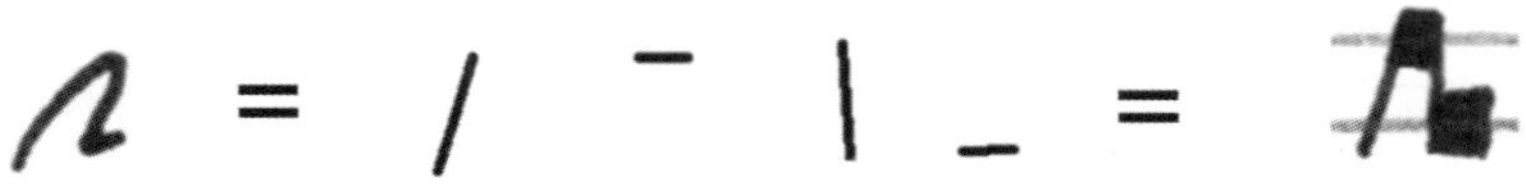

Figure 10. The *clivis*: neume to square

The characteristic 'hook' feature of the liquescent cannot be recreated using only the two models for square note/neume correspondence outlined above since *plicas* in square notation do not consistently represent liquescents.[28] However, in several manuscripts listed in Table 1, the shape of the liquescent *virga* is shown as a note-head with a slightly concave bottom edge leading into a small descender at the right edge.[29] It is tempting to understand this curve as a descendent of the 'hook' shape of early liquescent *virgae*. However, in square notation, such a curve rarely corresponds to the liquescent shape of the *pes* (at the bottom left), as shown in the example in Table 3,[30] nor to the *punctum*,[31] nor even to the *clivis*.[32] Perhaps the *plica*'s graphic connection to liquescents in square notation suggests that later scribes preferred standardization over graphic ancestry. The variety of liquescent neume shapes in early notations is striking whereas *plicas* are easily identifiable in square notation and consistently drawn.

---

[28] While it is generally held that liquescent neumes are rendered as plicas in square notation without exception, wide comparative studies will occasionally reveal liquescents and plicas that have been 'hardened' into regular pitches. See, for example, Eva Branda's discussion of the melodic variants in seventy-three versions of one Great Responsory for Thomas Becket, in which ten manuscripts do not present consistent uses of plicas in 'Melodic Variants in *Studens Livor Thome*' in *Les Traditions du Plain-Chant Occidental / Traditions in Western Plainchant: Proceedings of the Conference of the Gregorian Institute of Canada*, (Ottawa, 2010), 169-71.
[29] Three manuscripts included in my charts that show this clearly are: Vendôme 17E, Paris 1105, and Vienna 1793.
[30] Two manuscripts from the Schøyen Collection, MS 1664 and MS 1670, show this.
[31] This is found in the *puncta* in Cambrai 27 and 46.
[32] This is found in Vienna 1888 and Schøyen MS 1574.

It seems eminently reasonable that square notation be understood as the graphic heir of neume notation through the correspondence of neume lines with the two elements (note-head and stem) of square notation. However, this tells us little about the reasons why the shift—from neume notations in smaller books to square notation in larger, more standardized books—occurred at all.

Reasons for Change

Given that the earliest books containing musical notation are small and intended for personal use, they were probably not meant to have been sung from at all, but rather kept as a reference to which a singer might return if his memory failed him.[33] In some early books, neumes are even written above lines of chant text where notation was not originally planned, resulting in cramped, improvised, and in many cases, largely illegible neume forms. Most early books were planned to contain neumes above the text, but since the notation does not contain pitch information, whether legible or not, this notation could only be performed if the singer already knew the tune, using the notation only as a short-hand to remind him of the melody.

By the early thirteenth century, however, manuscripts containing notation were complex and the layout was carefully planned.[34] Consequently, the text was usually spaced so that it lines up vertically with the notes above, and the notation is clear and the note shapes relatively consistent. If the singer understood the conventions of square notation and read the staff correctly, he could accurately perform a melody even if he had never heard it before. Thus, the graphic shift in music notation opens up a new possibility for the *purpose* of notation and allows for the singer to have a new kind of relationship to it. From the early twelfth to late thirteenth centuries, when square notation was gradually replacing neumes, notation itself shifted from being solely a reminder to being an instruction as well as a reminder. When a singer reads notation in order to perform a melody he has not memorized, it is necessary for that notation to be consistent, and that the intervals and pitches are clearly represented. Square notation has the advantage over neumes in these respects, and it is easier to read when several singers are gathered around one choirbook in church. It should be mentioned here, however, that visual ambiguity remained in the area of rhythmic interpretation and it would require the efforts of later generations to invent further graphic distinctions, by altering the shape and visual character of each type of note, to reflect aspects of duration and metrical divisions.

In a discussion on the earliest neumes, Leo Treitler makes a general distinction between two types: symbolic and iconic.[35] Symbolic signs represent something without physically appearing to be like it, such as the triangle, used to mean 'yield' in traffic.

---

[33] Albi 44, a late ninth-century gradual and antiphoner from the cathedral of Sainte-Cécile in Albi, measures 225 x 165 mm. Vienna 1609, an early tenth-century troper from Freising, measures 125 x 185 mm. The missal fragment in the Schøyen Collection, MS 1275/19, from the mid tenth century, measures 90 x 120 mm. The St. Gallen antiphoner 390/391, written around 1000, measures 220 x 165 mm. These books are all small enough that it is not likely they were sung from by the choir during the liturgy.

[34] Andrew Hughes, 'The Scribe and the Late Medieval Liturgical Manuscript: Page Layout and Order of Work', in *The Centre and its Compass: Studies in Medieval Literature in Honor of Professor John Leyerle*, ed. Robert A. Taylor et al. (Kalamazoo, 1993), 151-224.

[35] Treitler, 'The Early History', 238-40.

Since symbols do not *look* like what they represent, their meanings must be learned. Contrastingly, iconic signs depict what they represent, such as a highway warning sign depicting the shape of a deer in mid jump. This sign can be interpreted immediately by drivers because it looks like what it means. Treitler applies these concepts to the earliest, unheightened neumes and the later, heightened neumes of the tenth and eleventh centuries to show how the increasing reliance on notation encouraged the shift from symbolic to iconic representation of music on the page.

The comparison of the symbolic vs. the iconic sign is useful in a discussion about the transition from neumes to notes as well. We might envision the early neume scribe as engaged in his own silent (graphic) performance; the shape of the neumes sketching the contour of a melody, his hand moving from left to right across the page in a two-dimensional, cheironomic representation of the melodic line.[36] Neumes can be seen to generally mimic, on parchment, the rise and fall of a melody as one might see hand-gesture in the air.[37] For example, the scribe, writing an early *clivis*, is engaged in producing a physically iconic symbol, because the 'upside-down U' shape is made by one rising stroke, representing the directionality of 'up', or 'higher', and one subsequent descending stroke, representing 'down' or 'lower'. In the act of writing neumes, scribes were showing the contour of the melody by tracing, with their quills, its trail in their musical memories. In the broadest sense, then, the writing of neumes is iconic. The singer of early neumes must also relate to the notation as iconic signs, in that the neumes depict the motion through time and space of a melody they already know. To interpret an iconic sign successfully, one must have *previously* acquired an understanding about whatever the sign represents; the aforementioned highway sign denoting 'beware of deer' can only be interpreted correctly if the driver has seen a deer before. Similarly, the only way to sing a melody written in early neumes properly is to know it well enough that the neumes act as reminders and not as an entirely new set of instructions.

The description of later scribal activity in the thirteenth century found in Anonymous IV (circa 1280) shows that scribes of square notation were engaged in a different sort of activity from that of earlier neume scribes. For example, the *clivis* in square notation is formed by four separate strokes: first the two note-heads, and then the stems.[38] This requires that the scribe move his hand to either side of the first note-head and that there is no sense of directionality in the production of the sign itself. While no one is sure precisely how quickly an experienced scribe could complete a melody in square notation, the separate strokes required suggests that it would have taken longer than to write the same melody in neumes. A scribe of square notation did not necessarily even make the note-heads in the order in which they were meant to be sung; a *pes* might be written by *first* making the top square (the second pitch), and *then* the bottom square (the first pitch), and finally connecting them with the thin stem, even though the pitches would have been

---

[36] In a discussion about early notation at the Gregorian Institute of Canada's 2009 conference at McMaster University, this vision was called in to question by James Borders, who wondered aloud how smooth this 'silent performance' could be when the scribe, working with a quill whose nib could not be forced in certain directions, was forced to draw neume shapes from right to left, thereby disturbing the direction of the silent melodic flow.

[37] The idea that neumes originate in hand gesture, the cheironomic theory, was first put forward by Fleischer in *Neumenstudien* (Leipzig, 1895), vol. 1, 25 ff., and mentioned by many other scholars, including Hucke in 'Toward a New Historical View of Gregorian Chant', in *Journal of American Musicology* 33 (1980), 437-67 at 449; and Hiley in 'Recent Research on the Origins of Western Chant', in *Early Music* 16 (1988), 202-13 at 210.

[38] John Haines, 'Anonymous IV as an Informant on the Craft of Music Writing', in *Journal of Musicology* 23 (2006), 375-425 at 385.

sung the other way around.[39] Increasing numbers of lay scribes and stationers in thirteenth-century cities probably thought of musical notation as a part of the expected skill set of graphic workmanship, and not as a musical activity at all. If their focus was primarily the look of the (increasingly standardized) notation on the page, it seems unlikely that their writing would have taken on the same musical performative quality that neumes convey.

Square notation, therefore, marks a significant contrast with the early neumed sources. In all probability, the scribes of square notation were not engaged in the same act of silent performance that the scribes of early neumes had been. Michael Gullick points out that 'by about the middle of the twelfth century uniformity in book production became more pronounced both regionally and nationally as well as internationally…It is striking…that the disciplined freedom enjoyed by those who worked in monastic scriptoria was replaced by the uniformity and constraint imposed by the conditions of the marketplace.'[40] This emphasis on standardization in the book-making process extended to musical books, of course. The resulting visual consistency of written music became necessary for singers who depended on it to interpret the notation correctly. Since they did not need to rely so heavily on their memories and could devote more time to learning how to *read* the new notation at sight, melodies did not have to be memorized or internalized to the same degree. Once begun, the reciprocal relationship between the clarity of the notation and the reliability of the singer's memory drove notation towards increasing standardization and visual clarity.

This discussion of graphic change spanning two centuries is necessarily broad and, as a consequence, the shift between neumes and note-heads might take on an appearance of universality. But this is not the case. In a few isolated regions, neumes remained the primary form of written music for several hundred years after square notation (or its 'German Gothic' equivalent) had replaced them in other areas. Regions where the early forms prevailed for longer, like Passau, St. Gallen, St. Florian, and Seckau, used the staffless Germanic neume, heavily slanted to the right, like cursive handwriting, even in graduals written in the fourteenth century.[41] The prolonged use of neumes also speaks to the ability of the singers in those regions to perpetuate the tradition of musical memory successfully enough to continue to use only memory aids and not employ complete instructions.[42] It is, of course, impossible to accurately compare what it would have been like to be a singer in one of the communities using square notation with a singer's experience in a tradition still using neumes, but the simple fact of the persistence of neumes in some areas reveals that chant tradition in the thirteenth and fourteenth centuries was not the same across the continent. This may also suggest that the concept of a musical manuscript as a reference work, and not a book to be sung from directly during the service, may have continued longer in what is now southern Germany and Austria than it did in the rest of Europe.[43]

Apart from the changing requirements of singers, there might have been other motivations encouraging this shift from neumes to square notes. Haines suggests an

---

[39] Haines, 'Anonymous IV as an Informant', 393.
[40] Michael Gullick, 'How Fast Did Scribes Write?', in *Making the Medieval Book: Techniques of Production*, ed. Linda L. Brownrigg (Los Altos Hills, 1995), 39-58 at 41.
[41] Hiley, *Western Plainchant*, 389.
[42] Inga Behrendt, 'Der Seckauer Liber ordinarius von 1345 (A-Gu 756) - Edition und Kommentar' (Ph. D. diss., Universität Graz, 2009), 437-39.
[43] I know of no study connecting the longevity of neumes with the liturgical or social history of a particular place. Such work might illuminate the influence of a given singing tradition on the scriptorium that produced its books.

interesting reason for the preference for square notes over neume forms, stemming from the writings of Franco of Cologne on mensural notation. Franco writes, 'the perfect long…is considered the first and principle note…since it contains all things and all things can be reduced to it.'[44] Of course, Franco's context is most probably thirteenth-century polyphony, but it should not be forgotten that square notation was used to notate both plainchant and polyphony at this time. Haines sees a more philosophical reason for Franco's use of the word 'perfection': 'Perfection, a notion ubiquitous in the thirteenth-century learned writings and theology, implies the ultimate perfection coming from God. The perfection of any worldly thing, including a musical note, must partake of the greatest perfection of all, God. So also go the graphics of music.'[45] Could it be that there are theological implications, or even Neoplatonist resonances, in the gradual shift from neumes to notes at this time? Certainly singers educated at the universities of the day would have made the connection between the invisible ideals of perfection with their visible incarnations in notation. It is unclear, however, whether this line of thinking sparked the change in the appearance of notation or simply evolved along with it.

There is evidence enough that the medieval mind typically entertained a plurality of explanations about the nature of the world, and perhaps the development of square notation from its neume ancestors is no exception. Where one scribe might well have understood the new kind of notation as a graphic form of divine perfection, another might have sought visual clarity, or perhaps simply standardization above all else. Another may have seen the importance of the new graphic aesthetic of sharp angles and thick/thin lines. Still another might have appreciated how the old neume shapes informed the new square notation. When asked about the meaning and usefulness of the new square notation, professional scribes in thirteenth-century French urban centres would answer differently from Austrian monks of the fourteenth century, steeped in a long tradition of memory and ritual.

Conclusion

Comparisons of the *virga*, the *clivis*, and the liquescent neume in three regions of Europe from 900 to 1500 show that the transition from neumes to square notation was gradual, and that it did not happen everywhere at the same time. This comparison was conducted between notations in manuscripts that were securely dated within a quarter-century in the descriptions of catalogues in which they are found today. Manuscripts from northern France show the beginnings of the shift towards more angular forms with more pronounced note-heads at the beginning of the twelfth century. The regions of southern Germany and Austria and the Czech lands begin the transition several generations later. Some geographical areas evolve a different form of notation from typical square notation (often called 'German Gothic'), which nevertheless consists of the same straight quill strokes, attention to verticality and horizontality, pitch placement on a staff, and a pronounced difference between thick and thin ink strokes. By the end of the thirteenth century, this transition was mostly complete, although it took another hundred years before neumes were no longer used anywhere.

---

[44] Haines, 'From Point to Square', 43.
[45] Haines, 'From Point to Square', 43.

For all three regions studied, the shape of the original neumes became incorporated into the final square notation form. The evolution in notation happened at the same time as a general increase in the size of manuscripts themselves. The role of the manuscript went from being one of personal use (a repository of information for periodic referral) to public display in a church. This change in the nature of the manuscript itself would have fostered a change in the scribe's method of performing his job, as well as the singers' relationship to the musical notation.

Since research in this area continues to produce an exciting number of sources which have until now lain largely unknown in archives and libraries across Europe, the number of precisely datable manuscripts continues to grow.[46] Studies focusing on individual scribal traditions may shed light on the way the graphic shift was understood by scribes within one school or tradition, and how the gradually shifting shapes were interpreted by singers throughout the twelfth and thirteenth centuries.

---

[46] For example, the Alamire Foundation's research project entitled Inventories of Antiphoners in Flemish Collections is now in the process of describing and cataloguing all office manuscripts held in Flemish libraries and archives. The results of these efforts will be published (Brepols) in multiple volumes according to geographical location in Flanders. Many of these sources were previously unknown to scholars and some are even securely datable.

Appendix. Methodological Appendix

I based my manuscript data collection method upon a model provided by the research project *Nota Quadrata*, the aim of which was the identification and study of the various forms of square notation. *Nota Quadrata* lists thirty-five manuscripts, mostly from France and Italy, which may be reliably dated within a twenty-five year period through the twelfth and thirteenth centuries.[1] The current database of 300 sources spans 700 years, from the ninth to the end of the fifteenth centuries.[2] The earliest manuscript in the database at present is dated between 817 and 835, and is a Welsh fragment containing the office for Easter Vigil. It is now held in the Bodleian library, Auct. F.4.32 (2176).[3] The latest manuscript included in the database was dated to the year 1539 and comes from the monastery of St. Truiden, Belgium. It is now held in the university library in Liège, Ms. 24. Only ten manuscripts (mostly English or northern French sources) could be reliably dated to before the end of the tenth century. Representing musical notation in the eleventh century are forty manuscripts, mostly from England, northern France or Germany/Switzerland. The highest proportion of datable manuscripts comes from the era of the graphic shift in the twelfth and thirteenth centuries: sixty-four manuscripts, mostly English, German/Swiss, French, or Italian come from the twelfth century, and eighty-five manuscripts, from mostly the same regions, with the addition of several from the Low Countries, in the thirteenth century. Representing the fourteenth century are another fifty-eight sources from the aforementioned regions, as well as central and eastern Europe. There are thirty-one mainly continental manuscripts from the fifteenth century, and only seven from the early part of the sixteenth century. Of the 300 manuscripts in the database, twenty-five have not been assigned a place of origin.

    A combination of online electronic inventories and traditional resources provided information to add manuscripts to the database. Among the traditional publications is the multi-volume *Catalogue des manuscrits en écriture latine, portant des indications de date, de lieu ou de copiste* by Samaran and Marichal, which contains thirteen French datable musical manuscripts.[4] Another resource is Solesmes' descriptions of various sources involved in their publication of *Le graduel romain,* four of which are precisely enough dated to be included in the database.[5] A more recent French publication that contributed a collection of seven manuscripts from Cambrai to the database is Denis Muzerelle's *Manuscrits datés des bibliothèques de France*.[6] The *Late Medieval Liturgical Offices* contributed another twelve manuscripts to the list.[7] Scholarly articles that list reliably dated musical manuscripts, such as Boynton's 'Orality, Literacy and the Early

---

[1] See <http://notaquadrata.ca>.
[2] See the PDF of this database, available at: <https://sites.google.com/site/katehelsen/academics/research-projects>.
[3] Oxford, Bodleian Library, Auct. F.4.32 (2176). Stephen Josef Peter van Dijk, *Handlist of the Latin Liturgical Manuscripts in the Bodleian Library Oxford*, 7 vols. in 8 (unpublished typescript, Bodleian Library, 1957-60), vol. 6, No. 311.
[4] Charles Samaran and Robert Marichal, *Catalogue des manuscrits en écriture latine, portant des indications de date, de lieu ou de copiste*, 5 vols. (Paris, 1962-84).
[5] *Le graduel romain: Edition critique par les moines de Solesmes*, vol. 2: *Les sources* (Solesmes, 1957).
[6] Denis Muzerelle, *Manuscrits datés des bibliothèques de France* (Paris, 2000).
[7] Andrew Hughes, *Late Medieval Liturigcal Offices* (Toronto, 1996).

Notation of Office Hymns'[8] or Baltzer's 'Thirteenth-Century Illuminated Manuscripts and the Date of the Florence Manuscript'[9] were also included.

Traditional resources are sometimes now searchable online. Particularly useful to this study was the Cantus Planus website, hosted by the University of Regensburg,[10] where David Hiley has posted databases of the information collected by Neil Ripley Ker in his *Medieval Manuscripts in British Libraries* and *Medieval Libraries of Great Britain: A List of Surviving Books*, Walter Howard Frere's *Bibliotheca Musico-Liturgica. A Descriptive Handlist of the Musical and Latin-Liturgical Mss. of the Middle Ages Preserved in the Libraries of Great Britain and Ireland*, and Stephen Josef Peter Van Dijk's *Handlist of the Latin Liturgical Manuscripts in the Bodleian Library Oxford*.[11] Not only is it possible to peruse these catalogues online, but an online query function is available as well. Between Ker, Frere, and Van Dijk, over eighty manuscripts in British libraries have been dated to within a quarter century, and were added to the database accordingly. Chief among online resources was the *Musikalische Quellen des Mittelalters in der Österreichischen Nationalbibliothek* begun by Robert Klugseder in 2008.[12] This project combines all the musical manuscripts compiled in the Schneider Database of 1928 with all other examples of medieval musical notation in the Austrian National Library, and lists them with links to detailed information about each source. In addition, images of the notation in over fifty of these sources may be viewed online. A total of seventeen of these manuscripts were datable precisely enough to become part of the database. The Bayerische Staatsbibliothek in Munich has also posted images of entire books in their medieval musical holdings in PDF format, available to download, as well as a summary of information about each one.[13] This provided another twelve manuscripts for the database. The Schøyen Collection's website provides images of forty-three of the musical items (fragments or manuscripts) in the collection, and basic information, including date and provenance, about each.[14]

Of course, this kind of database will always be a work in progress, as new research results in ever more datable manuscripts coming to light. The number of online databases which include manuscript images is increasing every year. Major libraries, such as the Bibliothèque nationale de France, now provide high-quality images of many of their most precious holdings online as part of their Gallica project.[15] Other research projects based at universities and research institutions, such as the Alamire Foundation's

---

[8] Susan Boynton, 'Orality, Literacy and the Early Notation of Office Hymns', in *Journal of the American Musicological Society* 56 (2003), 99-168.

[9] Rebecca Baltzer, 'Thirteenth-Century Illuminated Manuscripts and the Date of the Florence Manuscript', in *Journal of the American Musicological Society* 25 (1972), 1-18.

[10] This 'data pool for research on Gregorian chant' is found at:
<http://www.uni-regensburg.de/Fakultaeten/phil_Fak_I/Musikwissenschaft/cantus/>.

[11] Neil Ripley Ker, *Medieval Manuscripts in British Libraries*, I: London (Oxford 1969); II: Abbotsford-Keele (1977); III: Lampeter-Oxford (1983); IV: Paisley-York (1992) by Neil Ripley Ker and Alan J. Piper; Neil Ripley Ker, *Medieval Libraries of Great Britain: A List of Surviving Books* (first edition London 1941; 2nd revised edition 1964); Andrew G. Watson: Supplement to the second edition (1987); Walter Howard Frere, *Bibliotheca Musico-Liturgica: A Descriptive Handlist of the Musical and Latin-Liturgical Mss. of the Middle Ages Preserved in the Libraries of Great Britain and Ireland*, 4 fascicles in 2 volumes, London 1894, 1901, 1930, 1932 (reprint Hildesheim 1967); Van Dijk, *Handlist of the Latin Liturgical Manuscripts*.

[12] <http://www.oeaw.ac.at/kmf/cvp/en/index.htm>.

[13] <https://opacplus.bsb-muenchen.de>.

[14] <http://www.schoyencollection.com/music.htm>.

[15] <http://www.bnf.fr/en/collections_and_services/digital_libraries_gallica.html>.

Inventories of Antiphoners in Flemish Collections project, or the Portuguese Early Music Database (New University of Lisbon) aim to locate, catalogue, and display a certain selection of medieval sources.[16] More broadly, online research tools such as CANTUS provide an online nexus for information about the medieval source and links to library sites which display its images.[17]

The following table is taken from the database of 300 sources. Sources listed here are those with images available and from which the comparison tables for the *virga*, *clivis*, and liquescent neume forms are drawn.

---

[16] Inventories of Antiphoners in Flemish Collections: http://alamirefoundation.org/en/research/inventories-antiphoners-flemish-collections and the Portuguese Early Music Database: http://pemdatabase.eu/.

[17] http://cantusdatabase.org/.

Date	Manuscript		Abbreviation
933-36	Paris	Bibliothèque nationale de France	lat. 1240	Paris 1240
< 950	Vienna	Österreichische Nationalbibliothek	Cod. 1609	Vienna 1609
950 (approx.)	Oslo/London	Schøyen Collection	Ms. 1275/19	Schøyen 1275/19
>950	Vienna	Österreichische Nationalbibliothek	Cod. 1888	Vienna 1888
1000 (approx.)	Oslo/London	Schøyen Collection	Ms. 1665	Schøyen 1665
1000 (approx.)	Oslo/London	Schøyen Collection	Ms. 1664	Schøyen 1664
1000 (approx.)	St. Gallen	Stiftsbibliothek	390 / 391	St. Gallen 390 / 391
1000-50	Oslo/London	Schøyen Collection	Ms. 098	Schøyen 098
1030 (approx.)	Oslo/London	Schøyen Collection	Ms. 658	Schøyen 658
1050 (approx.)	Oslo/London	Schøyen Collection	Ms. 630	Schøyen 630
1050 (approx.)	Paris	Bibliothèque nationale de France	lat. 1092	Paris 1092
1050-72	Oxford	Bodleian Library	579 (2675)	Oxford 579
1050-1100	Munich	Bayerische Staatsbibliothek	Clm 29316(11	Munich 29316(11
1050-1100	Munich	Bayerische Staatsbibliothek	Clm 29316(6	Munich 29316(6
1065	Cambridge	Corpus Christi College	391	Cambridge 391
1065+	Vienna	Österreichische Nationalbibliothek	Cod. 1845	Vienna 1845
1075 (approx.)	Vienna	Österreichische Nationalbibliothek	Cod. 1043	Vienna 1043
1095	Toledo	Biblioteca capitular	44.2	Toledo 44.2
1100 (approx.)	Madrid	Biblioteca Nacional	289 (olim. C151)	Madrid 289
1100-30	Paris	Bibliothèque nationale de France	lat. 12044	Paris 12044
1100-50	Oslo/London	Schøyen Collection	Ms. 1574	Schøyen 1574
1020-30	Vienna	Österreichische Nationalbibliothek	Cod. 573	Vienna 573
1125-50	Piacenza	Duomo, Biblioteca e Archivio Capitolare	65	Piacenza 65
1130-38	Madrid	Biblioteca Nacional	Vitrina 20,4 (olim C.132)	Madrid Vitrina 20,4
1135 (approx.)	St. Gallen	Stiftsbibliothek	375	St. Gallen 375
1150	Oslo/London	Schøyen Collection	Ms. 1670	Schøyen 1670
1150+	Vienna	Österreichische Nationalbibliothek	Cod. 1826	Vienna 1826
1150-72	Cambrai	Bibliothèque municipale	27	Cambrai 27
1160 (approx.)	Vienna	Österreichische Nationalbibliothek	Cod. Ser. N. 2700	Vienna Ser. N. 2700
1173 (approx..)	Rouen	Bibliothèque municipale	209-210 (Y.175)	Rouen 209-210

Date	Manuscript		Abbreviation
1173-1228	Cambrai	Bibliothèque municipale	46	Cambrai 46
1175-1200	Oslo/London	Schøyen Collection	Ms. 2059	Schøyen 2059
1175+	Vienna	Österreichische Nationalbibliothek	Cod. 1355	Vienna 1355
1190 (approx.)	Vienna	Österreichische Nationalbibliothek	Cod. Ser. N. 2701 and 2702	Vienna Ser. N. 2701, Ser. N. 2702
1200 (approx.)	Munich	Bayerische Staatsbibliothek	Clm 2542	Munich 2542
1200 (approx.)	Vienna	Österreichische Nationalbibliothek	Cod. 1890	Vienna 1890
1200-50	Assisi	Biblioteca comunale	694	Assisi 694
1200-50	Assisi	Biblioteca comunale	693	Assisi 693
1200-50 and 1325-50	Vienna	Österreichische Nationalbibliothek	Cod. 1226	Vienna 1226
1224-35	Cambrai	Bibliothèque municipale	37	Cambrai 37
1225-50	Cambridge	University Library	Mm. 2.9	Cambridge Mm 2.9
1226-44	Naples	Biblioteca nazionale	Vittorio Emanuele III VI-E-20	Naples III VI-E-20
1230 (approx.)	Vienna	Österreichische Nationalbibliothek	Cod. 1799**	Vienna 1799**
1230 (approx.)	Worcester	Cathedral Library	F 160	Worcester F 160
1230-50	Cambrai	Bibliothèque municipale	38 (olim 40)	Cambrai 38
1230-50	Naples	Biblioteca nazionale	VI-G-38	Naples VI-G-38
1231-35	Rouen	Bibliothèque municipale	277 (Y.50)	Rouen 277
1233 (approx.)	Zürich	Zentralbibliothek	Rh. 14	Zürich Rh. 14
1235-38	Cambrai	Bibliothèque municipale	28	Cambrai 28
1235-45	Cambrai	Bibliothèque municipale	38	Cambrai 38
1240 (approx.)	Florence	Biblioteca Medicea-Laurenziana	Plut. 29.1	Florence 29.1
1245-66	Vendôme	Bibliothèque municipale	17E	Vendôme 17E
1250-75	Munich	Bayerische Staatsbibliothek	Clm 23083	Munich 23083
1250-75	Munich	Bayerische Staatsbibliothek	Clm 2643	Munich 2643
1250+	Vienna	Österreichische Nationalbibliothek	Cod. 1768	Vienna 1768
1250+	Vienna	Österreichische Nationalbibliothek	Cod. 1827	Vienna 1827
1256-59	Rome, Santa Sabina	Bibliotheca della Curia Generalizia dei Dominicani	XIV lit. 1	Rome XIV lit.1
1264	Vatican	Biblioteca Apostolica Vaticana	Vat. lat. 4756	Vatican 4756

THE EVOLUTION OF NEUMES INTO SQUARE NOTATION IN CHANT MANUSCRIPTS ■ 171

Date	Manuscript			Abbreviation
1265-72	Paris	Bibliothèque nationale de France	lat. 1105	Paris 1105
1266	Paris	Bibliothèque nationale de France	fr. 2163	Paris 2163
1270 (approx.)	Munich	Bayerische Staatsbibliothek	Clm 7907	Munich 7907
1275-1300	Cambridge	Trinity College	O.2.1	Cambridge O.2.1
1300	Paris	Bibliothèque de l'Arsenal	944	Paris l'Arsenal 944
1300 (approx..)	Vienna	Österreichische Nationalbibliothek	Cod. 14208	Vienna 14208
1300-19	Cambridge	University Library	2602	Cambridge 2602
1300-25	Vienna	Österreichische Nationalbibliothek	Cod. 1793	Vienna 1793
1300-25	Vienna	Österreichische Nationalbibliothek	Cod. 1774	Vienna 1774
1302-16	Cambridge	Fitzwilliam Museum	298	Cambridge 298
1310-20	Aberystwyth	National Library of Wales	15536	Aberystwyth 15536
1319	Sion, CH	Bibliothèque capitulaire	3	Sion 3
1323	Vienna	Österreichische Nationalbibliothek	Cod. 1813	Vienna 1813
1320-90 (approx.)	Aberystwyth	National Library of Wales	20541 E	Aberystwyth 20541 E
1323	Vienna	Österreichische Nationalbibliothek	Cod.1813	Vienna 1813
1324-33	Cambrai	Bibliothèque municipale	157	Cambrai 157
1340 (approx.)	Munich	Bayerische Staatsbibliothek	Clm 17003	Munich 17003
1347	Sion, CH	Chapter Library	1	Sion 1
1350-1400	Munich	Bayerische Staatsbibliothek	Clm 2542	Munich 2542
1350-1400	Vienna	Österreichische Nationalbibliothek	Cod. 12865	Vienna 12865
1350-1400	Vienna	Österreichische Nationalbibliothek	Cod. 1026	Vienna 1026
1360 (approx.)	Cambridge	University Library	Add. 710	Cambridge Add. 710
1381	Cambrai	Bibliothèque municipale	29	Cambrai 29
1400 (approx.)	Oslo/London	Schøyen Collection	Ms. 1275/28	Schøyen 1275/28
1400-1500	Munich	Bayerische Staatsbibliothek	Clm 6423	Munich 6423
1400-1500	Munich	Bayerische Staatsbibliothek	Clm 17010	Munich 17010
1410	Vienna	Österreichische Nationalbibliothek	Cod. 1462	Vienna 1462
1412-25	Douai	Bibliothèque municipale	116	Douai 116
1420	Florence	St. Mark's Monastic Library	571 (T)	Florence 571 (T)
1420-40	Vienna	Österreichische Nationalbibliothek	Cod. Ser. N. 4642	Vienna Cod. Ser. N. 4642

Date	Manuscript		Abbreviation
1430	Mainz	Erzbischöfliche Bibliothek	A	Mainz A
1433	Vienna	Österreichische Nationalbibliothek	Cod. 1848	Vienna 1848
1437	Frankfurt	Universitätsbibliothek	Carmelite 16	Frankfurt Carmelite 16
1450 (approx.)	Vienna	Österreichische Nationalbibliothek	Cod. 1824 and Cod. 1825	Vienna 1824, 1825
1459	Munich	Bayerische Staatsbibliothek	Clm 4305	Munich 4305
1459	Munich	Bayerische Staatsbibliothek	Clm 4303	Munich 4303
1477	Vienna	Österreichische Nationalbibliothek	Cod. 3079	Vienna 3079
1481-1500	Oslo/London	Schøyen Collection	Ms. 087	Schøyen 087
1491	Ljublijana	Archiepiscopal Archives	17	Ljublijana 17
1492	Vienna	Österreichische Nationalbibliothek	Mus. Hs.19179	Vienna Mus. Hs. 19179
1495	London	British Library	Printed Books, IB 6753	London, IB 6753
1499	Vorau	Stiftsbibliothek	253	Vorau 253
1501	Munich	Bayerische Staatsbibliothek	Clm 4306	Munich 4306
1508	Douai	Bibliothèque municipale	117	Douai 117
1509-16	Vienna	Österreichische Nationalbibliothek	Mus.Hs.15501	Vienna mus. hs. 15501
1519	Munich	Bayerische Staatsbibliothek	Clm 4304	Munich 4304

Abstract

The earliest form of musical notation, neumes, uses discrete or connected symbols to represent one or several pitches in a musical gesture. The next major stage in notation's development, square notes, presents the reader with a notation made up of variously shaped note-heads and stems or ligatures. The transition between these two forms of notation is the focal point of this study, which compares the virga, the clivis, and various alterations to represent liquescence, in three distinct geographical/scribal regions across Europe. Samples of notation were only taken from manuscripts that can be securely dated within a quarter-century, from 900 to 1500. Results of the comparison show that the transition from neumes to square notes begins first in northern France, at the beginning of the twelfth century. The Germanic and central European areas begin this transition slightly later. In all regions studied, the transition was complete by the end of the thirteenth century. Some reasons for this transition, including the role of the musical manuscript in liturgical culture and the function of notation for the singer, are discussed.

The Rhenish Heritage of the Preetz Antiphoner*

Alison Altstatt

Introduction

This study concerns the fifteenth-century antiphoner Preetz, Klosterarchiv Reihe V G1, from the former Benedictine convent of Preetz in the diocese of Lübeck (hereafter, the Preetz Antiphoner). While geographically distant from the Low Countries, evidence suggests that the convent's musical roots lead back to the Rhineland. This evidence is visible in both the convent's idiosyncratic notational style and its musical repertoire. The library at Preetz also preserves a gradual (Preetz, Klosterarchiv Reihe V G2; hereafter the Preetz Gradual). The earliest layer of musical repertoire in this source clearly originated in the Western region of the German-speaking area. The evidence for a Rhineland connection in the Preetz Antiphoner is more suggestive. Of particular interest is the antiphoner's transmission of a unique proper office for St. Blaise, a modally ordered office likely composed in the tenth century in a style of office composition established in the Rhineland by such composers as Stephen of Liège and Reginold of Eichstätt. The later addition of the office *Universa plebs fidelis* for St. Matthias most likely reflects a transfer of practice from Trier during the late fifteenth century during the time of the Bursfeld Reform of Benedictine monasticism.

The first mention of Kloster Preetz dates to the year 1211. Details of the cloister's founding, including the identity of its motherhouse, remain uncertain. Comprised primarily of noble women, the cloister flourished during the thirteenth through fifteenth centuries and grew to a community of seventy nuns. In the late fifteenth century, the cloister was reformed through the nearby male house of Kloster Cismar, which joined the Bursfeld Congregation in 1449 as a founding member.[1] The goals of the Bursfeld reform included a stricter observance of the Benedictine Rule, and the establishment of a standardized liturgy that adhered to the rule throughout its constituent houses.[2] Aside from the addition of the Matthias office, there is little evidence to suggest the influence

---

* This research was supported by grants from the Deutscher Akademischer Austauschdienst, the University of Oregon School of Music and Dance, The University of Oregon Center for the Study of Women and Society, and the American Musicological Society, and by a generous gift from Sachiyo Aoyama. I thank Kloster Preetz provost Graf Albrecht Brockdorff-Ahlefeldt and archivist Reinhard Schmidt-Supprian for generously allowing me to photograph the manuscripts Reihe V G1 and Reihe V G2, and to access the digital facsimile of Anna von Buchwald's *Initien Bok*. I am much obliged to Martin Dippon, director of the Bruno Stäblein Archive, for invaluable research assistance and to Lori Kruckenberg, Andreas Haug, and David Hiley for their advice and critique during the research and writing of this study.

[1] Johannes Rosenplänter, 'Kloster Preetz und seine Grundherrshaft. Sozialgefüge, Wirtschaftbeziehungen und religiöser Alltag eines holsteinischen Frauenklosters um 1210-1550' (Ph.D. diss., Christian-Albrechts-Universität zu Kiel, 2006), 20-44, 145-84.

[2] See Ulrich Faust, 'Bursfelder Kongregation' in *Lexicon für Theologie und Kirche*, ed. Walter Kasper, 11 vols. (Freiburg im Breigrau etc., ³1994), vol. 2, 815.

Table 1. Liturgical Manuscripts in the Preetz Cloister Archive

Siglum	Manuscript	Date
Preetz, Klosterarchiv, Hs. 01	The *Initien Bok* (*Buch im Chor*) of Prioress Anna von Buchwald	1471-87
Preetz, Klosterarchiv, Reihe V G1	Antiphoner (winter volume)	c. 1450
Preetz, Klosterarchiv, Reihe V G2	Gradual	c. 1450

of the Bursfeld reform on either the liturgical calendar or musical repertoire of Kloster Preetz, though the reform may have prompted changes in entrance rites and in the codification of previously unwritten customs.[3]

The three liturgical manuscripts that remain in the cloister's archive are listed in Table 1. Preetz, Klosterarchiv, Hs. 01 is cantrix, and later prioress, Anna von Buchwald's *Initien Bok*: a supplementary ordinal and convent chronicle written between the years of 1471 and 1487.[4] With this book, the author purported to instruct future cantrices in 'all that one should do, and how.'[5] Anna von Buchwald's book is an important source for understanding the convent's music and liturgy during the period of contact with the Bursfeld Reform movement.[6]

In addition to Anna's *Initien Bok*, the gradual with an intercalated sequentiary and the winter volume of the antiphoner, both copied circa 1450, remain in the cloister's archive. These two notated manuscripts preserve the convent's pre-Reformation musical practice, albeit in a fragmentary state: both books have been heavily damaged by the removal of decorated initials, marginal illuminations, and in some cases, entire leaves or gatherings. Rubrics in the Preetz Gradual referring to the *conventus*, female cantrices, and the male *prepositus* indicate without a doubt that the books were created for the use of a women's house.[7] Analysis of the gradual's sequence repertoire and its melodic variants has shown that the repertoire consists of multiple layers, the oldest of which originated in the Rhineland. This oldest Rhenish layer was eventually combined with newer elements of repertoire, including some regional pieces shared with Lübeck.[8]

The Preetz Antiphoner is of approximately the same age as the gradual, and is of the same scribal lineage. The winter part of a two-volume antiphoner, the manuscript contains the *Temporale* from Advent through Lent, interspersed with feasts of the *Sanctorale* from the octave of Andrew through the Annunciation. Table 2 gives a summary of its contents, with lacunae and additions noted. The summer volume of the antiphoner has been lost.[9]

---

[3] Alison Altstatt, 'The Music and Liturgy of Kloster Preetz: Anna von Buchwald's *Buch im Chor* in Its Fifteenth-century Context' (Ph.D. diss., University of Oregon, 2011), 34-35, 44, 89-103, 305-6, 325-29, 376-77.
[4] Anna von Buchwald's self-styled *Initien Bok* is better known as the *Buch im Chor*, a name that has been transmitted in the secondary literature since the nineteenth century. I advocate adopting Anna's own terminology and will thus refer to this source as the *Initien Bok*.
[5] D-PREk, Hs. 01, fol. 1r.
[6] See Altstatt, 'The Music and Liturgy of Kloster Preetz', 1-180.
[7] D-PREk, Hs. 01, fol. 33v, fol. 60v, fol. 81r.
[8] Altstatt, 'The Music and Liturgy of Kloster Preetz', 306-7, 343-437.
[9] A fourth source from Preetz, a sixteenth-century codex containing a combined antiphoner-gradual with sequentiary, is preserved in the Tallinn Historical Museum. See Victoria Goncharova (ed.), *Tallin, Eesti Ajaloomuuseum (Tallinn,*

Table 2. Collation and contents of the Preetz Antiphoner (Preetz, Klosterarchiv, Reihe V G1)

Location	Contents
Gathering 1	
fols. 1-3	Lacuna
fols. 4 (partial)-5	Advent I (continued) Octave of Andrew [7 December]
fols. 6-7	Lacuna
fol. 8	Advent II (continued)
fol. 9	Lacuna
fols. 10-12	Nicholas [6 December]
Gathering 2	
fols. 13-16	Nicholas (continued) - Lucy [13 December]
fols. 17-19	Lacuna
fols. 20-24	Advent III (continued), Quatember, Advent IV
Gathering 3	
fols. 25-29	Advent IV (continued), O antiphons, Vigil of Nativity [24 December]
fol. 30	Vigil of Nativity (continued) - Christmas Day [25 December]
fols. 31 (partial)-2	Christmas Day (continued)
fol. 33	Lacuna
fols. 34-36	Christmas Day (continued) - Stephen [26 December]
Gathering 4	
fols. 37-39	Stephen (continued)
fol. 40	Lacuna
fol. 41	Stephen (continued) - John the Evangelist [27 December]
fol. 42	Lacuna
fol. 43	John the Evangelist (continued) - Holy Innocents [28 December]
fol. 44	Lacuna
fols. 45-48	Holy Innocents - Silvester [31 December]
Gathering 5	
fol. 49	Lacuna
fols. 50-51	Circumcision [1 January], Octave of Christmas [1 January], Octave of John [3 January], Epiphany [6 January]
fols. 52-6	Lacuna
fols. 57-60	Epiphany (continued)

Historical Museum), MS 237.1.228a (XIX.184; 24075), Publications of Mediaeval Musical Manuscripts 35 (Ottawa, 2008). In her introduction, Goncharova concludes that the antiphoner, while written at Preetz, probably represented the musical practice of the convent's priests, and not that of the nuns, and is closely aligned with the musical practice of the diocese of Lübeck. My own comparison of notation, repertoire, and melodic variants from the Tallinn codex and from earlier cloister manuscripts supports the conclusion that the latter is from a different liturgical and musical tradition.

Table 2. (continued)

Location	Contents
Gathering 6	
fols. 61-67	Epiphany (continued)
fol. 68	Lacuna
fols. 69 (partial)-72	Sebastian [20 January] - Agnes [21 January]
Gathering 7	
fols. 73-75	Agnes (continued) - Conversion of Paul [25 January]
fol. 76	Lacuna (Conversion of Paul)
fols. 77-80 (partial)	Conversion of Paul (continued)
Gathering 8	
fols. 85 (partial)-7	Blaise [3 February]
fols. 88-89	Lacuna
fols. 90-95	Blaise (continued), Agatha [5 February], Sts. Vedastus and Amandus [6 February], Scholastica [10 February], Peter's Chair [22 February], Gregory [12 March]
fol. 96	Matthias [24 February] (first folio of inserted bifolio)
fol. 97	Lacuna (conjugate folio of inserted bifolio)
fol. 98	Gregory (continued from fol. 95)
Gathering 9	
fol. 99	Gregory (continued)
fol. 100	Lacuna
fols. 101-2	Gregory (continued) - Benedict [21 March]
fol. 103	Lacuna
fol. 104	Benedict (continued)
fol. 105	Lacuna
fols. 106-7	Annunciation [25 March] (continued)
fols. 108-9	Lacuna
fol. 110	Annunciation (continued)
Gathering 10	
fols. 111-20	Octave of Annunciation [1 April], Lent
fol. 121	Lacuna
fol. 122	Lent (continued)
Gathering 11	
fols. 123-27	Lent (continued)
fols. 128-29	Lacuna
fols. 130-31	Lent (continued)
fols. 132-34	Lacuna
Gathering 12	
fols. 135-46	Lacuna (stubs remaining)

Notation

The notation of the Preetz Gradual and Antiphoner may be described as a Rhenish-Gothic hybrid distinct from contemporaneous scripts of the surrounding diocese of Lübeck. Figure 1 gives the original hand of the Preetz Gradual (hereafter Hand A): a slender, flexible script that is tall and horizontally compact.

Figure 1. Preetz Gradual (Preetz, Klosterarchiv, Reihe V G2), fol. 67r, Hand A

Hand A is conservative in its maintenance of the pressus, oriscus, and liquesced forms.[10] It uses the German rounded clivis for downward two-note gestures, with the Messine square clivis reserved to indicate a repeated initial pitch. Hands B, C, D, E, F and G enter corrections and additions to the gradual. Figure 2 gives the original hand of the antiphoner (hereafter Hand H): less horizontally compact, and written with a slightly thicker pen than Hand A, resulting in diamond-shaped puncta and more articulated lines in the rounded forms of the clivis and torculus. Hands I and J are found in additions and corrections to the antiphoner.

Figure 2. Preetz Antiphoner (Preetz, Klosterarchiv, Reihe V G1) fol. 85v, Hand H

Figure 3. Berlin, Staatsbibliothek Preußischer Kulturbesitz, Musikabteilung, Ms. lat. 4° 664, Trier, c. 1120-1220

While it seems the scribe of the antiphoner is different from the scribe of the gradual, both hands appear to have been trained in the same scriptorium. The flexible, curved, connected strokes and vertical orientation of these hands are much closer to Rhenish scripts than to the blockier Gothic hands of fifteenth-century Lübeck: the diocesan seat and the origin of many of the priests who served at Kloster Preetz.[11] The Preetz hands are much more like the hands of twelfth- to thirteenth-century Trier (Figure 3) and fourteenth-century Aachen (Figure 4).

The use of a diagonally held pen in the Kloster Preetz hands results in the beginnings of a Gothic tendency.[12] Despite this modification, it appears that a notational style originally practiced in the Rhineland and abandoned by the mid-fourteenth century was preserved in Kloster Preetz as an 'island' of notational practice. As Ulrike Hascher-Burger has observed in her study of the manuscripts of the cloisters of the Lüneburger Heath, the notational style of convent manuscripts is an unreliable indicator

---

[10] This contrasts with those Messine traditions that lost the oriscus and all liquesced forms besides the epiphonus and cephalicus. See David Hiley and Janka Szendrei, 'Notation §III, 1. History of Western Notation: Plainchant', in *The New Grove Dictionary of Music and Musicians*, ed. Stanley Sadie and John Tyrell (London, ²2001), vol. 18, 103-4.

[11] See Hiley and Szendrei, 'Notation', 106-7.

[12] See Hiley and Szendrei, 'Notation', 110. The authors observe that 'Gothic notations were not a new notational type, but a change to the surface appearance of traditional neume shapes. Something similar had happened with the establishment of square notation, but whereas the pen was held parallel to the line, in gothic style it remained diagonal.'

Figure 4. Köln, Historisches Archiv der Stadt, Ms. W270, Aachen, c. 1339

of date due to claustration, the effects of which resulted in the persistence of styles that were abandoned elsewhere.[13]

The notation of Kloster Preetz furthermore developed certain features that may distinguish a specific notational lineage, as well as a 'house style'. Table 3 compares the original hands of the Preetz Gradual (Hand A) and Antiphoner (Hand H), as well as later cloister hands found in the same manuscripts, to hands from contemporary manuscripts copied in nearby Lübeck.

Two formal traits distinguish the Kloster Preetz hands from those active in Lübeck. The first is the use of the left-facing virga. The fifteenth-century manuscripts from Lübeck all use a right-facing virga, as typical of other Gothic scripts. Manuscripts that use the left-facing virga are significantly earlier Rhenish examples from the Mainz area: the late twelfth-century Dendermonde, Sint-Pieters-en-Paulusabdij, Ms. 9 (one of two surviving books containing Hildegard von Bingen's musical repertoire)[14] and the thirteenth-century Koblenz Missal.[15]

The second Preetz trait is the idiosyncratic use of a neume resembling a quilisma to indicate a two-note rising figure, created by a doubled initial stroke of the pes and torculus. Hands A and E from the gradual extend this scribal convention to the second pitch of the scandicus. While other stylistic elements, such as ductus, thickness of stroke, and degree of articulation of curved strokes vary between the cloister's hands, the near-ubiquity of the left-facing virga and quilisma-like rising figure points to a single scribal lineage. The exceptions are hands E and F: hand E, the scribe of a sixteenth-century replacement folio, uses a right-facing virga, yet maintains the quilisma-like form in the pes and scandicus. Hand F represents an addition of a pair of Sanctus and Agnus Dei melodies entered on a flyleaf. The right-facing virga and regular form of the square pes indicate that this is not a hand from Preetz, but rather that of a scribe trained in Lübeck or its environs—probably a priest who served the convent. In the antiphoner, two hands appear in addition to the original hand H. Hand I provides corrections on three folios.

[13] Ulrike Hascher-Burger, *Verborgene Klänge: Inventar der handschriftlich überlieferten Musik aus den Lüneburger Frauenklöstern bis ca. 1550. Mit einer Darstellung der Musik-Ikonographie von Ulrike Volkhardt* (Hildesheim etc., 2008), 10-17.
[14] See Peter Van Poucke (ed.), *Symphonia harmoniae caelestium revelationum: Dendermonde, St.-Pieters & Paulusabdij, Ms.Cod.9*, Facsimile Editions of Prints and Manuscripts (Peer, 1991).
[15] See Hiley and Szendrei, 'Notation', 107.

Table 3. Fifteenth-century hands from Preetz and Lübeck

Hand and manuscript	Virga	Pes	Torculus	Scandicus	German clivis	Messine clivis
Hand A: original hand of Preetz Gradual						
Hand B: Preetz Gradual, fol. 1r (addition)						
Hand C: Preetz Gradual, fol. 51v (margin)						
Hand D: Preetz Gradual, fol. 52v (margin)						
Hand E: Preetz Gradual, fol. 57 (replacement folio)						
Hand F: Preetz Gradual fol.1v (addition)						
Hand G: Preetz Gradual fol. 130v (correction)						
Hand H: Preetz Antiphoner original hand						
Hand I: Preetz Antiphoner fol. 8v, 23r, 36v (corrections, addition of verse)						
Hand J: Preetz Antiphoner (inserted Matthias office) fol. 96						…
Initienbok fol. 3v						
Initienbok fol. 122						
Tallinn, Historical Museum, Ms. 237.1.228a						
Lübeck, Bibliothek der Hansestadt Lübeck, theol. lat. 11						
Lübeck, Bibliothek der Hansestadt Lübeck, Ms. 12						
Lübeck, Bibliothek der Hansestadt Lübeck, Ms. 13					Used in torculus only	
Lübeck, Bibliothek der Hansestadt Lübeck, Ms. 16						
Lübeck, Bibliothek der Hansestadt Lübeck, Ms. 17						
Lübeck, Bibliothek der Hansestadt Lübeck, Ms. 18						
Lübeck, Bibliothek der Hansestadt Lübeck, Ms. 22						

Hand J is that of a scribe who notated an inserted office for St. Matthias, to be discussed further below.

In sum, the shared traits of the original and correcting hands indicate that Kloster Preetz maintained its own scriptorium and developed a distinctive house style, adapted from an earlier tradition of Rhenish notation The nuns of Preetz continued to use and alter the books they created in this distinctive notational style. At the same time, the increasingly Gothic tendencies in the notation suggest that the house scriptorium was not completely cut off from contemporary writing styles and technologies.

Repertoire of the Antiphoner

As mentioned above, an analysis of the gradual's sequence repertoire suggests that its oldest layer originated in the Rhineland. Can the same be said for the repertoire of the antiphoner? The identification of manuscript lineage using the analysis of the Advent Sunday responsory series pioneered by René-Jean Hesbert is hindered by the numerous lacunae in the manuscript.[16] It is nevertheless possible to compare the extant responsories from the third and fourth Sundays of Advent to Hesbert's lists in *Corpus Antiphonalium Officii*, as seen in Table 4.

An analysis of the antiphoner's extant repertoire of Advent Sunday responsories shows that the closest match is not with German monastic sources, but rather with monastic sources from Normandy and Brittany (monastic groups II and XXIV). Still, even these closest sources disagree regarding choice of the antepenultimate three responsories of the fourth Sunday, as is shown in boldface in Table 4. Given the fragmentary nature of the source, and the incomplete match, it is uncertain if these results can reliably indicate an origin in the southwest of the German-speaking area. It appears that the manuscript is derived from a German monastic lineage that has not been previously analysed.

While most of the music contained in the antiphoner is of international distribution, two unusual offices deserve special attention: a previously unknown office for St. Blaise that is contained in the original manuscript and an office for St. Matthias from Trier that appears as a later addition. The first office represents an older layer of material inherited from a secular cursus and which was adapted to Benedictine usage, and the second, a liturgical addition made during the time of the fifteenth-century Bursfeld reform.

I. The Proper Office for St. Blaise

The office for St. Blaise is of uncertain origin. While the cult of St. Blaise flourished at Lübeck cathedral from the second half of the thirteenth century, a different proper office for St. Blaise was in use there, as recorded in the antiphoner Lübeck, Bibliothek der

---

[16] René-Jean Hesbert (ed.), *Corpus Antiphonalium Officii*, Rerum ecclesiasticarum documenta Series maior Fontes 7-12 (Rome 1963-79), vol. 5, 411.

Table 4. Advent Sunday responsory assignments in the Preetz Antiphoner and in CAO monastic groups from Normandy and Brittany

Advent Sunday, responsory number	Responsory assignments in Preetz Antiphoner by incipit	Responsory assignments in Preetz Antiphoner by CAO number[a]	CAO Group II Normandy	CAO Group XXIV Brittany
I, 1.1 - III, 2.2	Lacuna			
III, 2.3	*Descendit dominus*	37	37	37
III, 2.4	*Ecce radix Jesse*	39	39	39
III, 3.1	*Docebit nos*	70	70	70
III, 3.2	*Veni Domine et noli tarde*	38	38	38
III, 3.3	*Festina ne tardaveris*	92	92	92
III, 3.4	*Ecce Dominus venit...tunc*	82	82	82
IV, 1.1	*Canite tuba in Syon vocate*	41	41	41
IV, 1.2	*Paratus esto*	94	94	94
IV, 1.3	*Me oportet*	44	44	44
IV, 1.4	*Non auferetur*	43	43	43
IV, 2.1	*Ecce iam veniet*	45	45	45
IV, 2.2	*Virgo Israel*	46	46	46
IV, 2.3	*Iuravi dicit Dominus*	47	47	47
IV, 2.4	*Intuemini quantus*	**49**	**48**	**48***
IV, 3.1	*Non discedimus*	**48**	**49**	**49**
IV, 3.2	*Egredietur virga*	**81**	**73**	**73**
IV, 3.3	*Radix Iesse*	59	59	59
IV, 3.4	*Nascetur vobis*	91	91	91

[a] Numerals in bold face indicate disagreements in liturgical assignment between the three groups.

Hansestadt Lübeck, theol. lat. 2° 6, copied in 1397 [D-LÜh 6].[17] Given the influence of Braunschweig on liturgies in Lübeck, Ratzeburg, and Kloster Cismar in the twelfth and thirteenth centuries, the cathedral of Sankt Blasius in Braunschweig would seem another logical place to look for an antecedent of the Preetz office for St. Blaise.[18] However, it appears that the widely disseminated proper office *Dum satellites* from Rheinau was in use in Braunschweig cathedral, suggesting that we must look elsewhere for the origin of the Preetz office.[19]

Table 5 lists the contents of the Preetz office for St. Blaise, with lacunae noted. The office originally consisted of first and second vespers, a matins following the monastic

---

[17] It is possible that the office transmitted in D-LÜh 6 was the new office first celebrated in Lübeck cathedral in 1284. See Jürgen Petersohn, *Der südliche Ostseeraum im kirchlich-politischen Kräftespiel des Reichs, Polens und Dänemarks vom 10. bis 13. Jahrhundert: Mission-Kirchenorganisation-Kultpolitik*, Ostmitteleuropa in Vergangenheit und Gegenwart 17 (Cologne, 1979), 132.
[18] Petersohn, *Der südliche Ostseeraum*, 126-44.
[19] Wolfenbüttel, Niedersächsisches Staatsarchiv, VII B Hs. 195, fols. 39r-45v.

Table 5. Contents of the proper office for St. Blaise, Preetz Antiphoner (Preetz, Klosterarchiv, Reihe V G1)

Folio	Office	Genre	Incipit	Mode	Cantus ID
85v	V1	M	[Blas]i martir inclite	4	
85v	M	I	Ad [confit]endum regi martirem	4	
85v	M	H	Martir [dei] egre[gie]*a	3	008346
85v	M	A 1.1	Beatus Blasius corporalis	1	
85v	M	A 1.2	Erat enim magne humilitatis	2	
85v	M	A 1.3	Instante persecution	3	
86r	M	A 1.4	Ibi magnis	4	
86r	M	A 1.5	Si qua ex illis	5	
86r	M	A 1.6	Hiis et talibus	6T	
86r	M	W	Gloria et honore	r[b]	008081
86r	M	R 1.1	Beatus Blasius Sebastea	7	
86r	M	V	Beatis meritorum	7	
86r	M	R 1.2	Cum duceretur vir	4	
86v	M	V	Tercio hac nocte	4	
86v	M	R 1.3	Cesus fustibus	3	
86v	M	V	Habeo enim	3	
86v	M	R 1.4	Presen[te] Blasius	2	
86v	M	V	Ecce tam caro	2	
87r	M	A 2.1	Idcirco hec tormenta	7	
87r	M	A 2.2	Cum videret preces	8	
87r	M	A 2.3	Ineffabile illud gaudium	1	
87r	M	A 2.4	Domine rex eterne	4	002374
87r	M	A 2.5	Sancte Blasi martir	4	
87r	M	A 2.6	Sancte Blasi intercede	4	
87r	M	R 2.1	Martir Blasius iterum	1	
87v	M	V	Tercia autem sessione	1	
87v	M	R 2.2	Vir domini cecitatem	6T	
87v	M	V	Quis enim nesciat	6T	
87v	M	R 2.3	Iussus autum sanctus	1	
87v	M	V	Ubi residens	1	
87v	M	R 2.4	Beatus Blasius*	8	006222 (contrafact)
87v	M	A 3	Adest veneranda nobis dies	4	
88			Lacuna		
89			Lacuna		
90r	L	B	Domine [...]die tue serviamus	6	
90r	P	A	Adest ve*	4	205663
90r	T	A	Adest nobis celeberrimus dies	4	001267
90r	X	R	Martir*	1	
90r	X	R	Vir domini*	6T	
90r	X	A	Domine*	6	
90r	S	A	Domine*	4	002374
90r	N	A	Sancte*	4	
90r	V2	A	Instante*	3	
90r	V2	A	Ibi*	4	
90r	V2	A	Si qua*	5	
90r	V2	A	Hiis*	6T	
90r	V2	R	Sancti Blasi martir Xristi*	2?	
90r	V2	M	Sacerdotem et martirem Blasius	4?	

[a] An asterik indicates pieces given in incipit only in the manuscript.
[b] r indicates a simple formula used for versicles to which no mode may be assigned.

cursus of twelve lessons, lauds, and pieces indicated by incipit for the little hours and for the pre-mass procession *per curiam*. Lacunae occur in the magnificat antiphon of the first vespers, in matins following the canticle antiphon of the third nocturn through lauds, and at the end of the second vespers.

II. Modally Ordered Matins Antiphons

As shown in Table 5, the first nine antiphons of matins from the Preetz office form a modally ordered series. Jean-François Goudesenne has identified the office for St. Amand as the first truly modally ordered office, and has suggested it may have been the prototype of offices written by Hucbald of St. Amand (850-930) and the three offices attributed to Messine-born Stephen of Liège (d. 920).[20] Later, the organizational principle of modal ordering appears in the St. Nicholas office of Reginold, Bishop of Eichstätt, who is believed to have hailed from the Rhineland.[21] Thus the later ninth and tenth centuries witnessed a northern diffusion through Metz and into the Rhineland of a compositional principle originally established in north-eastern France. It seems likely that the Preetz office was written following this transfer of compositional practice into the Rhineland and therefore may be a Rhenish composition, or an imitation thereof.

The narrative prose texts of modally ordered matins antiphons, as well as most of the matins responsories, were modelled on the *vita* BHL 1377.[22] The hagiographic narrative prose texts, the modal ordering of the antiphons, the adaptation of established antiphon melodies, together with the non-formulaic composition of its responsories, confirm that the earliest material in the Preetz office for St. Blaise belongs to the second stratum of office composition from circa 850-1050, referred to variously as the 'non-Gregorian' or 'transitional' stylistic era.[23] The earliest documented source of BHL 1377 is the late eleventh-century passionale München, Bayerische Staatsbibliothek, Clm. 14031, from Sankt Emmeram.[24] Despite the lack of an earlier source for the text of the *vita*, I

---

[20] Jean-François Goudesenne, *Les Offices historiques ou historiae composés pour les fêtes des saints dans la province ecclésiastique de Reims, 775-1030* (Turnhout, 2002), 233.

[21] Alfred Wendehorst, *Das Bistum Eichstätt*, Germania Sacra Neue Folge 45, Die Bistümer Kirchenprovinz Mainz 1 (Berlin, 2006), 45 n. 1.

[22] Société des Bollandistes, *Bibliotheca hagiographica latina antiquae et mediae aetatis,* Subsidia hagiographica 6/1-2 (Brussels, 1898-1901), Part 1(A-I), 205. The abbreviation 'BHL' stands for 'Bibliotheca Hagiographica Latina.' '1377' refers to the number assigned to the *vita* in the BHL edition. The vita BHL 1377, from which the text of the Preetz office for St. Blaise was adapted, begins with the incipit: 'Tempore Licinii imp. qui Constantini Augusti sororem'. The full text of BHL 1377 may be found in Johannes Bolland, Jean Baptiste Carnandet, Godefridus Henschenius, and Daniel van Papenbroeck (eds.), *Acta Sanctorum quotquot toto orbe coluntur: vel a catholicis scriptoribus celebrantur,* 68 vols. (Paris, 1863-), vol. 4, 343-48.

[23] For a discussion of stylistic periodization of office compositions, see Goudesenne, *Les offices historiques*, 153-63, 195-210, 213-78; Jean-François Goudesenne, 'A Typology of Historiae in West Francia (8-10 c.)', in *Plainsong and Medieval Music* 13 (2004), 1-31; Roman Hankeln, 'Properization and Formal Changes in High Medieval Saints' Offices: The Offices for Saints Henry and Kunigunde of Bamberg', in *Plainsong and Medieval Music* 10 (2001), 3-22; David Hiley, 'The Music of Prose Offices in Honour of English Saints', in *Plainsong and Medieval Music* 10 (2001), 23-37; Idem. 'Early Cycles of Office Chants for the Feast of Mary Magdalene', in *Music and Medieval Manuscripts: Paleography and Performance. Essays Dedicated to Andrew Hughes*, ed. John Haines and Randall Rosenfeld (Burlington, 2004), 369-400; László Dobszay and Janka Szendrei (eds.), *Antiphonen*, Monumenta monodica medii aevi 5 (Kassel, 1999); Richard Crocker, 'Matins Antiphons at St. Denis', in *Journal of the American Musicological Society* 39 (1986), 441-90.

[24] Elisabeth Wunderle, *Katalog der Lateinischen Handschriften der Bayerischen Staatsbibliothek München. Die Handschriften aus St. Emmeram in Regensburg. Band 1: Clm. 14000-14130*, Catalogus codicum manuscriptorium Bibliothecae Monacensis Tomus IV/2.1 (Wiesbaden, 1995), 74. See also *Bibliotheca Hagiographica Latina Manuscripta: Liste des témoins du texte 'BHL 1377'* <http://bhlms.fltr.ucl.ac.be/Nquerysaintsectiondate.cfm?code_bhl=1377>

contend that the musical setting of the Preetz office for St. Blaise dates to the late tenth century, and that the *vita* therefore must be as old or older.

The modally ordered set of nine matins antiphons transforms received Romano-Frankish antiphon melodies into the form László Dobszay and Janka Szendrei term the 'double antiphon'.[25] This form repeats an entire antiphon melody twice or more in the setting of a single text. The melody may be repeated exactly, extended, or abbreviated, creating longer, multi-part forms with elements of melodic parallelism that are inflected with subtle variants or ornamental elaboration.[26] In the double antiphons of the Preetz office, melodic repetition, parallelism, and variation mirror the phraseology of the text and underscore its meaning.

The first six antiphons of the modally ordered series narrate miracles from the saint's *vita*. In Example 1, the mode 1 *Beatus Blasius* that opens the series relates how St. Blaise, by merit of his talents as a healer, was unanimously elected as bishop.

Example 1. Antiphon 1.1 *Beatus Blasius*, office for St. Blaise, Preetz Antiphoner (Preetz, Klosterarchiv, Reihe V G1), fol. 85v

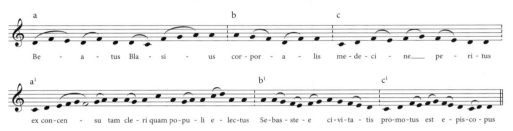

Beatus Blasius is a 'double antiphon' based on a common mode 1 melody that is not only ornamented, but repeated in its entirety, the first melodic iteration setting the first line of text, and the second accompanying the second and third lines. The first iteration of the melody prolongs the initial pitch d' before ascending to the reciting tone of a' in a typical mode 1 opening formula (a). The middle phrase (b), the most malleable part of the melody, travels from a' to a temporary cadence on f'. The closing section (c) is a cadential formula that centres on a shift from the structural note of f' to the *finalis* of d'.[27] Unlike the received melody, in which this formula begins simply e'-f', this elaborated version approaches from the lower fifth degree of the mode: c'-d'-$f'$$e'$-$f'$. Then, the same melody repeats in an expanded and embellished form. The opening (a^1) is reinterpreted as a scalar ascent from the undertone c' to the reciting tone a' that builds upward momentum. The melody then evades the expected undertone cadence[28] to a' (g'-a'-a'),

---

(Accessed 22 October, 2010). Another early example is found on fols. 87v-92v of the *passionale* Graz, Universitätsbibliothek Ms. 713, from the Benedictine house of St. Lambrecht.

[25] Dobszay and Szendrei (eds.), *Antiphonen*, 156.
[26] Dobszay and Szendrei (eds.), *Antiphonen*, 156.
[27] Because the Preetz antiphoner originates from a women's house and represents a tradition sung by women, I have transcribed musical examples in treble clef—the most appropriate modern clef for women's voices.
[28] I prefer the term 'undertone cadence' to the synonymous term 'Gallican cadence' for two reasons: its name reflects its structure as a proparoxytonic cadence built on the undertone (or *subfinalis*) of the mode, and, unlike the latter term, implies no connection to Gallican chant.

and instead ascends through these pitches, following the continuous syntax of the text. The parallel phrase, 'tam cleri quam populi', is set as an embellished recitation on *a'* that emphasizes the word *quam* with a leap up to *c"*. The repetition around *a'* builds a sense of urgency that culminates in the upward gesture *c"-d"* on 'electus', conveying elation over Blaise's unanimous election. The middle section (b¹) is re-interpreted as a downward descent from *a'* to *d'*, leading into the cadential formula (c¹), strengthened by an added undertone cadence.

In sum, in this careful setting, the repetition of the melody reacts not only to the longer length of the second and third textual phrases, but underscores their meaning and rhetoric through evaded cadences, motivic variation, and extended range. As seen in this example, double antiphons often expand in range in the second melodic iteration, usually coinciding with a rhetorically important point in the text, and thereby creating a dramatic peak that anticipates the imminent arrival of the final cadence.

The second through eighth antiphons in the modally ordered series are likewise double antiphons that repeat familiar Romano-Frankish melodies—sometimes two, sometimes three times in the setting of a single text—all with subtle variations that underscore both the structure and meaning of the text. The tessitura steadily rises with successive compositions built on *d'*, *e'*, and *f'* finals. The second nocturn begins with the mode 7 antiphon *Idcirco hec tormenta*, which narrates events from Blaise's martyrdom (transcribed as Example 2). Built on a familiar melodic type, this double antiphon represents the climax of the modally ordered set, in both tessitura and drama, coinciding with Blaise's statement of faith during his torture.[29] The mode 8 antiphon *Cum videret* that follows is a *depositio* (Example 3), a cathartic moment in the martyr's passion that is mirrored in the relaxation of tessitura that occurs in the plagal range.

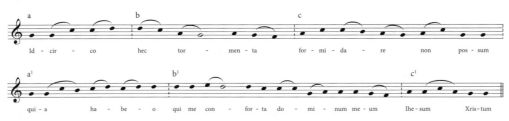

Example 2. Antiphon 2.1 *Idcirco hec tormenta*, office for St. Blaise, Preetz Antiphoner (Preetz, Klosterarchiv, Reihe V G1), fol. 87r

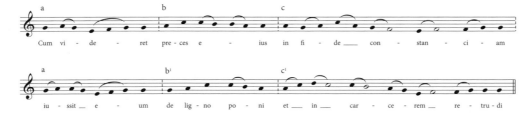

Example 3. Antiphon 2.2 *Cum videret*, office for St. Blaise, Preetz Antiphoner (Preetz, Klosterarchiv, Reihe V G1), fol. 87r

[29] See Dobszay and Szendrei (eds.), *Antiphonen*, No. 7018, for an example of this melody.

With the ninth and final antiphon, *Ineffabile illud gaudium* (see Example 4), the narrative comes to a resolution, and the modal order comes full circle to mode 1.[30]

Example 4. Antiphon 2.3 *Ineffabile illud gaudium*, office for St. Blaise, Preetz Antiphoner (Preetz, Klosterarchiv, Reihe V G1), fol. 87r

Unlike the narrative texts of the previous eight antiphons that were drawn from the *vita* BHL 1377, the ninth antiphon's description of heaven as 'that which eye has not seen, nor ear heard, nor has arisen in the heart of man' is based on Corinthians 2:9. This introspective text is uttered in the martyr's own voice, and its musical setting mirrors the paradoxical nature of the narrative of martyrdom. It seems fitting that the setting of a text that anticipates the indescribable joy of heaven should have no identifiable model. The melody inhabits an ambiguous plagal range, opening in phrase (a) on the fifth of the mode, a', and continuing through atypical descending gesture in phrase (b). By reversing the range and gestures that typify mode 1, the composer expresses the ineffable, thus resonating with the paradox of martyrdom, in which death is transformed into triumph. The overarching melodic motion, seen in the repeated (b) phrases, is one of descent, but just as the martyr's death is transformed, so too the melody unexpectedly reverses direction at the very end. As Blaise describes 'that which neither eye has seen nor ear has heard, nor has arisen in the hearts of men,' the melody takes an unexpected turn, arriving on the *finalis* of d' through a startling precadential figure that descends a minor seventh from a' to b. This move sets up an unanticipated ascent via an unusual variant of the undertone cadence: b-c'-d' on the text 'ascendit'. The juxtaposition of the mirror images of descent in the (b) phrases and ascent in the (c) phrases reflects the transformation of the martyr's impending death into triumph, and meditates on the ineffable through the reversal of typical modal characteristics.

These examples demonstrate the principles underlying the composition of the double antiphons in the St. Blaise office, and how the convention of modal ordering enhances their narrative trajectory.[31] In all but the final double antiphon, received melodic models are recast into longer, multi-part forms. Varied repetition simultaneously underscores syntactical divisions within the text, and allows for an expressive musical setting that heightens the text's rhetoric and meaning. As these examples show, double antiphons often expand in range in the second melodic iteration, usually coinciding

---

[30] It is not unusual for the ninth antiphon of a modally ordered set to return to mode 1. See Crocker, 'Matins Antiphons at St. Denis', 449.

[31] Crocker, 'Matins Antiphons at St. Denis', 489. Crocker claims that 'there are cases that suggest strongly that the numerical ordering was intended to have a musical effect through relative pitch—relative ascent to a climax, for instance'.

with a rhetorically important point in the text, and thereby creating a dramatic peak that anticipates the imminent arrival of the final cadence.

III. Mode 4 Antiphons

Following the modally ordered set appear antiphons 2.4 *Domine rex eterne*, 2.5 *Sancte Blasi martir*, and 2.6 *Sancte Blasi intercede*. These three antiphons (transcribed as Examples 5-7), form another distinct set, both modally and textually. The three antiphons are textually similar: all are petitions uttered by the singers in the here and now. The first of these three, the antiphon *Domine rex eterne*, first appeared as canticle antiphon in the widely-disseminated proper office for St. Blaise *Dum satellites* first recorded in the early twelfth century Rheinau *liber ordinarius*.[32] I hypothesize that *Domine rex eterne* was borrowed into the Preetz office no earlier than the twelfth century in the process of expanding a secular cursus of nine antiphons to a monastic cursus of twelve antiphons. In this scenario, the following two mode 4 antiphons, *Sancte Blasi martyr* and *Sancte Blasi intercede*, which do not appear in any other source, were newly composed in imitation of *Domine rex eterne* to complete the cursus of twelve antiphons.

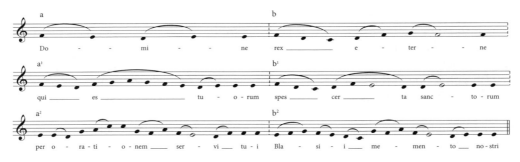

Example 5. Antiphon 2.4 *Domine rex eterne*, office for St. Blaise, Preetz Antiphoner (Preetz, Klosterarchiv, Reihe V G1), fol. 87r. Cantus ID 002374

Example 6. Antiphon 2.5 *Sancte Blasi martir*, office for St. Blaise, Preetz Antiphoner (Preetz, Klosterarchiv, Reihe V G1), fol. 87r

---

[32] Anton Hänggi (ed.), *Der Rheinauer Liber Ordinarius (Zürich Rh 80, Anfang 12. Jh.)*, Spicilegium Friburgense 1 (Fribourg, 1957), 85-86.

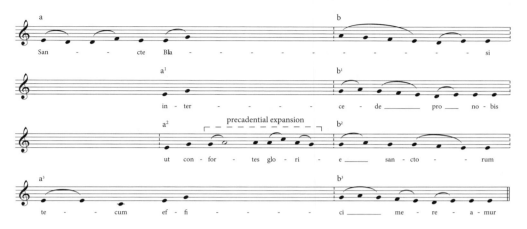

Example 7. Antiphon 2.6 *Sancte Blasi intercede*, office for St. Blaise, Preetz Antiphoner (Preetz, Klosterarchiv, Reihe V G1), fol. 87r

Melodically, the three antiphons are quite similar: they are neumatic in texture, generally inhabit the modest range of a fifth (d'-a'), and have a melodic centre on the e'-f'-g' trichord leading to frequent internal cadences to e'. In the last melodic iteration, prior to the final cadence, the melodies of Examples 5 and 7 expand in range, swelling upward along the pitch series c'-e'-g'-a'-c''-a'-g' before resolving into the final cadence on e'. As demonstrated in Examples 5-7, each of the antiphons can be analysed as a repeating multipart melody. However, the degree of variation and number of truncations and interpolations in the mode 4 set is greater than in the modally ordered set that precedes it. The consistency of style within the group of mode 4 antiphons could simply reflect general modal traits. However, the fact that *Domine rex eterne* first appeared in the Rheinau office suggests that the previously undocumented antiphons *Sancte Blasi martir* and *Sancte Blasi intercede* may have been written in imitation of the borrowed antiphon to fill out the monastic cursus of twelve antiphons.

IV. Canticle Antiphons

Three canticle antiphons in the Preetz office for St. Blaise appear to be from the earliest layer of composition in the office; unfortunately, all are fragmentary, due to damage inflicted on the manuscript. These three antiphons include the Magnificat antiphon for first vespers [*Blas*]*i martir inclite*, the Benedictus antiphon *Domine* […] *die tue serviamus* for lauds, and *Sacerdotem et martirem Blasium*, the Magnificat antiphon for second vespers. All three of these antiphons have longer texts that are not derived from the *vita*, but rather take the forms of petitions.

Formally, the three canticle antiphons, like the modally ordered series, are set as double antiphons consisting of multiple variations of a single melody. In comparison to the modally ordered matins antiphons, there is more variety between the melodic instantiations. As typical of the genre, the canticle antiphons tend to be wider in range than the matins antiphons, and while built on similar melodic gestures, their settings are ornate and melismatic, resulting in a slower pace and more solemn delivery of text.[33]

Example 8 transcribes the Benedictus antiphon *Domine* [...] *die tue serviamus* from lauds of the Preetz office for St. Blaise.[34]

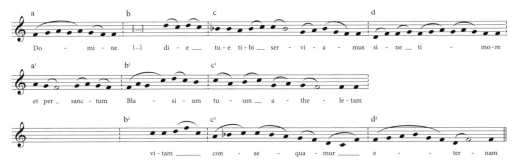

Example 8. Benedictus Antiphon *Domine* [...] *die tue serviamus*, office for St. Blaise, Preetz Antiphoner (Preetz, Klosterarchiv, Reihe V G1), fol. 90r

The Mode 6 antiphon *Domine* [...] *die tue serviamus* is written on f' with a $b\flat'$, having the range of an octave and a half, from c'-f''. While a lacuna in the manuscript prevents the transcription of the piece in full, the melody can be interpreted as three iterations of a tripartite melody, with variations, truncations, and interpolations. In the first iteration, the opening phrase (a) establishes the modal centre of f'. The second phrase (b) (the first part of which falls in a lacuna) rises to the fifth of the mode, c'' which is immediately decorated by its upper neighbour d''. The melody continues directly into the third phrase, (c): this phrase begins with a brief recitation on $b\flat'$, then lingers briefly on the second degree of the mode, g', before cadencing to f'. The phrase (d) that sets the text 'sine timore' extends the cadence on f' by dipping down to the sixth degree of the mode, d', before resolving in a decorated cadence that approaches the *finalis* from above.

In the second melodic instantiation, the phrase (a¹) succinctly establishes the modal final of f' through the falling trichord a'-g'-f'. In the phrase (b¹), the melody rises quickly to c'', decorated by its upper neighbour d'', before transitioning into the phrase (c¹). A short figure around reciting centre $b\flat'$ is followed by a variation of the cadence to f' via its upper neighbour g'.

The third statement of the melody eliminates the (a) portion of the melody and eschews the opening ascent typical of the (b) section, beginning immediately on the fifth of c''. The truncated (b²) section extends the range of the melody up to the octave f'': as noted above, the extension of the range in the last iteration of the melody seems to be typical in the double antiphons of the Blaise office. The (c²) closing phrase begins with a circling figure around the reciting centre of $b\flat'$, before a descent through f' that dips all the way down to c'. On the final word of the text, 'eternam', the final cadence on

---

[33] See David Hiley, *Western Plainchant: A Handbook* (Oxford etc., 1993), 96-98.
[34] The incipit of this antiphon falls in a lacuna (fols. 88 and 89) that extends from the third nocturn of matins through lauds. However, the incipit of the Benedictus antiphon is later repeated on fol. 90r for use as a processional antiphon *ad introitum*.

f' is confirmed first through a stepwise ascent from f' to $b\flat'$, and again from the lower sixth degree d'.

The sound of this piece is reminiscent of the famous canticle antiphon *O Christi pietas* from the mid-tenth century St. Nicholas Office, attributed to Reginold of Eichstätt.[35] The two pieces are both in mode 6, though *O Christi pietas* is transposed to c'' in the Preetz Antiphoner.[36] Both pieces occupy the same extended range of an octave and a half, from the lower fifth of the mode to its upper octave. Both similarly rely on the lower sixth degree of the mode in cadences, though *O Christi pietas*, unlike *Domine [...]die tue serviamus* does make use of the leading tone. While different in form, both pieces share the element of repetition and variation of structural melodic segments. The similarity between these two antiphons, combined with other formal likenesses between the St. Nicolas and St. Blaise offices, may suggest a similar date of composition, or a close imitation of the former office.

V. Later borrowings

Two canticle antiphons were later added to the Preetz St. Blaise office from other sources. The antiphon *Adest nobis celeberrimus dies* (Example 9) represents another borrowing from the Rheinau office for St. Blaise *Dum satellites*.[37] The sources from Rheinau, along with the other Austrian and southern German monastic sources that transmit the office, assign *Adest nobis celeberrimus dies* as a Magnificat antiphon. At Preetz, it was reassigned to the office of terce.

The mode 4 *Adest nobis celeberrimus dies* bears typical markers of a late style that emerged c. 1050. These include a version of the typically late modal structure built on the final, fifth, and octave of the mode, the use of recurrent formulae without any specific structural function, and extended runs and large leaps in close proximity to one another.[38]

Modally, *Adest nobis celeberrimus dies* alternates between a typical mode 4 focus on the e'-f'-g' trichord and the pitch series c'-e'-g'-a'-c''. It appears as if this latter series of pitches, used in the older mode 4 antiphons described above as a pre-cadential pitch space, took on a more central melodic function in the later mode 4 antiphon. Perhaps a peculiarity of mode 4, this pitch series, built on the sixth degree of the mode, seems to occupy the same structural role as a more typical late modal structure built on the final, fifth, and octave.

---

[35] Cantus ID 004008. See David Hiley, *Western Plainchant*, 205.
[36] Preetz, Klosterarchiv, Reihe V G1, fol.13v.
[37] Cantus ID 001267. *Adest nobis celeberrimus dies* was also borrowed into the Lübeck proper office for St. Blaise recorded in D-LÜh 6.
[38] See Roman Hankeln, 'Properization and Formal Changes', 11-21.

Example 9. Terce Antiphon *Adest nobis celeberrimus dies*, office for St. Blaise, Preetz Antiphoner (Preetz, Klosterarchiv, Reihe V G1), fol. 90r. Cantus ID 004008

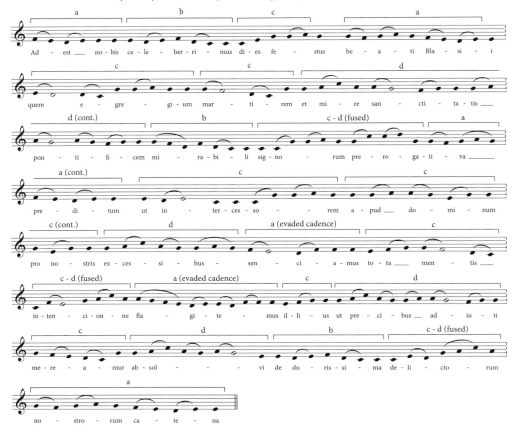

The formulaic nature of *Adest nobis celeberrimus dies* is demonstrated in Example 9. Formula (a) designates short and long forms of undertone cadence to the *finalis* of e'. Versions of this formula are found in the first phrase of the piece, and at its end. In certain cases, the formula is altered to create unexpected cadences to f'. Formula (b) consists of a cadence to c'. This cadential formula is encountered for the first time in the second phrase of the piece. Formula (c) consists of the ascent of a fifth from c' to g', often triadic, and usually ending in the pitches g'-a'-g'. The formula may be varied, inverted, or extended to include the upper octave c''. Formula (d) is essentially a decoration of a recitation on the note g', built around the kernel g'-a'-c''-a'-g'. The formula may be abbreviated or extended. The formula (c) (rising from c' to g') and (d) (decorating g') are also found fused together, elided through the note g'.

When these extended motives are mapped onto the antiphon, it becomes clear that *Adest nobis celeberrimus dies* is constructed almost exclusively of non-structural formulae that are repeated with variations: a completely different style of composition, distinct from that seen in the earliest layer of the Preetz office for St. Blaise.

Another concordance is seen in the case of the mode 4 antiphon *Adest veneranda nobis dies* assigned as the Canticle antiphon for Matins in the Preetz antiphoner[39]. In three known concordances, *Adest veneranda nobis dies* appears as a vespers antiphon for the feast of St. Martin.[40] Because this antiphon is not associated with a unique proper office for St. Martin, it is uncertain in which direction the borrowing took place. However, two points of evidence support that it was borrowed into the Preetz office, and not vice versa. First, the antiphon exists in multiple sources assigned to St. Martin, suggesting that this was its usual liturgical assignment. Second, the process of expanding a secular office to a monastic cursus would have necessitated the addition of a canticle antiphon. For these reasons, it seems more likely that *Adest veneranda nobis dies* represents a later addition to the Blaise office than an antiphon borrowed from it into the office for St. Martin.

In sum, the canticle antiphons in the Preetz Antiphoner consist of three pieces that appear to be from an original layer of composition, along with two later additions borrowed from other offices. It appears that *Adest nobis celeberrimus dies* and *Adest veneranda nobis*, together with *Domine rex eterne,* were borrowed in the expansion of an earlier secular tradition to conform to the longer monastic cursus. This is consistent with the observation that Preetz may have descended from a liturgical lineage that was not Benedictine in origin, but rather originated in a secular foundation that later adopted the Benedictine rule.[41]

VI. Matins Responsories

Due to the lacuna in the third nocturn, it is impossible to know if the series of responsories was originally modally ordered, or to determine with certainty which responsories are part of an original layer, and which may have been borrowed or newly composed in the expansion to a monastic cursus. Seven responsories survive in full, two in mode 1, and one each in modes 2, 3, 4, 6, 7, and 8. All but two of the responsory texts are adapted from the *vita* BHL 1377. The text of responsory 1.1, *Beatus Blasius Sebastea*, derives from an independent origin. Responsory 2.4, *Beatus Blasius,* given in incipit only, appears to be a contrafact of the responsory *Beatus Nicolaus jam triumpho,* which shares the same position (2.4) in the office for St. Nicholas in the Preetz Antiphoner.[42] Thus we may assume that these two responsories are later additions to the office.

The verses of the fully notated responsories are completely formulaic. The same may not be said for the responsories themselves, which contain few if any typical compositional formulae. The responses furthermore contain lengthy melismas of 21-28 notes preceding the final cadence, a marker, according to Frere, of later composition.[43]

---

[39] Cantus ID 205663.
[40] The three documented concordances for *Adest veneranda nobis dies* are: Fulda, Hessische Landesbibliothek, Hs. Aa 55 (a fourteenth- to fifteenth-century antiphoner); Erfurt, Domarchiv und Bibliothek, Hs. Liturg 6a (antiphoner, c. 1390); and Stuttgart, Württembergische Landesbibliothek, Hs. HB I. 159 (fifteenth-century breviary). For an index of the last source, see Virgil Ernst Fiala, Hermann Hauke, and Wolfgang Irtenkauf (eds.), *Die Handschriften der Württembergischen Landesbibliothek Stuttgart. Zweite Reihe. Die Handschriften der ehemaligen Königlichen Hofbibliothek*, 3 vols. (Wiesbaden, 1963-), vol. 1, pt. 2, 13.
[41] Altstatt, 'The Music and Liturgy of Kloster Preetz', 441, 537-39.
[42] Cantus ID 006222 Preetz. Klosterarchiv Reihe V G1, fol. 12r.
[43] Walter Howard Frere (ed.), *Antiphonale Sarisburiense: A Reproduction in Facsimile of a Manuscript of the Thirteenth Century* (Farnborough, 1966), 58.

The absence of typical modal formulae and the inclusion of lengthy end melismas distinguish these compositions from the earliest layer of responsory repertoire composed in a formulaic style, and from later pieces that emulate that style. Most significantly, with the exception of the responsory *Martyr Blasius iterum*, the responsories of the office for St. Blaise exhibit a compositional structure of varied repetition, a trait shared with certain responsories from the office for St. Nicholas.

Like the antiphons original to the Preetz St. Blaise office, the responsories use a similar compositional principle of repetition and variation of one or more melodic elements. For example, the mode 3 responsory *Cesus fustibus* from the Preetz office for St. Blaise, shown in Example 10, may be understood as five variations of the same essential melody.

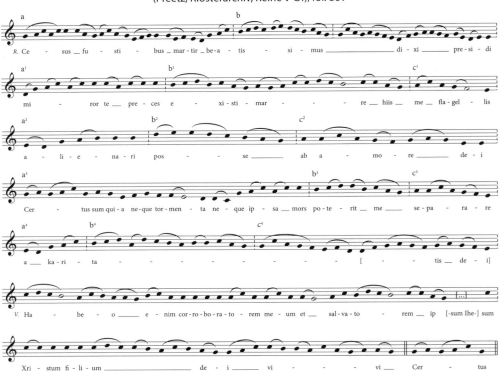

Example 10. Responsory 1.3, *Cesus fustibus*, office for St. Blaise, Preetz Antiphoner (Preetz, Klosterarchiv, Reihe V G1), fol. 86v

The underlying melodic form, built around the central pitches of *e'*, *g'*, *a'*, and *c"* consists of three phrases. Phrase (a) descends from the *finalis* of *e'* one step to *d'*, before ascending through *g'* and *a'* to the theoretical tenor of *c"*. Phrase (b) ascends and descends through the trichord of *b'-c"-d"*, before resolving to *g'*. Phrase (c) ascends momentarily from *a'* to *c"* and back, before descending via the trichord *g'-f'-e'* to a final cadence on *e'*.

Other responsories in the St. Blaise office likewise vary a single melody, or alternate between two repeated melodic segments. David Hiley has described a similar repetitive structure that orders the responsory *Lugens pie defunctum* from a Norman office for St. Mary Magdalene.[44] Certain matins responsories from the St. Nicholas office also share this structure of varied repetition, offering yet another point of comparison with the St. Blaise office.[45]

In sum, the composition of the St. Blaise office is consistent with the second epoch of chant composition, c. 850-1050. Its formal and stylistic similarities to the St. Nicholas office suggest a more specific date of the late tenth century. The St. Blaise office represents an example of the trend towards modal ordering in office composition that originated in northeast France and was transmitted northward to Metz and into the Rhineland. The evidence suggests that this office, and possibly the congregation of nuns in whose antiphoner it was preserved, also originated in the Rhineland. Further research is needed to test this hypothesis.

Figure 5. Proper office *Universa plebs fidelis* for St. Matthias, Preetz Antiphoner

---

[44] Hiley, 'Early Cycles of Office Chants', 381, 383 Example 14.3a, 398. While Hiley does not offer a date of composition for the Norman series, he implies that its composition may have been contemporaneous with abbacies of such German-born authors as Isembert, abbot of St. Cathérine-du-Mont, Rouen (1033-54) and Ainard, abbot of St. Pierre-sur-Dives (1046-48).

[45] See, for example, R. *Qui cum audissent sancti* from the St. Nicholas office, Cantus ID 007474.

VII. A Late Addition: The office *Universa plebs fidelis*

I will now turn briefly to the second unusual proper office contained in the Preetz Antiphoner, the historia *Universa plebs fidelis* for St. Matthias. As reproduced in Figure 5, the office was notated on a single bifolio that was awkwardly inserted into the original manuscript in the middle of the Office for St. Gregory. The second leaf of the bifolio is lost.

In a recent study, Zsuzsa Czagány has shown that the historia *Universa plebs fidelis* was likely written in Trier between 1309 and 1329, with the first manuscript instantiation dating to 1345. Versions of the office survive in three Trier sources, one each from Liège and Hildesheim, as well as six sources from Prague.[46] In the Preetz Antiphoner, the office appears to have been expanded to a monastic cursus with additions from the common of apostles. What can account for the addition of *Universa plebs fidelis* to the Preetz Antiphoner? I suggest that the most likely explanation is that the office was transmitted to the convent during the period of contact with the Bursfeld reform in the late fifteenth century, a movement that drew heavily on previous reform efforts that took place at St. Matthias Abbey in Trier.[47] Kloster Preetz was reformed through the nearby men's house of Kloster Cismar, a founding member of the union from 1449, providing a *terminus post quem* for the adoption of the St. Matthias office into the Preetz liturgy.

Conclusion

Numerous strands of evidence point to a Rhenish inheritance in the musical repertoire of Kloster Preetz. First, the scribal evidence supports the argument that the cloister maintained its own scriptorium and developed a distinctive house style, adapted from an earlier tradition of Rhenish notation. Second, as witnessed in the tenth-century office for St. Blaise, the convent inherited at least one proper office influenced by the modally ordered offices of Stephen of Liège and Reginold of Eichstätt, suggesting another point of contact with Rhineland repertoires. Judging by the date and origin of the added material, it appears that the office was adapted to a monastic cursus no earlier than the twelfth century, possibly coinciding with the community's adoption of the Benedictine rule. This suggests that we might search for the origins of Kloster Preetz, a convent whose motherhouse has never been identified, in a foundation of canonesses from the western part of the German-speaking region. A final phase of Rhenish musical influence visible in the Preetz Antiphoner likely occurred during the Bursfeld reform, as evidenced by the addition into the Preetz Antiphoner of the proper office *Universa plebs fidelis* for St. Matthias.

---

[46] Zsuzsa Czagány, 'Historia sancti Mathiae apostoli. Wege eines spätmittelalterlichen Reimoffiziums zwischen Prag und Trier', in *Papers Read at the Thirteenth Meeting of the IMS Study Group Cantus*, ed. Barbara Haggh and László Dobszay (Budapest, 2009), 143-56. A third manuscript source from Trier may be added to the two identified by Czagány: the fifteenth-century notated breviary Trier, Bistumsarchiv, Hs. 480, 370-76.

[47] Johannes Dederoth, abbot of Klus, was charged in 1433 with the reform of Bursfeld Abbey. He visited St. Matthias Abbey in Trier in 1434 to ask the advice of Abbot Johannes Rode, and returned with four monks from St. Matthias, along with their reformed *consuetudines*, to revitalize the communities of Klus and Bursfeld. While there is no direct evidence that *Universa plebs fidelis* for St. Matthias was transmitted at this time, this seems a likely explanation for the entry of the office into the Preetz repertoire. See Pegeen Mary Connolly, 'Servare Unitatem in Vinculo Pacis: The First Century of the Bursfeld Congregation, 1433-1530' (Ph.D. diss., University of California, Los Angeles, 1999), 68-70.

Abstract

This paper examines the fifteenth-century antiphoner Preetz, Klosterarchiv Reihe V G1, from the former Benedictine convent of Preetz in the diocese of Lübeck. Scribal evidence and elements of the convent's musical repertoire together indicate that the community's musical roots lead back to the Rhineland. The convent appears to have maintained its own scriptorium that developed a distinctive adaptation of an earlier Rhenish notational tradition. A previously unknown office for St. Blaise represents the oldest layer of the convent's repertoire. Its hagiographic narrative prose texts, the modal ordering of its antiphons, its adaptation of established antiphon melodies into the form of the 'double antiphon', and the non-formulaic composition of its responsories confirm that the office for St. Blaise belongs to the second stratum of office composition (c. 850-1050.) The office appears to have been adapted from a secular cursus to Benedictine usage, possibly indicating that the predecessor of the Preetz community was a secular foundation that later adopted the Benedictine rule. The addition into the Preetz antiphoner of the proper office *Universa plebs fidelis* for St. Matthias that originated in Trier may reflect a final phase of Rhenish musical influence that took place during the Bursfeld Reform of the late fifteenth century.

The Relationship between the Festal Office and the New Sequence: Evidence from Medieval Picardy

Lori Kruckenberg

The 'new sequence' emerged in the final decades of the eleventh and first half of the twelfth century as a poetic and musical renewal of a long-established proper chant of the mass.[1] These new specimens of the genre demonstrate that their poet-composers turned to accentual verse for technical and formal inspiration and away from a pre-existing melody as the structural source and supplier of the text. Furthermore, the authors of these new works sought out different approaches to modality, melodic vocabulary, text-music relationships, and the established structural conventions. While scholars have looked closely at stylistic developments in the new sequence, they have given far less attention to the contexts giving rise to these pieces, their individual transmission histories, their likely places of origin, and their specific liturgical uses.[2]

In this essay, I will introduce *Celeste organum* from c. 1100,[3] a new sequence whose context and transmission history point to the area of modern-day northeast France and southwest Belgium—roughly medieval Picardy—as a likely region of origin. Moreover, in a handful of its earliest witnesses, *Celeste organum* had particularly strong ties to the

---

[1] The older secondary literature on the sequence divided the history of the genre into three basic chronological-stylistic categories: (1) artistic prose style or *Kunstprosa* of the first epoch (roughly before 1050); (2) transitional style of an intermediary phase (roughly 1050-1150); and (3) the rhymed, rhythmic poetry of the second epoch (after 1150). More recent scholarship treats the so-called transitional sequence and the second-epoch rhymed sequence as belonging to a common initiative. As Margot Fassler has noted, the twelfth-century sequence connected to Paris represents 'only the most famous of the poetic styles that emerged from the various late eleventh- and twelfth-century experiments in writing rhythmic poetry'; see 'Who Was Adam of St. Victor? The Evidence of the Sequence Manuscripts', in *Journal of the American Musicological Society* 37 (1984), 237, n. 20. See also Lori Kruckenberg, 'The Sequence from 1050-1150: Study of a Genre in Change' (Ph.D. diss., University of Iowa, 1997); eadem, 'Two *Sequentiae novae* at Nidaros: *Celeste organum* and *Stola iocunditatis*', in *The Sequences of Nidaros: A Nordic Repertory and Its European Context*, ed. Lori Kruckenberg and Andreas Haug (Trondheim, 2006), 297-342. In the latter, I use 'new sequence' to draw attention to stylistic traits similar to those found in the contemporaneous 'new song' tradition. See below n. 4.

[2] Scholarship focusing on contexts, origins, and especially the transmission of new sequences can be found in Kruckenberg, 'The Sequence from 1050-1150', 226-79, 337-407; eadem, 'Two *Sequentiae novae* at Nidaros'; and Philipp Zimmermann, 'Zur Überlieferung der Sequenz *Sacrosancta hodierne festivitatis preconia* nach Nidaros,' in *The Sequences of Nidaros*, ed. Kruckenberg and Haug, 341-65. Fassler offers a rich evaluation of the ecclesiastical and re-form-related milieu connected to the regular, rhymed type of new sequences found in Paris in *Gothic Song: Victorine Sequences and Augustinian Reform in Twelfth-Century Paris* (Notre Dame, ²2011). Wulf Arlt's study on the new sequence *Letabundus exultet fideles chorus*, moreover, serves as model of tracking dissemination and ensuing changes. His study is also one of the first to call for a rewriting of 'the history of the sequence in the central and late Middle Ages'. See Arlt, 'Sequence and *Neues Lied*', in *La sequenza medievale: Atti del convegno internazionale, Milano, 7-8 aprile 1984*, ed. Agostino Ziino (Lucca, 1992), 3-18, esp. 17.

[3] I published an earlier case study on *Celeste organum* as it relates specifically to its reception and likely path of transmission to the archdiocese of Nidaros. In this earlier study, I consulted forty sources, especially concentrating on England (the likely supplier for the Nidaros tradition) as well as several sources from modern-day France. For the present article, I have examined seventy-six readings of *Celeste organum* (nearly double the previous study), and my interests here take into account the possible origins of the work, and its overall paths of dissemination, rather than concentrating on its relationship to the Nordic tradition. See Kruckenberg, 'Two *Sequentiae novae* at Nidaros', 371-87.

Divine Office rather than to the mass, the normal liturgical locus of the genre. The office hours in question were especially vespers and matins of what are called the festal offices (*Festoffizien*), especially the clerics' offices occurring between Christmas and the octave of Epiphany; other special Christmastide commemorations come into the frame as well. To this end, I will offer some brief observations concerning the textual, melodic, and liturgical histories of several other new sequences denoting an attachment to votive liturgies and clerics' offices emanating from medieval Picardy.

This study will offer evidence showing that when and where new sequences were sung is often a good predictor of the degree of musical novelty discernible in these pieces. When assigned to clerics' festivals—including the controversial Feast of the Fools—their 'newfangledness' is most evident, for these new sequences more closely resemble *Benedicamus domino* tropes, versus, conductus, and other Latin songs than earlier sequences. Votive chants like *Benedicamus domino* tropes, versus, conductus, and other Latin songs—known collectively as 'new songs' or *nova cantica* (to use the coinage of Wolfram von den Steinen and popularized by Wulf Arlt)—were strongly connected to and identified with the festal offices and other special liturgies of Christmastide. Certain new-style sequences might be viewed, then, as counterparts to the new songs, as 'novae sequentiae' to the 'nova cantica'.[4] When assigned as the single sequence of a given mass, tamer versions of that sequence are in evidence, with these redactions looking and sounding more like the genre's forebears. The detachment of new sequences from the festal offices and other special liturgical occasions, then, and a reassertion of the mass as the genre's appropriate liturgical locus would seem to accompany the stylistic 'domestication' of these works. Their early association with the oft-derided special post-Christmas celebrations suggests that the more 'permissive' environment of these liturgies (or paraliturgies) provided the creators of new sequences a venue for renewing and reinventing the genre, and safe harbour for singing the 'nova sequentia'.

A New Sequence of c. 1100: The Example of *Celeste organum*

In order to understand what constitutes the new sequence, let us begin by looking at one such example in depth, that of *Celeste organum* (Example 1). *Celeste organum* bears all the marks of the new understanding of the genre around 1100. First, its text was clearly conceived as poetic verse that was then set to a new melody. Various types of rhythmic stress—imitative of trochaic verse interspersed with iambs and dactyls—are present, and these versified units are further marked off by rhymes. Couplet 10a/b, for instance, is organized as pair of trochaic septenarii (i.e., twice 8p+7pp); these versicles are framed

---

[4] Wolfram von den Steinen used the phrase 'das neue Lied' in *Der Kosmos des Mittelalters: Von Karl dem Grossen zu Bernhard von Clairvaux* (Bern, 1967), 231-52, and Wulf Arlt has subsequently rendered the term *novum canticum* or (the plural form *nova cantica*) in writings such as 'Sequence and *Neues Lied*'; idem, 'Das eine Lied und die vielen Lieder: Zur historischen Stellung der neuen Liedkunst des frühen 12. Jahrhunderts', in *Festschrift Rudolf Bockholdt zum 60. Geburtstag*, ed. Norbert Dubowy and Sören Meyer-Eller (Pfaffenhofen, 1990), 113-27; idem, 'Neues zum neuen Lied: Die Fragmente aus der Handschrift Douai 246', in *Sine musica nulla disciplina...Studi in onore di Giulio Cattin*, ed. Franco Bernabei and Antonio Lovato (Padua, 2006), 89-110. See also Gunilla Björkvall and Andreas Haug, 'Altes Lied - Neues Lied: Thesen zur Transformation des lateinischen Liedes um 1100', in *Poesía latina medieval (siglos V-XV): Actas del IV Congreso del "Internationales Mittellateinerkomitee", Santiago de Compostela, 12-15 de septiembre de 2002*, ed. Manuel C. Díaz y Díaz and José M. Díaz de Bustamante (Florence, 2005), 539-50.

not only by the concluding rhymes of 'ecclesia' and 'vitia', but also with each 8p unit subdivided as 4p+4p, and marked with the internal rhymes 'maris'-'paris' and 'nostra'-'pia':[5]

/	-	/	-	/	-	/	-	/	-	(/)	-	/	-	-
Stel-	la	ma-	ris	Quem	tu	pa-	ris	co-	lit	hunc	ec-	cle-	si-	a
Ip-	si	nos-	tra	Per	te	pi-	a	pla-	ce-	ant	ser-	vi-	ti-	a

In addition to the more traditional '-a' assonance that rings throughout this text, the writer has delighted in setting off his poetic segments with a variety of single syllable and two-syllable rhymes as with 'sonuit'-'cecinit', 'homo'-'caro', 'gregum'-'ortum', 'dona'-'bona', 'data'-'prolata', 'divisa'-'promissa', and 'maris'-'paris'. These poetic effects serve as reminders that the author has moved away from the artistic prose style *(Kunstprosa)* so common to early sequences of the ninth through eleventh centuries. In *Celeste organum*, the rendering of the normal three-syllable 'bethleem' in 8b as a two-syllable 'bethlem' (or 'bellem' in the Laon version represented in Example 1) denotes that even small matters of versification—here syllable count and rhythmic stress—guided the poet's choices in writing the text.

While the author certainly approached the text with versification in mind, he also took care to preserve the structural essence of the genre, with the coupling of versicles often articulated in syntactic and semantic pairings. For instance, the paired questions of versicle 3a ('Quid facis humana turba? Cur non gaudes cum supera?') are countered by short declarative bursts of 3b ('Vigilat pastorum cura; vox auditur angelica'). In 5a and 5b the versicles are launched by the negation words 'Nec' and 'Non' respectively, while 7a and 7b begin with the twin phrases 'Gaude homo' and 'Gaude caro'. The word order of 8a and 8b is strikingly similar as well. Overall, tight poetic construction indicates the text to be the starting point of this chant.

The melody of *Celeste organum* is new to the musical tradition of the genre as well. First of all, the tune is not found among the repertorial core of first-epoch melodic families. More indicative, the fluctuating note-syllable ratios and thorough eschewing of syllabicism demonstrate that the compositional procedure was not one of texting a pre-existing melody.

---

[5] For a point of contrast, one can compare a similar juncture (i.e., the closing versicles) of a sequence in the early style. For instance, the final versicles (9a, 9b, and 10) of *Ecce iam votiva festa*, a 'prosulation' to the well-known sequence tune known variously as MATER, MUSA, CHRISTI HODIERNA, and SIRENA, read: 'Naturam dum hominis induit deitas / Non tamen diminuens deitatem suam / Conserva hec quesumus Christe nobis munera tanta a te prerogata'. Though there is a strong use of a-assonance here and throughout the entire text, from the point of view of prosody, the text of *Ecce iam votiva festa* is devoid of regular stress patterns and dissyllabic rhymes. When analysing medieval Latin prosody, scholars commonly use paroxytone and proparoxytone to denote words or verse, versicle or phrase endings having an acute accent on the penultimate syllable and the antepenultimate syllable, respectively; by extension, verses and verse units ending with paroxytonic and proparoxtonic accents are represented by 'p' and 'pp'. For a thorough discussion and application of these and related terms see the seminal study: Dag Norberg, *An Introduction to the Study of Medieval Latin Versification*, trans. Grant C. Roti and Jacqueline de La Chapelle Skubly and ed. with an introduction by Jan Ziolkowski (Washington D.C., 2004); originally published as *Introduction à l'étude de la versification latine médiévale* (Stockholm, 1958).

Example 1. *Celeste organum* in Laon, Bibliothèque municipale, fols. 125r-126r

The oldest extant version of *Celeste organum* is found in Ms. 78 of the Médiathèque municipale in Cambrai [F-CA 78], a source copied before 1100, perhaps by 1092 (see Figure 1).[6]

---

[6] For the most recent assessment, see Denis Muzerelle (ed.), *Manuscrits datés des bibliothèques de France. I Cambrai* (Paris, 2000), 15. Muzerelle dates F-CA 78 as 'XIe s., fin'. The presence of certain sequences in this manuscript suggests that its primary copying occurred between 1087 and 1092. For instance, the presence of *Congaudentes exultemus*, a sequence for Nicholas, makes F-CA 78 one of the earliest, if not the earliest, extant witnesses to this chant. Although sequences for St. Nicholas are occasionally found before 1087, the spectacular *translatio* of the saint's relics in that year clearly sparked the advance of his rapidly growing cult in the Latin West and possibly the composition of *Congaudentes exultemus*. Moreover, the ambitious collection of sequences in F-CA 78, and the main scribe's clear juggling of multiple exemplars recommend that the contents were far more likely to have been assembled and copied during the favourable conditions of the episcopacy of Gerard II (bishop 1076-92), whose tenure oversaw the reconstruction of

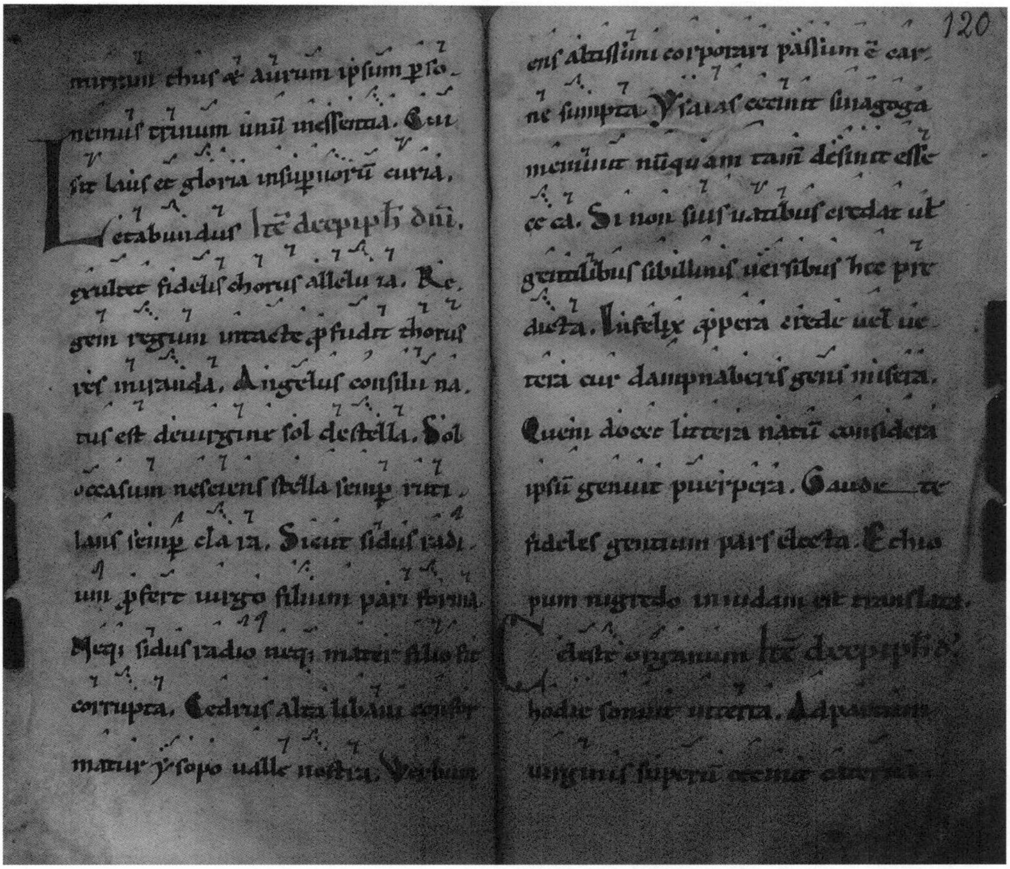

Figure 1. The new sequences *Letabundus exultet fidelis chorus* and the beginning of *Celeste organum* in Cambrai, Médiathèque municipale, Ms. 78, fols. 119v-120r

Although this Cambrai reading is adiastematic, the partial heightening of the neumation allows for a secure comparison (if not a solid reconstruction) when compared to the fifty-five diastematic readings thus far collected and consulted.[7] Example 1 presents the reading from Ms. 263 from Laon, Bibliothèque municipale [F-LA 263], a late twelfth-century codex from Laon cathedral. The version in F-LA 263 represents an early diastematic concordance, and its text and musical readings are quite representative of the Cambrai tradition.

Based on the seventy-six readings (notated and unnotated) of *Celeste organum* thus far compiled, transcribed, and analyzed, nearly the whole of this sequence's

cathedral and enlargement of fortifications, the building and endowing of several abbeys in the diocese, the strengthening of episcopal holdings, and the flourishing scribal activity in the Cambrai scriptorium of St-Sépulchre. Beginning in 1093/94, the episcopal stability of Cambrai eroded precipitously, with opposing candidates representing papal and imperial interests. The dispute lasted from 1093-1105 and beyond, and resulted in the siege of Cambrai and the authoritative as well as economic decline of the bishopric. Thus, I propose conditions more conducive to the creation of this book likely took place before 1093. For a description of the sequence repertory in F-CA 78 and the multiple exemplars, see Kruckenberg, 'The Sequence from 1050-1150', 189-225.

7   Of the seventy-six readings of *Celeste organum*, sixty-two are notated, fourteen are unnotated. Of the sixty-two notated readings, fifty-five are diastematic, seven are adiastematic.

transmission can be securely divided into two basic groups, hereafter labelled the 'alpha' (α) and 'beta' (β) traditions.[8] These two main traditions can be further subdivided, but let us begin by first identifying the primary features of the basic α and β groups. The primary distinguishing features for these traditions are both of a textual and melodic nature. Table 1 presents a summary of the principal textual indicators.

Table 1. Summary of significant text variants between α and β sources

	α readings	β readings
Versicle 8a	'ethera' or 'sidera'	'sidera'
Versicle 8b	'subeunt'	'ineunt'
Versicle 9b	'cingit'	'fecit'
Conclusion	Couplet 10a/b or coda 'Iam dicantur...'	Coda 'Resonent cuncta...'

As can be seen in Table 1, toward the end of *Celeste organum*, the two traditions show strong preferences for particular verbal choices: α versions typically give the verbs 'subeunt' in 8b and 'cingit' in 9b to the β's employment of 'ineunt' and 'fecit' in the equivalent places. The β sources consistently give the adjective 'sidera' in 8a, while most (but not all) α readings present 'ethera'. Beta sources dependably conclude the sequence with some version of the coda phrase 'Resonent cuncta redempta amen'. Almost all of the α sources either conclude with versicle 10b, 'Ipsi nostra per te pia placeant servitia', or offer some version of the coda phrase 'Iam dicantur alia'.

Particular melodic readings similarly corroborate the basic α-β divisions. On two occasions in *Celeste organum* (couplets 5 and 6), the α sources demonstrate more florid musical treatment than the β ones. Thus, in the first half of 5a/5b, the setting of the syllables 'sunt'/-'lu'- is strikingly more melismatic in the α reading, typified by Abbeville, Bibliothèque Municipale, Ms. 7 [F-AB 7] compared to that in the representative β source, Sens, Bibliothèque Municipale, Ms. 46 [F-SEm 46] (see Example 2).

Example 2. Comparison of α and β readings in couplet 5

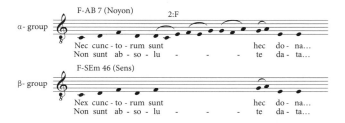

In the closing phrase of couplet 6, the α reading of F-LA 263, for instance, has a great deal more surface detail than the purely syllabic rendering in the β version of F-SEm 46 (Example 3).

---

[8] As will be discussed in due course, there are a few exceptions to these basic α and β groupings, signalling a contact with both traditions and as a result, a mixing of textual and melodic variants.

Example 3. Comparison of α and β readings in couplet 6

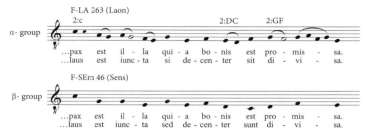

Moreover, in the α readings in general, the melodic setting shows greater variety on the concluding eight syllables of couplets 4, 5, and 6 respectively (Example 4).

Example 4. Cadential ending of couplets 4, 5, and 6 in the α source F-LA 263

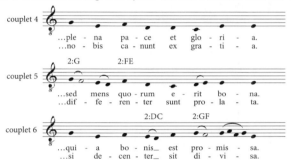

The β sources, by contrast, tend to show a uniform treatment of the concluding eight syllables of these three successive paired versicles (Example 5).

Example 5. Cadential ending of couplets 4, 5, and 6 in the β source F-SEm 46

In versicles 9a/b however, it is the β sources that record a slightly more elaborate treatment of text (Example 6), while most α sources, here represented by Brussels, Bibliothèque Royale, II 3823 (Fétis 1172) [B-BR 3823] from Souvigny for Sauxillanges, present a flattened melodic contour.

Example 6. Comparison of α and β readings of couplet 9

THE RELATIONSHIP BETWEEN THE FESTAL OFFICE AND THE NEW SEQUENCE ■ 207

Moreover, in the β sources, couplet 9 commences on *c* (not shown here), while the α sources typically begin a third lower on *a* (as can be seen in Example 1 above). In versicle pair 10a/b the β sources invariably present the cadential figure *F-F-F-D-E-E-E*. The α readings, by contrast, present a variety of melodic treatments of this couplet. Table 2 serves as a summary of these melodic distinctions.

Table 2. Summary of significant musical variants between α and β sources

	α readings	β readings
Versicles 5a/b	Florid setting of 'sunt (hec)/-lu(te)'	Syllabic setting of 'sunt (hec)/-lu(te)'
Versicles 4a–6b	Cadential endings of couplets 4, 5, and 6 are often distinct from one another	Uniform endings of versicle pairs 4, 5, and 6
Versicles 6a/b	Greater melodic inflection for the recitational figure of the first 9 syllables	Often less melodic inflection for the recitational figure of the first 9 syllables
Versicles 6a/b	More florid setting of final 12 syllables	Syllabic setting of final 12 syllables
Versicles 9a/b	The phrases 'Invenitur rex celorum/Arto iacet in presepi' begin on an *a* and end on an *F*	The phrases 'Invenitur rex celorum/Arto iacet in presepi' begin on a *c* and end on an *E*
Versicles 9a/b	Syllabic setting of 'inter animalia/rex qui cingit omnia'; also different contour from β	Florid setting of 'inter animalia/rex qui fecit omnia'; also different contour from α
Versicles 10a/b	A range of melodic treatments of 'colit hunc [hec] ecclesia/placeant servitia'	A consistent setting (*F-F-F-D-E-E-E*) of 'colit hunc [hec] ecclesia/placeant servitia'

In addition to the melodic variants given above, on the whole the α readings tend to present far more surface detail than the relatively syllabic melodies of the β ones.

The distribution of α and β readings is largely a regional one. The α tradition can be found throughout modern-day France, Spain, and Switzerland. There is also one α reading attested to in England, two in Germany, and one in Bratislava. The β tradition is concentrated at Sens cathedral (though an α version is found at the Benedictine abbey of St-Pierre-le-Vif in Sens). The β tradition is also found throughout England, in the archdiocese of Nidaros (modern-day Norway and Iceland), and in the house of Augustinian canons in Seckau (Austria).

The question arises then: which version, α or β, has priority? Which tradition more closely resembles the earliest manifestation of this new kind of sequence? From the melodic perspective, was the more syllabic melody of the β tradition subsequently ornamented—sometimes more, sometimes less—to render the readings among the α group? Or was *Celeste organum* conceived of as a more florid chant like those of the α tradition, and subsequently simplified to produce the β tradition? Are there any verbal variants suggesting one of the traditions to be a deviation from the other?

Fortunately the word choices in two places in the text of *Celeste organum* give some hint. In versicle 8b, the reading 'subeunt' of the α tradition can be argued to be the better word to the slightly awkward 'ineunt' of the β version. With the α reading 'cingit' in versicle 9b we have arguably an example of a *lectio difficilior* to the perfectly acceptable but more mundane 'fecit' of the β sources. Melodically the α reading on the syllables 'sunt'/'-lu-' of couplet 5a/b (given above) might be viewed as the more challenging gesture than that of the β, hence the α group presents a musical *lectio difficilior* as well. Overall, in couplets 4, 5, and 6 of the α tradition (see Example 4), distinct cadential approaches are found at the end of the pairs. By contrast, at the same junctures in the β readings, the cadential approaches in these three couplets are undifferentiated, suggesting signs of levelling.

The external evidence of the witnesses further bolsters the primacy of the α tradition. By conservative estimates, no fewer than a dozen α sources can be securely dated to before c. 1200; their places of origin range from northern, central, and southern France as well as Spain and Worcester. By contrast, the earliest β sources date to c. 1200 and come from the Augustinian house at Seckau (Hs. 479, Hs. 1584, and Hs. 769, all in the Universitätsbibliothek in Graz [A-Gu 479, A-Gu 1584, and A-Gu 769]). The oldest β sources from Sens cathedral are just a little later, dating to the first half of the thirteenth century; they are Sens, Bibliothèque Municipale, Ms. 46 [F-SEm 46] and Paris, Bibliothèque Nationale de France, Fonds latin 10502 [F-Pn lat. 10502].[9] Thus, taken together, the internal evidence of the musical and verbal texts (including consideration of the melodic *lectio difficilior* and the textual *lectio difficilior*) and the external evidence of the readings (relative antiquity of sources and relative diversity of geographical transmission) point to the α tradition as the primary one, the β as the secondary one.

From the forty-five α concordances thus far collated, is it possible to pinpoint the place, or at least region, of origin of *Celeste organum*? Of these forty-five readings, two are clear outliers and will be excluded from further consideration in the present study.[10] On the whole, however, the α readings can be divided into four distinct subgroups. These subgroupings are largely regional in nature, and will be designated accordingly as α-north, α-central, α-south, and α-east. Before we consider the melodic and textual differences between the four α subgroups, let us take note of their sources and provenances.

Sources and Provenances for the α-North Version of *Celeste organum*

The first subgroup of the α tradition—hereafter designated as α-north—is made up of seven concordances: two from Cambrai, one from Laon, two from Beauvais, one from

---

[9] The earliest extant β witnesses from England date to the mid or second half of the thirteenth century; these include Cambridge, University Library, Add. 710 [GB-Cu 710]; Manchester, John Rylands Library, lat. 24 [GB-Mr 24]; and Oxford, University College Ms. 148 [GB-Ouc 148].

[10] These are Bratislava, Archív mesta Bratislavy, E.C. lat. 3/EL 18, a missal dated to before the year 1341, and from Bratislava (Pressburg) [SK-Brm E.C. lat. 3/EL 18]: fol. 331r; and Munich, Bayerische Staatsbibliothek, clm. 23027, from the fifteenth century, of unknown origin (possibly with a German Carmelite affiliation) [D-Mbs clm. 23027]: fols. 148v-149r. While these sources' respective readings of *Celeste organum* were clearly derived from the α tradition (probably the α-central one), several textual and melodic variants demonstrate notable independence from the general α tradition. For more on SK-Brm E.C. lat. 3/EL 18, see Janka Szendrei and Richard Rybarič (eds.), *Missale notatum Strigoniense ante 1341 in Posonio*, Musicalia Danubiana 1 (Budapest, 1982).

Noyon, and a source once used at the Church of the Holy Sepulchre in Jerusalem, but presumably drawing on a tradition from somewhere in northern France (see Table 3).[11]

Table 3. Sources of the α-north tradition

RISM siglum	Source	Provenance and date
F-AB 7	Abbeville, Bibliothèque Municipale, Ms. 7, fols. 10v-11r	Noyon cathedral, 1240-1260
F-CA 78	Cambrai, Médiathèque Municipale, Ms. 78, fols. 120r-121r	Cambrai cathedral, late 11th century (1087-92?)
F-CA 60	Cambrai, Médiathèque Municipale, Ms. 60, fols. 125r-v	Cambrai cathedral, c. 1100-25
F-LA 263	Laon, Bibliothèque Municipale, Ms. 263, fols. 125r-126r	Laon cathedral, c. 1173-87
F-Pn lat. 1140	Paris, Bibliothèque Nationale de France, Fonds latin 1140, fols. 35r-v	Beauvais, 15th century
GB-Lbl 2615	London, British Library, Egerton 2615, fols. 21r-22r	Beauvais cathedral, 1227-34
I-Ra 477	Rome, Biblioteca Angelica, Ms. 477, fols. 198v-199r	N. France (?) for Church of the Holy Sepulchre in Jerusalem, 12th century (c. 1140?)

While the α-north tradition is comprised of a relatively small group of sources, it is distinguished by claiming the two earliest extant readings of *Celeste organum*: the late eleventh-century F-CA 78 and the early twelfth-century F-CA 60. Two more manuscripts have been dated to the twelfth century: I-Ra 477, for Jerusalem, c. 1140; and F-LA 263, from Laon cathedral, c. 1173-1187. Two are from the thirteenth-century, GB-Lbl 2615 from Beauvais, and F-AB 7 from Noyon, while the youngest source is from fifteenth-century Beauvais (F-Pn lat. 1140).

None of the α-north sources are connected to Benedictine traditions: four of the five institutions represented are cathedrals (Cambrai, Laon, Beauvais, and Noyon), and the fifth a secular church with Augustinian canons. With the exception of the Jerusalem source and its unknown place of origin, the provenances of the α-north sources are confined to the northeast corner of modern-day France.

Sources and Provenances for the α-Central Version of *Celeste organum*

The α-central sources constitute by far the largest subgroup of the α tradition with, thus far, nineteen readings identified (see Table 4).

---

[11] It is uncertain where this manuscript was copied, but both notation and concordances of certain items in the sequentiary suggest an origin in north France, possibly with Norman connections.

Table 4. Sources of the α-central tradition

RISM siglum	Source	Provenance and date
B-Br II 3823	Brussels, Bibliothèque Royale, II 3823 (Fétis 1172), fols. 158v-159v	Souvigny for Sauxillanges, 12th century
F-AM 132	Amiens, Bibliothèque Municipale, Ms. 132, fols. 5v-6v	Celestine Priory of Sts. Antoine and Martin, Amiens, 16th century
F-AUT S 10	Autun, Bibliothèque Municipale, Ms. S 10 (8), fols. 36v-37r (first entry)	Autun, 12th century; additions 15th century
F-AUT S 10	Autun, Bibliothèque Municipale, Ms. S 10 (8), fol. 297v (second entry)	Autun, 12th century; additions 15th century
F-AUT S 143	Autun, Bibliothèque Municipale, Ms. S 143, II, fols. 3r-4r	Autun, 15th century (2nd half)
F-CF 62	Clermont-Ferrand, Bibliothèque Municipale et Interuniversitaire, Ms. 62 (57), fols. 11r-v	Clermont, 13th century
F-E 124	Épinal, Bibliothèque Intercommunale Épinal-Golbey, Ms. 124 (20), fol. 251r	Toul *usus*, Abbey of Saint-Pierre of Senones, 15th century
F-O 129	Orléans, Bibliothèque Municipale, Ms. 129, fol. 144v-145r	Fleury-sur-Loire, 1218-1238
F-Pn lat. 865[A]	Paris, Bibliothèque Nationale de France, Fonds latin 865[A], pp. 716-717	Troyes, 15th century
F-Pn lat. 1086	Paris, Bibliothèque Nationale de France, Fonds latin 1086, fols. 28v-30r	St-Léonard-de-Noblat, c.1200
F-Pn lat. 1087	Paris, Bibliothèque Nationale de France, Fonds latin 1087, fols. 118r-v	Cluny, 11th century (last quarter); additions 12th century (1st quarter)
F-Pn lat. 1119	Paris, Bibliothèque Nationale de France, Fonds latin 1119, fol. 3v	St-Martial; mid 11th century; additions 12th century (2nd half)/c.1200
F-Pn lat. 1139	Paris, Bibliothèque Nationale de France, Fonds latin 1139, fols. 151r-152v	Aquitaine, c. 1200; in St-Martial by 13th century (1st quarter)
F-Pn lat. 13252	Paris, Bibliothèque Nationale de France, Fonds latin 13252, fols. 65v-66r	St-Magloire, end 11th/ start 12th century; additions mid 12th century
F-Pn n.a.lat. 1871	Paris, Bibliothèque Nationale de France, Nouv. acq. latin 1871, fol. 99v	St-Pierre of Moissac, 11th century (3rd quarter); additions 13th century
F-SEm 18	Sens, Bibliothèque Municipale, Ms. 18, pp. 349-50	St-Pierre-le-Vif of Sens, 13th century
GB-Lbl A.xiv	London, British Library, Cotton Caligula, Ms. A.xiv, fols. 44v-45r	Worcester, 12th century (2nd half)
I-Ac 695	Assisi, Biblioteca del Sacro Convento, Ms. 695, fols. 63r-v	Reims, later Paris, 1230s
I-Tn D. I.7	Turin, Biblioteca Nazionale Universitaria, D. I.7, fols. 348r-v	Amiens, 15th century

As can be seen in Table 4, the Autun manuscript F-AUT S 10 reports two entries of *Celeste organum*, a scribal detail the importance of which will become apparent in due course.

Save for the α-north's Jerusalem witness, the regional reach of the α-central tradition is far wider than that of α-north sources tradition with α-central readings from Amiens, St-Magloire in Paris, and Reims in the north; Toul in the east; and Moissac in the south. While the α-central tradition spans much of modern-day France, the strongest concentration is found between the Loire Valley, Burgundy, Auvergne, and Limousin, with representatives from Fleury-sur-Loire, St-Pierre-le-Vif of Sens, Cluny, Autun, Clermont, Souvigny for Sauxillanges, St-Léonard-de-Noblat, and St-Martial. One α-central source, GB-Lbl A.xiv, is from Worcester, and while it is the only non-β source in England thus far identified, it is also the earliest extant testimony to the presence of *Celeste organum* in the British Isles.

The relatively broad dissemination of the α-central version may have been aided in part by the reform network connected to Cluny: sometime between 1130 and 1146, Peter the Venerable, abbot of Cluny, mandated in his statutes the adoption of *Celeste organum* for the second mass of Christmas Day.[12] Indeed, the oldest known α-central reading of *Celeste organum* is as a twelfth-century addendum entered on a formerly empty folio near the end of F-Pn lat. 1087, a late eleventh-century gradual from Cluny. Other α-central sources with a Cluniac affiliation include B-Br II 3823, copied at the Cluniac priory of Souvigny for the Cluniac abbey at Sauxillanges; F-SEm 18 for the abbey of St-Pierre-le-Vif in Sens; F-Pn lat. 1119 and F-Pn lat. 1139 from St-Martial; and F-Pn n.a.lat. 1871 from St-Pierre-de-Moissac.[13]

A handful of the α-central sources can be dated to the twelfth century, all about a generation or more later than the two earliest extant α-north sources from Cambrai. What further distinguishes several of the oldest α-central readings from the four oldest α-north readings is that, with the former, *Celeste organum* was often added to chant books at a later time, frequently without any rubric or liturgical assignment. This is the case with F-Pn lat. 1087, F-Pn lat. 13252 (from St-Magloire), F-Pn lat. 1119, as well as F-Pn n.a.lat. 1871; the liturgical assignment of the added rubric of F-Pn lat. 1139 is surely a mistake. Furthermore, some of these earliest readings are incomplete (as in the case of F-Pn lat. 1119 and GB-Lbl A.xiv), while the version in F-Pn lat. 13252 breaks off, with later hands completing both text and music. By contrast, of the four α-north readings dating from the late eleventh or twelfth centuries, none are added entries or incomplete. The external source evidence for the earliest α-central sources strongly suggests that *Celeste organum* was a relative newcomer to the twelfth-century liturgical traditions at Cluny,

---

[12] Giles Constable (ed.), *Consuetudines Benedictinae variae (saec. XI-saec. XIV)*, Corpus consuetudinum monasticarum 6 (Siegburg, 1975), 88.

[13] For the influence of Cluny with regard to B-Br II 3823, see Michel Huglo, 'Trois anciens manuscrits liturgiques d'Auvergne', in *Bulletin historique et scientifique de l'Auvergne* 77 (1957), 81-104, reprinted in *Les sources du plain-chant et de la musique médiéval*, Variorum Collected Studies Series 17 (Aldershot and Burlington, 2004), 81-104; for Cluniac influence in St-Martial (thus, F-Pn lat. 1119) see, for example, James Grier, *The Musical World of a Medieval Monk: Adémar de Chabannes in Eleventh-Century Aquitaine* (Cambridge and New York, 2006), 317-18; for that of F-Pn n.a.lat. 1871, see the introduction to Marie-Noël Colette with Marie-Thérèse Gousset (eds.), *Tropaire séquentiaire prosaire prosulaire de Moissac (troisième quart du XIe siècle): Manuscrit Paris, Bibliothèque nationale de France, n.a.l. 1871* (Paris, 2006), esp. p. 18. It is unknown where F-Pn lat. 1139 originated, but the bound manuscript was in St-Martial by the beginning of the thirteenth century. Here I wish to thank Konstantin Voigt and David Catalunya for sharing with me their recent codicological and palaeographic findings (including dating, binding, provenance) on F-Pn lat. 1139.

St-Magloire, St-Martial, Worcester, and Moissac, and an afterthought to the principal manufacture of these books. Even so, this version of *Celeste organum* can claim staying power, with several witnesses dating to the fifteenth and sixteenth centuries including F-AM 132, F-AUT S 143, F-E 124, F-Pn lat. 865[A], and I-Tn D. I.7 as well as several ordinals, and printed missals.[14]

The Sources and Provenances for α-South Version of *Celeste organum*

The *Celeste organum* readings from Spain (Huesca, Toledo, Tortosa, Seville, and Zamora) and a band along the southern border of modern-day France (vicinities of Bazas and Saugnac, Saint-Guilhem-le-désert, Narbonne, and the region of Toulouse) share enough small variants to set them apart from the α-central group.[15] These nine readings constitute the α-south subset and are as follows (see Table 5).

Table 5. Sources of the α-south tradition

RISM siglum	Source	Provenance and date
E-H 4	Huesca, Biblioteca Capitular, Ms. 4, fols. 16r-v	Huesca, 12th century (1st quarter)
E-MO 73	Montserrat, Biblioteca de la Abadía de Montserrat (Barcelona), Ms. 73, fols. 17r-18r	Region of Toulouse, end 12th century
E-Tc 35-10	Toledo, Biblioteca Capítular, 35-10, fols. 123r-v	Toledo, c.1200
E-TO 135	Tortosa, Biblioteca Capitular, Ms. 135, fols. 39r-40r	Tortosa, c. 1254
E-Zaahp 52	Zamora, Archivo Historico Provincial, fragment 52, fols. 1r-v	Zamora (?), 12th/13th century
F-LANs 126	Langres, Bibliothèque Diocésaine, Fonds de la Bibliothèque du Grand Seminaire, 126 (anc. 312), fols. 287r-v	Southwest France (Bazas?), c. 1220; in Saugnac by end 13th century
F-MOv 20	Montpellier, Médiathèque Emile Zola, Ms. 20, fols. 91r-92v	St-Guilhem-les-désert, 14th century
F-Pn lat. 778	Paris, Bibliothèque Nationale de France, Fonds latin 778, fols. 41v-42v	Narbonne, 12th century (2nd half)/c. 1200
US-NYcubc 3	New York City, Columbia University, Barnard College, Ms. 3, fols. 33v-35v	Seville, 16th century

[14] Ordinals and printed missals uphold this testimony of longevity; compare the inventories of printed missals in Eugène Misset and W. H. James Weale, *Pars ii: Thesaurus hymnologicus…Supplementum amplissimum…notulisque illustraverunt*, Analecta liturgica, 3 vols. (Lille, 1888-92), vols. 2-3. See also Kruckenberg, 'Two *Sequentiae novae* at Nidaros', 372.

[15] I wish to thank Susan Boynton for kindly providing me with photocopies of the version of *Celeste organum* in US-NY cubc 3, a sixteenth-century gradual-sequentiary most likely from Seville, as well as a list of pieces in the sequentiary in that source. I would also like to thank David Catalunya for providing me with images of several notated fragments from Zamora, including E-Zaahp 52.

While E-H 4 has been dated to the first quarter of the twelfth century, and E-MO 73 (from the Toulouse region) to the end of the twelfth century, most of these readings date to after c. 1200.[16] The institutional proveniences and liturgical traditions represented in these manuscripts include Benedictine houses, cathedrals, and secular churches. Several scholars have noted however, that the liturgical traditions of Cluniac affiliates from France became the basis of late eleventh- and twelfth-century Spanish liturgies.[17] Thus, as with several of the α-central readings of *Celeste organum*, the version of the sequence found in the α-south group may in part be dependent upon this specific Benedictine network.

The Sources and Provenances for α-East Version of *Celeste organum*

The final a subset—the α-east group of eight readings—is concentrated in modern-day Switzerland. These are given in Table 6.

Table 6. Sources of the α-east tradition

RISM siglum	Source	Provenance and date
CH-GSBh 6	Congrégation du Grand-St-Bernard, Großer St. Bernhard, Bibliothek, Ms. 6 (ancient 1983), pp. 24-26	Bourg-St-Pierre, end 15th/start 16th century
CH-SGs 383	St. Gall, Stiftsbibliothek, Codex 383, pp. 40-42	Lausanne, c. 1250
CH-SGs 546	St. Gall, Stiftsbibliothek, Codex 546, p. 742; fol. 338v	St. Gall, 1507-1514
CH-Sk 29	Sion, Archives du Chapitre de la Cathédrale, Ms. 29, fols. 139r-v	Valeria, Sion (Sitten), mid 13th century
CH-Sk 48	Sion, Archives du Chapitre de la Cathédrale, Ms. 48, fols. 5v-6v	Sion (Sitten) cathedral, 14th century (1st half)
CH-Sk 49	Sion, Archives du Chapitre de la Cathédrale, Ms. 49, fols. 93v-94v	Valeria, Sion (Sitten), 13th century (2nd half)/start 14th century
CH-Sk 78	Sion, Archives du Chapitre de la Cathédrale, Ms. 78, pp. 95-98	Sion (Sitten), 16th century (1st half)
D-KA 102	Karlsruhe, Badische Landesbibliothek, Codex 102, fols. 163r-v	Southwest Germany (Black Forest region?), end 14th/start 15th century

The oldest of this group is CH-SGs 383, a troper-sequentiary thought to have originated in Lausanne around 1250, before coming to Saint Gall around 1300, where it

---

[16] See Eva Castro Caridad, *Tropos y troparios hispanicos* (Santiago de Compostela, 1991), 127-39, 143-55, 177-83, and 189-97; eadem and Susana Zapke, individual entries in Susana Zapke et al. (eds.), *Hispania Vetus: Musical-liturgical Manuscripts from Visigothic Origins to the Franco-Roman Transition (9th-12th Centuries)*, (Bilbao, 2007), 344-35, 356-37. See also Lorenzo F. Candelaria, 'Tropes for the Ordinary in a Sixteenth-Century Chantbook from Toledo, Spain', in *Early Music* 34 (2006), 609, n. 15.

[17] See Kathleen E. Nelson, *Medieval Liturgical Music of Zamora* (Ottawa, 1996), 12-38. Nelson has also transcribed *Celeste organum* from the Zamoran fragment E-Zaahp 52. See pp. 280-81.

remains today.[18] The youngest α-east source, CH-SGs 546, was copied in Saint Gall between 1507 and 1514, and its *Celeste organum* was undoubtedly copied directly from CH-SGs 383.[19] Four representatives from the α-east tradition are found in Sion (Sitten): two from the cathedral there, two from St. Valeria.[20] Another witness is the sequentiary from Bourg-St-Pierre, located at the Great St-Bernard Pass, and dated to the end of the fifteenth or beginning of the sixteenth century. The fourteenth-century manuscript D-KA 102 has been localized to southwest Germany, possibly the Black Forest region, and it is the only α-east source whose provenance lies beyond the borders of modern-day Switzerland. Compared to the other three α subsets, the oldest α-east source (CH-SGs 383) is notably younger than its counterparts in the α-north, α-central, and α-south traditions.

The α Traditions Compared

The categories of variants distinguishing α and β groups from one another are also the types distinguishing the α-north concordances from the other three α subgroups. For instance, six of the seven α-north sources end with couplet 10a/b; one α-north reading, F-AB 7 from Noyon, reports the coda 'Ipsi laus et gloria Amen'. That this ending is unique among all seventy-six concordances of *Celeste organum* suggests the coda of F-AB 7 is not original to the piece, rather put together from a basic formulaic peroration (see Table 7). By contrast, the overwhelming majority of α-central, α-south, and α-east readings end with a coda containing some form of the phrase 'Iam dicantur'.[21]

Table 7. Summary of codas with the phrase 'Iam dicantur'

Coda text	Sources
Iam dicantur alia (Amen)	B-Br II 3823, CH-SGs 383, CH-SGs 546, CH-Sk 29, CH-Sk 48, CH-Sk 49, CH-Sk 78, D-KA 102, E-H 4, E-MO 73, E-TO 135, F-AM 132, F-LANs 126, F-MOv 20[a], F-Pn lat. 778, F-Pn lat. 1086, F-Pn lat. 1139
Iam dicantur alia amen amen eia	F-Pn lat. 13252, F-Pn n.a.lat. 1871, I-Ac 695
Iam dicantur alleluia	E-Tc 35-10
Iam dicatur alleluia (Amen)	CH-BSBh 6, US-NYcubc 3
Iam dicat turba alleluia Amen[b]	F-Pn lat. 865[A]
Cui laus et gloria. Iam dicantur alia[c]	F-E 124

[a] F-Mov 20 has 'Nam' for 'Iam'.
[b] This reading is likely a misreading or mishearing of 'dica[n]tur'.
[c] This reading is also found in the outlier α source D-Mbs clm. 23027.

---

[18] For some comparison of this source to liturgical books from Fribourg and St. Gall, see Gabriel Zwick (ed.), *Les Proses en usage à l'église de Saint-Nicolas à Fribourg jusqu'au dix-huitième siècle*, 2 vols. (Fribourg, 1950) and Frank Labhardt, *Das Sequentiar Cod. 546 der Stiftsbibliothek von St. Gallen und seine Quellen*, 2 vols. (Bern, 1959-63), vol. 1, 27, 36-37, and 48.
[19] See Labhardt, *Das Sequentiar Cod. 546*, vol. 1, 168-73.
[20] Jürg Stenzl, *Repertorium der liturgischen Musikhandschriften der Diözesen Sitten, Lausanne und Genf*, vol. 1: *Diözese Sitten* (Fribourg, 1972).
[21] Other than the Noyon source, two other α sources have a coda not containing some form of the 'Iam dicantur' conclusion. They are: the Bratislava source, SK-Brm E.C. lat. 3/EL 18, i.e., 'Per eterna secula'; and I-Tn D. I.7, which presents a version of the β coda, namely 'Resonent cuncta redempta alleluya'.

Several α-central readings, however, conclude as the α-north tradition, that is, with couplet 10a/b (sometimes appended with a closing 'Amen'). These are F-AUT S 10 (first entry), F-AUT S 10 (second entry), F-AUT S 143, F-CF 57, F-O 129, F-Pn lat. 1087 and F-SEm 18.[22] These 'coda-less' α-central concordances include the Cluny source, the earliest representative of the α-central tradition.

In terms of other text variants distinguishing the α groups from one another, the α-north and α-central subsets mostly present 'terra' as the concluding word of versicle 1. By contrast, seven of the eight α-south sources prefer 'terris' (or 'terras' in one case) to the standard singular form 'terra' in versicle 1, a clear disruption of the assonantal rhymed ending with versicle 2. Alpha-east versions likewise mostly have 'terris'. The α-east sources consistently give 'turma' for the standard 'turba' (3a); 'pax' for the standard 'laus' (6b). Only among α-south sources (some but not all) do we find the reading 'nisi quorum mens est bona' for the 'sed mens quorum erit bona' (5a). In 8a, all α-east have 'sidera'; all α-south readings have 'ethera' as do the majority of α-north and α-central subsets. Moreover, all α-east witnesses offer a transposed order of the second halves of couplet 8a/8b, thus 'bethleem usque previa'/'lucis per indicia', rather than the reverse.

A few textual variants of minor significance further unify the regional subgroups. While the α-north and α-east sources consistently have 'pax est illa' in 6a, α-central sources either report the inverted word order 'est pax illa' or have rendered the phrase as 'et pax illa'. Six of the eight α-south readings also have 'est pax illa'. Of course, these changes are minute in and of themselves, but their occurrence is consistent regionally, reinforcing these subtraditions. Similarly the α-south *Celeste organum* readings are also unanimous in their reading 'colit hunc ecclesia' in versicle 10a, while the α-central and α-east traditions unvaryingly have 'colit hec ecclesia'. Only the α-north examples are split on the treatment of this demonstrative (as either the feminine singular adjective for 'ecclesia', or masculine accusative pronoun for the aforegoing 'quem').

The α-north sources are singular in preferring a clear two-syllable reading of 'bethle(h)em' in 8b.[23] As mentioned above, the poetic elision of 'bethlem' is necessary to uphold the verse form, in this case, 7p+3pp+7pp; the extra syllable and musical note of 'bethle(h)em'—arguably a negligible detail—would nevertheless mar the versification of the couplet.

From a musical standpoint, α-south versions of *Celeste organum* frequently report a few melodic idiosyncracies: the delay of the internal cadence in versicle 2 (shifted from 'virginis' to 'superum'); an inflected opening in 4a/b; and in some, a compressed range and registral transposition in couplet 6. In the α-east sources, the concluding 7pp of couplet 9 is set to a melodic arch (e.g., *a-a-G-a-b-c-a-G*); the α-central and α-south subsets generally have a flattened profile, hovering between *a* and *G*. Melodically the α-east are relatively uniform in their conclusion of couplet 10 on *E* and beginning of the following phrase 'Iam dicantur alia' on *G*. The α-south sources typically conclude the final couplet on *C*, and begin the coda on either *C* or a fifth higher on *G*. By contrast,

---

[22] The readings of *Celeste organum* in F-Pn lat. 1119, GB-Lbl A.xiv, and E-Zaahp 52 are fragmentary or incomplete, and therefore these sources are silent on the matter of conclusion to the piece.

[23] Musically the six notated α-north sources are plain on this matter, providing just two notes for the word, regardless of spelling. Thus, F-CA 78, F-CA 60, and GB-Lbl 2615 have 'bethlem', F-LA 263 'bellem', while I-Ra 477 and F-AB 7 have 'bethleem', but according to the notational coordination, the double 'ee' should be read as an elision.

the α-north and α-central readings vary far more on the cadential endings of versicle pair 10 (thus, *C*, *D*, *E*, or *G*); when a coda is present, these begin either on the *C* or *G*.

Overall, α-north sources are more ornate than other α subsets. Alpha-north sources are alone in offering—and consistently so—a long flourish on 'sunt'/'-lu-' in 5a/b (usually nine notes but just seven in F-LA 263). In the α-central, α-south and α-east traditions, this flourish usually consists of two or three notes, more rarely four. Compare the A-north reading of F-AB 7 to that in I-Ac 695, an α-central concordance and a fair representative of the α-south and α-east traditions as well (Example 7).

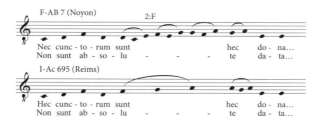

Example 7. Comparison of α-north (F-AB 7) and α-central (I-Ac 695) readings of couplet 5

Moreover, the α-north sources are more likely to have greater surface detail compared to other α traditions, with the α-central, α-south, and α-east traditions occupying a kind of middle ground between the more ornate melodies in the α-north tradition and the bare bones framework of the β tradition.

There are several more distinctions between these α groups, but for the current study, suffice it to say that generally the witnesses of *Celeste organum* at Cambrai, Laon, Beauvais, Noyon, and Jerusalem—though not identical—reveal a common aesthetic: a relaxed relationship towards the 'Isonian ethos' of syllabicism and the strict one-to-one text-music relationship characteristic of the early sequence. In terms of the general relationship of subsets, the α-north group can claim the earliest sources, the musical *lectio difficilior*, the textual *lectio difficilior*, as well as a kind of *lectio brevior* insofar that six of seven readings conclude with couplet 10 and lack a coda.

Sources and Provenances for β Subgroups and Hybrid Versions of *Celeste organum*

Before I propose a scenario for the possible place and conditions giving rise to the production, circulation, and reception of *Celeste organum*, let me offer a few brief observations concerning the β subgroupings and four sources presenting α-β hybrid versions of this sequence. While it is beyond the scope of the current study to provide an in-depth analysis of the β tradition, in short, this secondary tradition can be further divided into three subgroups according to melodic and textual variants. Compared to the α subgroups, provenances of two of these β subgroups are localized. One β sub-tradition is represented by seven concordances, all from Sens, in particular the cathedral or as representative of the cathedral *usus*; I refer to this as the β-Sens tradition.[24] Another

---

[24] It is worth noting here that the version of *Celeste organum* found in F-SEm 18, from the Benedictine monastery of Pierre-le-Vif of Sens, is clearly not from the same tradition as that of the cathedral use, and as discussed previously, it belongs instead to the A-central tradition.

β subgroup is comprised of eight sources specific to the Augustinian house of Seckau, thus the β-Seckau tradition.[25] The third group, hereafter β-England, claims several locales, including Chichester, Exeter, London, Oxford, Hanley Castle (near Malvern in Worcestershire), the diocese of Lincoln, Hereford, Norwich or Bury St. Edmunds, and East Drayton in Nottinghamshire (York use). There is also one Irish representative, GB-Cu 710, the so-called Dublin troper in this subset. Several in the β-England group are illustrative of the Sarum use; these include F-Pa 135, GB-Cu 710, GB-Mr 24, I-Bu 2565, GB-Lbl 11414, and GB-Lbl 462. According to one extant concordance from Iceland and the printed missal of 1519 for Trondheim cathedral, the β-England version of *Celeste organum* is that found in the liturgy of the archdiocese of Nidaros.[26] The sources of the β-Sens, β-England (including Nidaros), and β-Seckau readings are given in Tables 8, Table 9, and Table 10, respectively.

Table 8. Sources of the β-Sens tradition

RISM siglum	Source	Provenance and date
F-Pn lat. 10502	Paris, Bibliothèque Nationale de France, Fonds latin 10502, fols. 29r-v	Sens cathedral, 13th century (1st third)
F-PR 11	Provins, Bibliothèque Municipale, Ms. 11, fols. 162v-163r	Sens, 13th century
F-PR 13	Provins, Bibliothèque Municipale, Ms. 13, fols. 13v-14v, (also cued 22v)	Sens (cathedral?), 13th century (2nd third)
F-SEm 16-17	Sens, Bibliothèque Municipale, Ms. 16, fols. 24r-v	Sens, 13th/14th century
F-SEm 46	Sens, Bibliothèque Municipale, Ms. 46, pp. 17-18	Sens cathedral, 1200-1222
GB-Lbl 30058	London, British Library, Add. 30058, fol. 22v	Sens, 14th century (2nd half)
P-Ln 84	Lisbon, Instituto da Biblioteca Nacional e do Livro Iluminado 84, fols. 29v-30v	Sens *usus*, c. 1400

---

[25] I have also consulted another Seckau book, the *Directorium-Cantionarum* of c. 1345, Graz, Universitätsbibliothek, Ms. 756 [A-Gu 756] where unnotated incipits of *Celeste organum* are cued on fol. 38r and again on fol. 47r, once for the Sunday within the octave of Christmas, and the second time for Marian masses between Christmas and the feast of the Purification. Franz Karl Praßl also reports the occurrence of *Celeste organum* in a few other thirteenth- and fourteenth-century Seckau books that I have not yet been able to consult; these are Graz, Universitätsbibliothek, Ms. 281 [A-Gu 281], fols. 52v-53r; Graz, Universitätsbibliothek, Hs 474 [A-Gu 474], fol. 332r; Graz, Universitätsbibliothek, Hs 469 [A-Gu 469], fols. 91r-91v; and Graz, Universitätsbibliothek, Hs 197 [A-Gu 197], fols. 75v-76r. See Praßl, 'Psallat Ecclesia Mater: Studien zu Repertoire und Verwendung von Sequenzen in der Liturgie österreichischer Augustinerchorherren vom 12. bis zum 16. Jahrhundert', 2 vols. (Ph.D. diss., Karl-Franzens-Universität zu Graz, 1987), vol. 1, 56-62, 67-71, and 77-80.

[26] Nidaros is both the medieval name for the northern Norwegian town of Trondheim, and for the ecclesiastical territories of current-day Norway, Iceland, the Orkneys, Faroe Islands, Greenland, and Western Isles of Scotland. From 1152–1537 these territories were known as the archdiocese of Nidaros. As has been determined in a prior study, the two Nidaros witnesses of *Celeste organum* show that they were dependent on the β-England tradition; see Kruckenberg, 'Two *Sequentiae novae* at Nidaros', 368-71.

Table 9. Sources of the β-England tradition (with Nidaros)

RISM siglum	Source	Provenance and date
F-Pa 135	Paris, Bibliothèque de l'Arsenal, Ms. 135, fols. 237r-v	London (?), end 13th century
GB-Cu 6	Cambridge, University Library, Kk. ii 6, fols. 116v-117r	Hanley Castle (near Malvern in Worcestershire), 14th century
GB-Cu 710	Cambridge, University Library, Add. 710, fols. 43r-v	Dublin, 13th century (2nd half)
GB-Lbl 11414	London, British Library, Add. 11414, fols. 278r-v	Diocese of Lincoln, 14th century
GB-Lbl 3965	London, British Library, Harley 3965, fols. 103r-104r	Hereford, 14th century
GB-Lbl 462	London, British Library, Lansdowne 462, fol. 5r	Norwich or Bury St. Edmunds, 15th century (3rd quarter)
GB-Mr 24	Manchester, John Rylands Library, lat. 24, fol. 234v	Exeter, 13th century (2nd half)
GB-Ob liturg. b.5	Oxford, Bodleian Library, Ms. Lat. liturg. b.5, fols. 11r-v, (also cued 13v)	East Drayton in Nottinghamshire (York use), 15th century
GB-Ouc 148	Oxford, University College Ms. 148, p. 34	Chichester, 13th century (2nd half)
I-Bu 2565	Bologna, Biblioteca Universitaria, Ms. 2565, pp. 602-603 (also cued p. 41)	Oxford (?), end 13th century
DK-Kar frag. 249	Copenhagen, Det Arnamagnæanske Institut, frag. 249 r-v	Iceland, 15th century (?)
MN 1519	*Missale Nidarosiense* (Copenhagen, 1519), fol. B22r	Archdioces of Nidaros *usus*, 1519

Table 10. Sources of the β-Seckau tradition

RISM siglum	Source	Provenance and date
A-Gu 17	Graz, Universitätsbibliothek, Ms. 17, fols. 379v-380v	Seckau, 1480-1510
A-Gu 285	Graz, Universitätsbibliothek, Ms. 285, fols. 88v-89r	Seckau, c. 1300
A-Gu 417	Graz, Universitätsbibliothek, Ms. 417, fol. 2v	Seckau, 1164-1171; additions 13th century
A-Gu 444	Graz, Universitätsbibliothek, Ms. 444, fol. 257r	Seckau, 12th century (3rd quarter); additions 14th century
A-Gu 456	Graz, Universitätsbibliothek, Ms. 456, fols. 116v-117r	Seckau, before 1339
A-Gu 479	Graz, Universitätsbibliothek, Ms. 479, fols. 110r-v	Seckau, 1171-1196
A-Gu 769	Graz, Universitätsbibliothek, Ms. 769, fols. 93r-v	Seckau, c. 1200
A-Gu 1584	Graz, Universitätsbibliothek, Ms. 1584, fols. 1v-2r	Seckau, c. 1200

Several variants distinguish the β subgroups from one another, including some minor ones, the occurrences of which are so consistent that they warrant notice. For instance, in versicle 6a, all seven β-Sens sources present the verb 'deserat' to the fairly standard plural form 'deserant'. In versicle 8a, the Sens sources give 'nati per indicia' for 'lucis per indicia', a reading nearly unique to the β-Sens witnesses save for β-England reading from Hereford, GB-Lbl 3965. About half of all β-England sources have the reading 'Nec sunt absolute data sed decenter' for the standard 'Non sunt absolute data differenter'. In 6b, six of seven Sens sources are alone in having the plural form 'sunt', thus 'sed decenter sunt divisa' (to the singular forms of 'sit', 'fit', or 'est' found elsewhere).[27] The β-Sens and β-Seckau traditions consistently have 'colit hec ecclesia' in 10b, while four β-England have 'colit hec ecclesia' to six β-England readings of 'colit hunc ecclesia'.

As noted in Table 1, the β sources typically have a coda with a formulation containing the words 'cuncta' and 'redempta'. More specifically, all seven witnesses from Sens report the formula 'Resonent cuncta amen redempta'. The β-England witnesses, on the other hand, typically conclude the sequence either with 'Resonent cuncta redempta' or 'Resonent cuncta redempta amen'.[28] The Seckau sources always have 'Iubilent' for 'Resonent', thus 'Iubilent cuncta redempta'. While these slight rewordings are utterly minor in terms of meaning, and consistent with the flexibility of Latin word order, they do underscore the general stability as well as static nature (even insularity) of the β subsets in their respective institutional or regional traditions.

The textual variants in Seckau's *Celeste organum* are so numerous (and at times extensive) that we might presume a transmission marked by either significant disruption or an intentional reworking. A representative version of the Seckau reading based on A-Gu 479, one of the four oldest sources (all dated c. 1200) is provided in Appendix 1.[29] Compare the text of the β-Seckau to the α-north version in F-LA 263 (Example 1).

Melodically the β-Sens and β-England sources are quite similar, but there are a few musical deviations. For instance, in couplet 4, the β-Sens concordances present a small embellishment on 'carmina'/'propria', while the β-England witnesses generally report a syllabic treatment.[30] The 'reciting tone' gesture that launches couplet 6 is routinely inflected with a *b* in the Sens tradition; the English sources commonly remain on *c* at the beginning of this couplet. Overall, the English readings favour a heavier use of the *oriscus* figure.

Three of the consulted Seckau readings of *Celeste organum* are unnotated (A-Gu 769, A-Gu 479, and A-Gu 444). Four others—including two of the earliest concordances—are notated with neumes *in campo aperto* (A-Gu 1584, A-Gu 417, A-Gu 285, and A-Gu

---

[27] The Icelandic fragment of the Nidaros tradition, DK-Kar frag. 249, has the exceptional 'si decenter sint divisa'.
[28] GB-Ouc 148 has the unique word order 'Resonent redempta cuncta amen'; GB-Cu 710 commences the coda with the initial P, to create 'Personent cuncta redempta amen', a reasonable substitution (there is little difference in meaning between the *verba canendi* 'personare' and 'resonare'), though it could be a mistake made by the scribe responsible for entering initials. See Gunilla Iversen, '"Verba canendi" in Tropes and Sequences', in *Latin Culture in the Eleventh Century: Proceedings of the Third International Conference on Medieval Latin Studies, Cambridge, September 9-12, 1998*, ed. Michael W. Herren et al., 2 vols. (Turnhout, 1998), vol. 1, 444-73.
[29] The codices A-Gu 1584 and A-Gu 769 have been dated to c. 1200; the main of manuscript A-Gu 417 was written between 1164 and 1171, but *Celeste organum* belongs to a group of added sequences. Praßl gives A-Gu 479, a gradual-sequentiary-sacramentary-lectionary, the dates 1171-96. Praßl, 'Psallat Ecclesia Mater', vol. 1, 43-45, 48-51, 53-56.
[30] One notable exception is GB-Ob liturg. b.5 from East Drayton in the archdiocese of York. A few of the English readings also have G-G (often notated with an *oriscus*) on the first syllable of 'propria', but not on the first syllable of 'carmina'.

456). The youngest reading, A-Gu 17 from c. 1480-1510, is notated on a four-line staff with *Hufnagel* notation. While the contours and compound figures of the adiastematic neumes of the pre-1300 Seckau readings agree generally with the melodic tradition of the β-Sens and β-England versions, the melody of A-Gu 17 is clearly unrelated to any other known *Celeste organum* reading.[31] It is a D-mode melody, rather than an E-mode; it may have been newly composed around the time that this late source was copied, perhaps because of a disruption in the use of *Celeste organum* in the Seckau liturgy.[32]

Whereas the β tradition—especially the β-Sens and β-Seckau subsets—demonstrates a certain isolation and independence, a few concordances present something of a mixture of the α and β traditions, suggesting contact between the two principal traditions and perhaps some kind of interference or attempt at reconciliation.[33] These are listed in Table 11.

Table 11. Sources showing a mix of α and β traditions

RISM siglum	Source	Provenance and date
F-Pn lat. 1106	Paris, Bibliothèque Nationale de France, Fonds latin 1106, fols. 28r-29r	St-Laurent-des-Aubats, near Nièvre, 14th century
F-Pn lat. 10513	Paris, Bibliothèque Nationale de France, Fonds latin 10513, fols. 5v-6v	Nevers, 14th century
F-Pn n.a.lat. 3126	Paris, Bibliothèque Nationale de France, Nouv. acq. 3126, fols. 8r-v	Nevers, 12th century (2nd half); additions 13th century
CH-Val d'Illiez	Val d'Illiez, Archives Paroissiales, *sine numero*, fols. 186r-187r	Val d'Illiez, c.1354

Two 'mixed tradition' readings are from Nevers (F-Pn n.a.lat. 3126 and F-Pn lat. 10513) and one from St-Laurent-des-Aubats, near Nièvre. The β-Sens tradition seems to be the basis of these three hybrid versions, though each shows clear contact with the α tradition, especially the α-central testimonies. Both Nevers and Nièvre fall in the archdiocese of Sens, and of the many loci represented by the seventy-six readings of *Celeste*

---

[31] The Toledo source E-Tc 35-10 has several distinct melodic variants, suggesting a certain divergence from the rest of the α-south tradition; even so, the melody is clearly derived from the *Celeste organum* musical tradition common to α and β groups alike.

[32] The liturgical tradition of Salzburg appears to have had an increased influence on the Seckau tradition by the second half of the fifteenth century. A set of books including a 'Direktorium' of 1468/69 (A-Gu 332), *Missale Plenarium Salisburgense* of 1474-1477 (A-Gu 74), and three late fifteenth-century full missals of the Salzburg use (A-Gu 109, A-Gu 112, and A-Gu 131) came into the abbey's possession at that time. None contain *Celeste organum*. The gradual-sequentiary A-Gu 17, copied in the final two decades of the fifteenth or first decade of the sixteenth century, is unusual in that it carries diastematic notation, while other sequentiaries from Seckau are notated with German neumes *in campo aperto* (i.e., from the 1170s up through the 1470s). Compare the inventories in Praßl, 'Psallat Ecclesia Mater', vol. 1, 83-104, as well as his discussion on repertorial and notational developments at Seckau as well as at other Austrian Augustinian houses; ibid., vol. 1, 345-464.

[33] It should be noted that a few β-England sources also present some α variants, including 'cingit' for 'fecit' (GB-Lbl 11414, GB-Lbl 462, GB-Ob liturg. b.5, I-Bu 2565); on the other hand, two English sources offer unique readings for the verb in 9b, namely 'regit' (F-Pa 135), and 'augit' (GB-Cu 6). This may show that singers and scribes working in English institutions had access to α versions of *Celeste organum*, and were harmonizing or combining particular readings as well as introducing new variants. Similarly the printed missal for the archdiocese of Nidaros has the α reading 'subeunt' rather than the β 'ineunt'. The blending of β features in an otherwise α version has already been noted in the late fifteenth-century missal from Amiens, I-Tn D. I.7, which presents a version of the β coda. See n. 21.

organum, those from Nevers and Nièvre claim the greatest proximity to the cathedral town of Sens, save, of course, for that of St-Pierre-le-Vif. The fourth witness to record a mixed version of *Celeste organum* is found in CH-Val d'Illiez, a mid fourteenth-century gradual-sequentiary-troper from Val d'Illiez, today in the Swiss canton of Valais. Val d'Illiez has numerous variants in common with the α-east readings as well as β-Sens.

A Scenario for the Emergence of *Celeste organum* and the Significance of Liturgical Use

Based on an analysis of text and melodic variants of seventy-six readings of *Celeste organum* as well as the relative dates and manuscript traditions of each of the source subgroups, I hypothesize that this particular new sequence originated in the α-north region, an area roughly corresponding to medieval Picardy. In the thirteenth century, Picardy was defined as the dioceses of Beauvais, Noyon, Amiens, Laon, Thérouanne, Arras, Cambrai, and Tournai, along with parts of the dioceses of Liège and Utrecht.[34] Notable representatives of the α-north version of *Celeste organum* are found in chantbooks from Cambrai (the earliest witnesses of all seventy-six readings), Laon, Beauvais, and Noyon.

I propose, then, that an α-north version of *Celeste organum* migrated southward from Picardy. Certainly it had arrived in Cluny by no later than the second quarter of the twelfth century. Perhaps it was at Cluny that it was ever so lightly revised, with a slight reduction of the florid texture, some levelling of cadential distinctions, and softening of verse elements (as with a three-syllable 'bethleem'). Wherever these changes might have been introduced, a lightly redacted version became the basis for the α-central tradition, and came to represent the main tradition found throughout much of hexagonal France. It should be remembered that the α-central *Celeste organum* of the Cluniac tradition was likely transmitted further afield thanks to Peter the Venerable. His statute required that *Celeste organum* replace the 'rough', 'unpolished' *Nostra tuba nunc tua clementia* as the sequence for the second mass of Christmas.[35] Especially through its Cluniac affiliates, *Celeste organum* of the α-central tradition spreads throughout France.

I put forward, furthermore, that again, aided in part by the Cluniac network, this new sequence circulated along Franco-Iberian border and into Spain, where some small variants (noted in the α-south subset) materialize. It was probably the α-central version that likewise moved eastward, perhaps from Burgundy into the Swiss Jura, where it was

---

[34] 'Picard' and 'Picardy' emerge as cultural, linguistic, and regional terms of identity in the twelfth and thirteenth centuries, with the first reference linked to a certain Guillaume le Picard, a crusader who died in 1098. See Serge Lusignan, 'L'aire du picard au Moyen Age: Espace géographique ou espace politique?', in *Évolutions en français: Etudes de linguistique diachronique*, ed. Benjamin Fagard (Bern, 2008), 274.

[35] The statute reads: 'Statutum est, ut solemni nocte Natalis Domini, ad missam de luce cantetur prosa, cuius initium Celeste organum. Causa instituti huius fuit, quia illius cuius principium erat *Nostra tuba* series verborum incompta nihilque paene ad nativitatem salvatoris pertinens, longe amplius incomptiore cantu, cunctis hoc advertentibus displicebat' ('It is decreed that on the solemn night of the Nativity of Our Lord, the sequence [*prosa*] with the opening words *Celeste organum* is to be sung for mass at daybreak. The reason this was decreed was because that [sequence] whose beginning is *Nostra tuba* is an unpolished chain of words not at all pertaining to the saviour's birth [and] with a melody much rougher still. This was displeasing to all who heard it.'); Constable (ed.), *Consuetudines Benedictinae variae (saec. XI-saec. XIV)*, 88. While *Celeste organum* is found in later sources from Cluny (in a thirteenth-century list of sequence incipits used at Cluny, as well as in a fifteenth-century missal), I was not able to consult these sources for text variants. See Michel Huglo, 'Le répertoire des proses à Cluny à la fin du XIIIe siècle', in *Revue Mabillon* 11 (2000), 39-55.

adopted in the liturgies of Val d'Illiez, Sion, Fribourg, Lausanne, Bourg-St-Pierre, and eventually at St. Gall; again variants specific to the region surface, hence the α-east tradition.[36]

Perhaps the α-central version formed the basis for the β tradition as well. Certainly an α-central reading of *Celeste organum* can be found in a thirteenth-century missal from the Senonense abbey of St-Pierre-le-Vif. Moreover, extant testimonies of the α-central tradition blanketed most of hexagonal France, and they 'encircled' Sens.

The β-Sens version of *Celeste organum* appears to be another redaction, one with an even more syllabic texture than that of the α-central tradition. Might this revision have been made in Sens around 1200 at the behest of the archbishop of Sens, Pierre de Corbeil? And from Sens cathedral, might this β-Sens version have arrived in England (perhaps introduced into the north around York, Lincoln, or Hereford), perhaps owing to Pierre de Corbeil's connections to England?[37] I will return to this hypothesis shortly.

The liturgical destinations and usage for *Celeste organum* strengthen the regional subgroups, and tell us about the relationships between them. Alpha-central sources most typically assign the sequence to the second Christmas mass, while the α-south and α-east manuscripts mostly assign *Celeste organum* to the first. The β-England sources generally designate either the second or third mass of Christmas Day. The β-Seckau sources prescribe this chant as the sequence for the main mass of Christmas, for the Sunday within the octave, or, more unusually, as a Marian sequence within the octave or from Christmas up to Purification. Among the β-Sens sources we find that Christmas, its octave, or the Sunday within the octave is rubricated—with one notable exception. We will return to the 'Sens exception' presently.

In terms of liturgical assignment, the α-north group is more diverse, and certainly trickier in terms of identifying a universal rule from their festal rubrics. The two youngest sources, F-AB 7 and F-Pn lat. 1140, are similar to nearby α-central traditions where *Celeste organum* is sung at the second mass of Christmas. By contrast, the Jerusalem source I-Ra 477 designates this chant for the feast of the Annunciation (25 March), a somewhat odd assignment in the twelfth century, since sequences were not at that time normally sung during Lent.

Four of the earliest five witnesses to the α-north group are even more unusual because they connect *Celeste organum* to a group of extra liturgical materials for either the feast of the Circumcision or Epiphany. At Beauvais, according to GB-Lbl 2615 (probably copied between 1227 and 1234), *Celeste organum* was to be sung as a hymn for the second nocturn of matins on the feast of the Circumcision.[38] The liturgy presented

---

[36] Although I have not yet seen the Fribourg witnesses to *Celeste organum*, the variants reported by Zwick correspond precisely with the subgroup of the α-east tradition. See Zwick (ed.), *Les Proses en usage à l'église de Saint-Nicolas à Fribourg*, 48.

[37] The sources from Sens and two from England (GB-Lbl 3965 and GB-Ob liturg. b.5) share several additional significant textual and melodic variants. The 'path' of a β version to Seckau is unclear; the numerous idiosyncratic verbal variants in the Seckau sources point to the isolation and foreignness of the piece in the regional context. It is worth noting that a fragment (Fragm. 660) containing the Sens's version of the Feast of Fools office has been identified in the Österreichischen Nationalbibliothek in Vienna. No explanation has been suggested for its deposit there but this fragment was in Austria no later than the sixteenth century, though there is no Seckau connection. See Robert Klugseder (ed.), *Ausgewählte mittelalterliche Musikfragmente der Österreichischen Nationalbibliothek Wien*, Codices Manuscripti Supplementum 5 (Purkersdorf, 2011), 92-95.

[38] The central study of this manuscript and its contents remains Wulf Arlt, *Ein Festoffizium des Mittelalters aus Beauvais in seiner liturgischen und musikalischen Bedeutung*, 2 vols. (Cologne, 1970). For his discussion of scribal hands, notation, dates, and the cathedral school of Beauvais, see esp. pp. 13-37.

in this festal book was not that of the typical liturgy for the hours of the Divine Office, but rather the special ceremonies in GB-Lbl 2615 exemplify the so-called clerics' offices.[39] While this source dates to the early thirteenth century, it is believed to be a copy of a now-lost mid twelfth-century book.[40] The use of this sequence during matins, then, may reach back to c. 1160 at Beauvais cathedral; likewise this α-north witness to *Celeste organum* might be chronologically closer to the Cambrai testimonies than the actual age of the GB-Lbl 2615 copy reports.

In the Laon manuscript, *Celeste organum* is not among the fifty-eight sequences in the troper-sequentiary (fols. 34r-81v); rather it appears in a section containing clerics' offices for the period between Christmas and Epiphany (fols. 91r-141v).[41] Here *Celeste organum* is sung in the third nocturn of matins of Epiphany, and again for the second vespers of that day, as a *prosa post tertium psalmum*. While the copying of this Laon codex has been dated to the final quarter of the twelfth century, Robert Lagueux has proposed that the special liturgical materials and dramas redacted in F-LA 263 were created between 1111 and 1138, during the tenure of the cantor Blihard.[42] If Lagueux's supposition is correct, then *Celeste organum*—and thus another α-north specimen—may have already existed at Laon in the first decades of the twelfth century, a date comparable to that of F-CA 60 from Cambrai.

As with the Laon source, the two Cambrai manuscripts assign *Celeste organum* to the feast of Epiphany. However, unlike either F-LA 263 or GB-Lbl 2615, the sequence serves its customary liturgical function, that is, as a chant of the mass, rather than as a hymn, conductus, or some other votive *canticum* sung within the clerics' office.

Even so, there are a few peculiarities in the two Cambrai sequentiaries that bespeak a higher degree of solemnity for the mass of Holy Innocents and Epiphany than almost any other time of the liturgical year.[43] For the other major holy days of the year—each of the three Christmas masses, Easter, Pentecost, and the Assumption of Mary—only one sequence is given. In other words, the cantor and his scribes were generally selective. For most other days on which sequences were sung, the masses have similarly been fitted with only one sequence. There are a couple of exceptions when two sequences have been provided; one of these exceptions is the feast of St. Stephen, the first of the four clerics' days.[44] Indeed, in F-CA 78, it is apparent that the clerics' days of St. Stephen, Holy Innocents, and Epiphany have been elevated ceremonially.

---

[39] For an overview of this phenomenon, see David Hiley, *Western Plainchant: A Handbook* (Oxford, 1993), 39-42. In addition to Arlt, *Ein Festoffizium*, esp. chapters 3 and 4; see also Margot Fassler, 'The Feast of Fools and *Danielis Ludus*: Popular Tradition in a Medieval Cathedral Play', in *Plainsong in the Age of Polyphony*, ed. Thomas Forrest Kelly (Cambridge, 1992), 65-99; Robert Charles Lagueux, 'Glossing Christmas: Liturgy, Music, Exegesis, and Drama in High Medieval Laon', 2 vols. (Ph.D. diss., Yale University, 2004); and Max Harris, *Sacred Folly: A New History of the Feast of Fools* (Ithaca and London, 2011).

[40] Arlt, *Festoffizium*, 30-32.

[41] Folios 85r-90v comprise an added gathering of five sequences, copied in the late thirteenth or fourteenth century. Concerning the four clerics' feasts, these are: the festal office for deacons, on the feast of St. Stephen (26 December); the festal office for priests, on the feast of St. John the Evangelist (27 December); the festal office for acolytes, on the feast of the Holy Innocents (28 December); and the festal office for subdeacons, celebrated at Laon on Epiphany (6 January), but elsewhere for the feast of the Circumcision (1 January).

[42] Lagueux, 'Glossing Christmas', vol. 1, 135-36. It was likely copied after 1172, but the text and notational hands correspond to twelfth-century styles.

[43] In F-CA 78 and F-60 there are three sequences for the Dedication of the Church.

[44] Two sequences have been provided for St. Mary Magdalene and St. Laurence in F-CA 78, while in F-CA 60, two sequences are given for the Holy Cross and St. Laurence (albeit with second one left unneumed).

I will return shortly to the sequences of Holy Innocents and Epiphany, but in order to gain a greater understanding of the oldest Cambrai chantbook, let us consider more closely its make up. F-CA 78 is essentially a cantor's book, comprised of a processional (1r-49r); a divided kyriale (58v-68v, 221v-223v); a cycle of alleluias with verses for the liturgical year (74v-100v); a sequentiary (100v-160v); and an offertoriale with verses (161r-203v).[45] On folios 49r-58r, we find a small provision of special ceremonial materials. These have been summarized in Table 12.

Table 12. Summary of special ceremonial materials in F-CA 78, fols. 49r-58r

Main festal rubric	Summary of contents, performance instructions, and additional rubrics
IN NOCTE NATALE DOMINI	Three prosulas for the *Fabrice mundi* melismas and one for the *Descendit* melisma of the matins responsory *Descendit de celis*; the prosula *Letemur gaudiis*
LECTIO AD PRIMAM MISSAM NOCTIS	The introductory verse *Laudes deo dicam per secula* to the farsed epistle *Lectio Ysaiae prophete/In qua Christi lucida*; POST NONAM LECTIONEM CANTATUR ISTUD EWANGELIUM; the short versicle *Dominus vobiscum* and its response *Et cum spiritu*, etc; the genealogy from Gospel of Matthew, i.e., *Liber generationis*; *Te deum* (as neumed incipit)
IN DIE AD MISSAM	The introit trope *Hodie cantandus est* with instructions for the deacons to sing the 'versicle' beginning 'Quis est iste puer', and to intone the introit *Puer natus est* (presumably the cantor was to begin the trope and resume at the final 'versicle' portion 'Hic enim est')
DE SANCTO STEPHANO	The instructional rubric ANTE SEPTIMAM LECTIONEM VENIAT DIACONUS IN SIMILITUDINE SANCTI STEPHANI DALMATICA INDUTUS CUM PALMA IN MANU ITA DICENS followed by the antiphon *Filie Ierusalem venite et videte*; the rubric CHORUS followed by the antiphon *Ave senior Stephane, ave martyr paradoxe*; the benediction *Dominus omnipotens benedicat vos*; the instructional rubric MOX LEGAT LECTIONEM SEPTIMAM
IN EPIPHANIA	POST NONUM RESPONSORIUM LEGATUR HOC EWANGELIUM: the short versicle *Dominus vobiscum* and its response *Et cum spiritu*, etc; the baptism and genealogy from the Gospel of Luke *Factum est autem cum baptizaretur*; *Te deum* (as neumed incipit)

Except for these ten folios, most of the materials found throughout F-CA 78 are for the mass. Yet here we find a small bundle of ceremonial materials where chants are assigned to, or at the very least associated with, matins of Christmas, matins of St. Stephen, and matins of Epiphany. Moreover, the majority of these items—*Fabrice mundi* prosulas to *Descendit de celis*, the prosula *Letemur gaudiis*, the introductory song *Laudes deo dicam*,

---

[45] For a short description on the overall contents of F-CA 78 as well as an inventory and analysis of the sequentiary, see Kruckenberg, 'The Sequence from 1050-1150', 189-222. In the present text, I have amplified my 1997 discussion of the processional, and I now consider the chants and liturgical items on fols. 49r-58r to comprise a liturgical section distinct from the processional. Alejandro Planchart calls F-CA 78 a 'cantatorium' and provides a rationale for the lack of gradual chants common to this book type; see Planchart, 'Choirboys in Cambrai in the Fifteenth Century', in *Young Choristers, 650-1700*, ed. Susan Boynton and Eric Rice (Woodbridge, 2008), 123-45, here esp. 130 and 133.

the farsed epistle *Lectio Ysaiae/In qua Christi lucida*, a set of introductory versicles and responds, the *Liber generationis*, *Te deum*, and *Factum est autem cum baptizaretur*—were used in the clerical offices of Holy Innocents, Circumcision, or Epiphany as attested to by the books of Laon (F-LA 263) and Beauvais (GB-Lbl 2615), as well as Sens (F-SEm 46).[46] According to one set of instructional rubrics in F-CA 78, toward the end of matins for St. Stephen, prior to the reading of the seventh lesson, a deacon, in imitation of the protomartyr, was to wear a dalmatic as he carried a palm in his hand, while singing the chant *Filie Ierusalem venite et videte*. To this the choir responded with the antiphon *Ave senior Stephane, ave martyr paradoxe*, petitioning the saint—or rather his surrogate the deacon—for a blessing, which he grants by singing the benedictio *Dominus omnipotens benedicat vos*. Afterwards the seventh reading was immediately read.

There are relatively few surviving chantbook preserving the clerics' offices and comprehensive collections of related votive materials. Is it possible that these ten leaves in this late eleventh-century cantatorium from Cambrai represent short versions of clerics' offices and other votive materials common to the customs at Laon and Beauvais? Certainly the strong emphasis on St. Stephen and Epiphany on these folios in F-CA 78 is sustained in its sequentiary. Moreover, does the sequentiary in F-CA 78 as well that in F-CA 60, with their inclusion of three sequences for Holy Innocents and four for Epiphany, corroborate the importance of those clerics' days in the liturgical tradition of the cathedral?[47] It is worth noting that during the period between Christmas and Epiphany we find an unmistakable concentration of new sequences. For St. Stephen, there is the new sequence *Unus amor* in addition to the early sequence *Magnus deus* while for Holy Innocents, there are the two new pieces *Laus tibi Christe quem magi deferentes* and *Misit Herodes innocentum* in addition to the early-style sequence *Pura deum laudet innocentia*. For the Octave of Christmas, we find the unusual *Verbum legibus* with its emphasis on the New Covenant, a typical theme in *nova cantica*. For Epiphany, three of the four sequences are in the new style: *Exultemus hodie*, *Letabundus exultet fidelis chorus*, and *Celeste organum*; *Festa Christi* is an early sequence by Notker. Except for perhaps *Misit Herodes innocentum*, this trio of *novae sequentiae* for Epiphany are perhaps the most novel and boldly inventive of the entire collections attested to by the two Cambrai books.

Moreover, of these seven sequences for Innocents and Epiphany, five of which are in the new style, four are used as votive songs in the Laon and Beauvais clerics' offices.[48]

Beyond the α-north *Celeste organum* of medieval Picardy where *Celeste* so clearly had a connection to special liturgies of Christmastide including the festal offices for Circumcision and Epiphany, we find a few traces of a similar use at thirteenth-century Sens as well as at Autun. F-SEm 46, the famous festal book of c. 1200-20, is thought, in

---

[46] For identifying concordant readings for most of the items found on fols. 49r-58r in F-CA 78, Arlt's *Editionsband* is an indispensable starting place. See Arlt, *Ein Festoffizium*, vol. 2.

[47] Similarly F-CA 78 provides two alleluias and three alleluias for St. Stephen and Epiphany, respectively. In the gradual of F-CA 60, we still find two alleluias for St. Stephen, but there is only one alleluia for Epiphany.

[48] The two Cambrai sources are also, in effect, the two earliest witnesses for yet another new sequence, *Gaudete vos fideles*, albeit in its incomplete form. Both F-CA 78 and F-CA 60 have the unusual coda 'Gaudete fideles pars electa'/ 'Ethiopum nigredo in iudam translata' as the conclusion of their version of *Letabundus exultemus*. This couplet is normally the opening couplet of the new sequence *Gaudete vos fideles*, which was commonly used as a sequence for mass on Epiphany, but which was used as a votive song for vespers in the Epiphany festal office in F-LA 263. See Appendix 2 below for the Laon context.

fact, to represent a reformed and redacted version of the Feast of Fools produced at the behest of Archbishop of Sens, Pierre de Corbeil.[49] Containing the earliest of the Sens readings for *Celeste organum*, F-SEm 46 is arguably the oldest surviving occurrence of the β version. Might it signal that this sequence belonged to those pieces reformed and edited for (and possibly by) Archbishop Pierre de Corbeil?

Another tantalizing piece of evidence linking this new sequence to the clerics' offices is found in the Autun source F-AUT S10, where *Celeste organum* is, in fact, written out twice in full. Its first occurrence is on fol. 36v within the revised gradual portion of the manuscript; there it is assigned to the first Christmas mass. The other entry (fol. 297v) happens within the sequentiary, where it receives the rubric DE FESTO FOLORUM. Here *Celeste organum* falls between the sequences assigned to the Sunday after Christmas and the sequence for Epiphany, suggesting that at Autun, the *festum folorum* occurred on the feast of the Circumcision. Though these two fifteenth-century Autun readings of *Celeste organum* clearly belong to the α-central recension, the festal designation 'for the Feast of Fools' for the second entry signals that, as at Sens cathedral, a connection of *Celeste organum* to 'Twelve Days' celebrations was known beyond medieval Picardy, the area of the α-north tradition. Moreover, Autun was one site where such special ceremonies were not without controversy, for, as E. K. Chambers noted in 1903, 'At Autun, the chapter forbade the *baculus anni novi* in 1230'.[50] While the portions of manuscript F-AUT S10 containing both occurrences of *Celeste organum* date to the fifteenth century, is it possible that, like the main of the manuscript, they date back to the twelfth century and before the prohibition of 1230?[51] Moreover, might these Autun rubrics betray yet another clue to the migration of *Celeste organum* outside of medieval Picardy? Initially might *Celeste organum* have served primarily as a votive chant in clerics' offices, only to be 'repatriated' as a traditional sequence of the mass? Is the version of *Celeste organum* found at Autun (including the contemporary notated witness of F-AUT S 143) a reminder of revision that provided a more orthodox text-music relationship typical of early specimens of the genre? As noted previously, the more radical stylistic departures of the new sequence are not unlike those found among the *nova cantica*—verse technique, novel melodic vocabulary, and textural variety ranging from melismatic to mildly florid to syllabic, all in the same piece.

Indeed, *Celeste organum* is in many ways emblematic of other new sequences emerging at the close of the eleventh and beginning of the twelfth century. I will close this essay with some brief observations concerning other such pieces, particularly as they relate to melodic versions, liturgical functions, and the geography connected to the transmission histories of new sequences.

---

[49] Henri Villetard (ed.), *Office de Pierre de Corbeil (Office de La Circoncision) Improprement Appelé 'Office Des Fous'* (Paris, 1907), see esp. 51-73.
[50] Edmund Kerchever Chambers, *The Mediaeval Stage*, 2 vols. (Oxford, 1903), vol. 1, 289.
[51] The oldest layer of the manuscript has been dated to the twelfth century. See Éric Palazzo's entry on this source in Claire Maître (ed.), *Catalogue des manuscrits conservés à Autun. Bibliothèque municipale, Société Eduenne* (Turnhout, 2004), 63-64. Palazzo dates the added portions containing the entries of *Celeste organum* to the fifteenth century.

Some Preliminary Conclusions on the New Sequence of c. 1100

In my on-going work on the new sequence, I have focused on almost two dozen examples where the earliest witness can be roughly dated to c. 1100.[52] Like *Celeste organum*, these new sequences frequently present one or more of the following traits.

First, several of them demonstrate that, early on, their respective melodies existed in more than one version, often strikingly divergent in their details of ductus and shape. Some of these musical variants can be understood in terms of surface detail, with one version of a given sequence more ornate (or at least portions of it), while another version of the same piece presents a nearly one-to-one note-syllable ratio. In other cases, one musical version might be more unconventional in terms of range, intervallic contents, and melodic gestures, while the other version of the same conforms to the eight ecclesiastical modes in the strictest interpretation of finalis and compass, and uses more acceptable intervals, standard melodic patterns, and stereotypical cadential approaches.

Second, a handful of these new sequences can be shown to have had in their earliest sources liturgical contexts different from the common prescription as a mass chant following the Alleluia and preceding the gospel. As with *Celeste organum*, new sequences in their oldest extant manifestations were occasionally used for clerics' offices and other enriched or extended liturgies. They could function as hymns, conductus, versus, or other types of new song. For a point of reference, a summary of the use of sequences (both early and new types) in the clerics' office for Epiphany in F-LA 263 that for Circumcision in GB-Lbl 2615 can be found in Appendix 2 and Appendix 3, respectively. Moreover, there are a few cases where new sequences are found in collections of *nova cantica*, for which the function or liturgical use is unclear, and genre-bending is in evidence.[53]

A final characteristic of the new sequence concerns relationships between geography and transmission histories. Of the nearly two dozen examples forming the core of my ongoing investigation, almost all point to the vicinity of northeast France, and to a lesser extent southwest Belgium, as either a possible place of origin, or, at least, as an important region for the cultivation of these pieces, in terms of composing, circulation, and revision. Again, although these individual chants were often widely transmitted, how they were known in medieval Picardy early on often differed significantly with how they were known later on and farther afield. Indeed, in some instances, the more novel musical aspects of the new sequence—their boldly flexible, often florid, untraditional melodies—appear to have been unsuccessfully transmitted, and these 'disruptions' at times suggest that there was deliberate editing. As in the case of *Celeste organum*, witnesses from Cambrai, Laon, Beauvais, and Noyon provide vital

---

[52] These are (alphabetically): *Alto consilio, Celeste organum, Clara chorus, Concurramus devoti, Congaudentes exultemus, Diem natalem, Ecce gratulemur, Excita domine, Exultemus hodie, Gaude canora curia, Gaudete vos fideles, Hec dies gratissima, Iubilemus cordis voce, Laudes cruces attolamus, Laudes deo devotas, Letabundus exultet fidelis, Mane prima sabbati, Misit Herodes innocentum, Novum canticum cantemus, Sacrosancta hodierna, Stola iocunditatis, Trinitatem reserat aquila,* and *Unus amor*. The majority can be shown to have existed by 1100, though the oldest extant readings for a few are from the latter half of the twelfth century or the beginning of the thirteenth century. Most of these were influential and boasted staying power in some fashion in sequence repertories, but a few were apparently more restricted in their transmission and did not survive more than a century.

[53] For the principal study on the *nova cantica* in the Norman-Sicilian source Madrid, Biblioteca Nacional, 289 [E-Mn 289], see David Hiley, 'The Liturgical Music of Norman Sicily: A Study Centred on Manuscripts 288, 289, 19421 and Vitrina 20-24 of the Biblioteca Nacional, Madrid' (Ph.D. diss., University of London, 1981), 376-83; 692-700. See also idem, *Western Plainchant*, 241-50; and Arlt, *Ein Festoffizium*, vol. 1, 175-90.

information about the renewal of the genre of c. 1100, but other places come into play as well: Amiens, Lille, Arras, St-Amand, Anchin, Marchiennes, Compiègne, Reims, and occasionally Tournai, Liege, and Utrecht. Thus, the region of modern-day northeast France and southwest Belgium—the liturgical soundscape of medieval Picardy—may very well have provided a liberal venue for introducing the new sequence into musical practices of the twelfth and early thirteenth centuries, and played a seminal role in a major stylistic changes that left a deep and abiding imprint on the history of the genre.

Appendix 1. *Celeste organum*: β-Seckau version [A-Gu 479]

1. Celeste organum hodie sonuit in terra
2. Et partum virginis superna cecinit caterva
3a. Quid vacas humana turba cur non gaudes cum celica
3b. Vigilat pastorum cura vox auditur angelica
4a. Cantabant inclita carmina plena pace et gloria
4b. Ad Xpistum referunt propria nobis canunt ex gracia
5a. Non sunt absolute data differenter sunt prolata
5b. Nec cunctorum sunt hec dona sed mens quorum extat bona
6a. Affectus deserant vicia et sic nobis pax est illa quia bonis est promissa
6b. Iunguntur infimis ardua fortis sumit hec infirma immortalis mortalia
7a. Gaude homo cum perpendis talia
7b. Gaude caro facta verbi socia
8a. Nunciant eius ortum sydera lucis per indicia
8b. Secuntur ducis reges lumina bethlehem usque previa
9a. Invenitur rex celorum inter animalia
9b. Arto iacet in presepi rex qui fecit omnia
10a. Stella maris quem tu paris colit hec ecclesia
10b. Ipsi nostra per te piam placeant obsequia
Coda. Iubilent cuncta redempta

Appendix 2. Sequences used in the Laon festal office for Epiphany [F-LA 263]Lbl 2615]

Sequence	Type of Sequence	Rubric in F-LA 263	Liturgy	Use or Function
Letabundus exultet fidelis	New	--	First vespers	Conductus (?)
Iubilemus cordis voce	New	AD MATUTINAS...PROSA	Matins	Invitatory (?)
Misit Herodes innocentum	New	IN PRIMO NOCTURNO POST TRES PS. PROSA	Matins	Hymn for first nocturn (?)
Gaudete vos fideles	New	IN IIo No PROSA	Matins	Hymn for second nocturn (?)
Celeste organum	New	IN IIIo No PROSA	Matins	Hymn for third nocturn (?)
Festa Christi	Early	SEQUENTIA	Mass	Sequence
Misit Herodes innocentum	New	PROSA POST PRIMUM PSALMUM	Second vespers	Votive song
Laudete vos fideles [sic]	New	PROSA POST SECUNDUM PSALMUM	Second vespers	Votive song
Celeste organum	New	PROSA POST TERTIUM PSALMUM	Second vespers	Votive song
Potestate non natura	New	PROSA POST QUARTUM PSALMUM	Second vespers	Votive song
Promissa mundo gaudia	New	PROSA POST QUINTUM PSALMUM	Second vespers	Votive song
Ave Maria...virgo serena	New	VERSUS.. REQUIRE IN ANNUNTIATIONE	Second vespers	Versicle (?)
Alma chorus domini	Early	COMPLETORIUM INFINITUM... PROSA POST PRIMUM PSALMUM	Compline	Votive song
In sapientia disponens	New	ITEM ALIA	Compline	Votive song
Epiphaniam domino	Early	POST SECUNDUM PSALMUM COMPLETORII PROSA	Compline	Votive song
Hac clara die turma	New	POST TERTIUM PSALMUM	Compline	Votive song
Alto consilio	New	ITEM ALIA PROSA	Compline	Votive song
Salus eterna	Early	POST IIII. PSALMUM COMPLETORII SEQUENTIA	Compline	Votive song
Area virga	Early	SEQUENTIA POST HYMNUM	Compline	Hymn
[L]etabundus exultet fidelis	New	[POST COMPLETAM ORATIONEM SUBDIACONI IN MEDIO CHORO DICANT]	Compline	Conductus (?)

Appendix 3. Sequences used in the Beauvais festal office for the Feast of the Circumcision [GB-Lbl 2615]

Sequence	Type of Sequence	Rubric in GB-Lbl 2615	Liturgy	Use or Function
Letabundus exultet fidelis	New	TENENTES CHORUM	First vespers	Hymn
Qui regis sceptra	Early	HYMNUS	Compline	Hymn
Salus eterna	Early	SEQUITUR HYMNUS	Matins	Hymn for first nocturn
Extract of Sancti spiritus adsit	Early	TERCIA BENEDICTIO	Matins	Benediction
Extract of Laudes deo devotas	New	PRIMI	Matins	Versified doxology for responsory
Celeste organum	New	SEQUITUR PROSA	Matins	Hymn for second nocturn
Laudes deo devotas	New	PROSA	Matins	Alternate conductus (?)
Extract of Rex omnipotens	Early	QUINTA BENEDICTIO	Matins	Benediction
Extract of Laudes deo devotas	New	SEXTA BENEDICTIO	Matins	Benediction
Extract of Sancti spiritus adsit	Early	VEL <SEXTA BENEDICTIO>	Matins	Benediction
Area virga	Early	SEQUITUR PROSA	Matins	Hymn for third nocturn
Regine nunc celorum	Early	HYMNUS	Lauds	Hymn
Alle celeste necnon	Early	SEQUITUR PROSA	Mass	Sequence
Christi hodierne	Early	SEQUITUR PROSA	Second vespers	Votive song
Hac clara die turma	Early	HYMNUS	Second vespers	Hymn
Ave Maria...virgo serena	New	SEQUITUR <PROSA>	Second vespers	Votive song / Marian antiphon or suffrage
Alto consilio	New	CONDUCTUS	Second vespers	Conductus

Abstract

The new sequence emerged in the decades around 1100 as a poetic and musical renewal of a long-established proper chant of the mass. These new specimens of the genre demonstrate not only that their poet-composers turned to accentual verse for technical and formal inspiration and away from pre-existing melodies as the structural source and supplier for the text, but also that they sought out different approaches to modality, melodic vocabulary, and text-music relationships in their musical settings. A close analysis of the melodic and textual variants as well as the transmission history of *Celeste organum* demonstrates that how new sequences were known in their earliest iterations and how they initially functioned liturgically often differed significantly from later instantiations. In many cases, the most innovative melodic features of the new sequence appear to have been unsuccessfully transmitted. These 'disruptions' suggest conscious redacting of received models in order to make the pieces conform better to the musical style of the early sequence and the established context of the Gregorian mass. Furthermore, medieval Picardy appears to have been an important region for the production, circulation, and reception of the new sequence in its earliest phase of transmission.

Free Papers

Das „Gaudeamus omnes"-Zitat in Lassos Motette *Nunc gaudere licet* und sein Kontext – Aspekte der geistlichen Parodie bei Orlando di Lasso[*]

■

BERNHOLD SCHMID

Für Reinhold und Roswitha Schlötterer

Erstmals in den *Selectissimae cantiones* im Jahr 1568[1] erschien Lassos *Nunc gaudere licet*, ein Trinklied, das mit einem Gelage zu Fastnacht in Verbindung gebracht werden kann, da im Text von den „Bacchanalia" die Rede ist. Dabei handelt es sich um ursprünglich heidnische nächtliche Riten zu Ehren des Dionysos, die vom Christentum in der Zeit von Weihnachten bis zu Beginn der vorösterlichen Fastenzeit geduldet wurden.[2] Die Verbindung der Fastnacht mit Trinken ergibt sich aus der Erklärung des Wortes: Das mittelhochdeutsche „vast-schanc", aus dem die in Süddeutschland und Österreich gebräuchlichen Ausdrücke „Faschang" und „Fasching" abzuleiten sind, steht für Ausschank und Trunk vor der Fastenzeit.[3] Der Text des Stücks lautet:

---

[*] Dem Beitrag liegt ein Referat zugrunde, das der Verfasser bei der Tagung *European Sacred Music, 1550-1800. New Approaches* (Fribourg, 9.-12. Juni 2010) gehalten hat. Für die Druckfassung wurde der Text erheblich erweitert. Für zahlreiche Hinweise und Hilfestellung danke ich Barbara Eichner, Theodor Göllner, Franz Körndle und Jan Kuswari ganz herzlich.

[1] In der Bibliographie der Lasso-Drucke (zugleich Werkverzeichnis) trägt der Druck die Sigle 1568-3; vgl. Horst Leuchtmann und Bernhold Schmid, *Orlando di Lasso: Seine Werke in zeitgenössischen Drucken 1555-1687*, 3 Bde. (Kassel etc., 2001). Die im Folgenden erwähnten Drucke werden stets nach den Siglen bei Leuchtmann und Schmid zitiert.

[2] Zum Stück, seinen Texten – im *Magnum opus musicum* (= 1604-1,472), einer von seinen Söhnen erstellten „Gesamtausgabe" der Motetten Lassos, wird der Text durch geringe Änderungen zu einem Lied verändert, das die Freude der Schüler über den Ferienbeginn ausdrücken soll – und ihrer Funktion vgl. Bernhold Schmid, „Lassos ‚Nunc gaudere licet': Zur Geschichte einer Kontrafaktur", in *Compositionswissenschaft. Festschrift für Reinhold und Roswitha Schlötterer zum 70. Geburtstag*, hrsg. von Bernd Edelmann und Sabine Kurth (Augsburg, 1999), 47-56; dort 50 über den Zusammenhang mit Fastnacht. *Nunc gaudere licet* ist mit seinem originalen Text ediert in Orlando di Lasso, *The Complete Motets 6: Motets for Four to Eight Voices from Selectissimae cantiones (Nuremberg, 1568)*, hrsg. von Peter Bergquist, Recent Researches in the Music of the Renaissance 110 (Madison, 1997), 87-90. Das im *Magnum opus* (1604-1) überlieferte Kontrafakt ist ediert in Orlando di Lasso, *Sämtliche Werke*, Band 19: *Magnum opus musicum … Lateinische Gesänge für 2, 3, 4, 5, 6, 7, 8, 9, 10 u. 12 Stimmen. In Partitur gebracht von Carl Proske, kritisch durchgesehen und redigiert von Franz Xaver Haberl*, Teil X: *Für 6, 7 und 8 Stimmen* (Leipzig, [1908], Nachdruck: New York, 1973), Nr. 472, 66-68. (Im Folgenden zit. als GA XIX; von diesem Band liegt die zweite, nach den Quellen revidierte Auflage noch nicht vor.)

Das Bacchanal spielt auch in der zeitgenössischen Kunst eine Rolle: So schuf Albrecht Dürer 1494 eine Federzeichnung mit dem Titel *Bacchanal mit Silen*, im internet einsehbar unter <http:// http://uploads7.wikipaintings.org/images/albrecht-durer/bacchanal-with-silenus.jpg> (zuletzt aufgerufen am 18. Juli 2013). Vorlage Dürers ist ein Stich von Andrea Mantegna aus den 1470er Jahren (New York, The Metropolitan Museum of Art; <http://www.metmuseum.org/toah/works-of-art/29.44.15>, zuletzt aufgerufen am 22. August 2012).

[3] Harry Kühnel, „Fastnacht", in *Lexikon des Mittelalters* (München etc., 1980-99), Bd. IV (1989), Sp. 313-14, hier 313.

Nunc gaudere licet, dolor hinc et cura. Bibendum est, ut lex Posthumiae iubet magistrae laetitiae, quoniam patri rediere sacrata bacchanalia. Gaudeamus omnes.	Jetzt darf man sich freuen. Fort mit Schmerz und Sorge! Man soll trinken, wie die es Vorschrift Posthumias, der Herrin der Freude, befiehlt, da die dem Vater geweihten Bacchanalia wiedergekehrt sind. Lasst uns alle froh sein.

Der Satz „ut lex Posthumiae iubet magistrae laetitiae" entstammt dem Gedicht Nr. 27 von Catull.[4] Diversen Kommentaren zu Catull ist zu entnehmen, dass Posthumia möglicherweise die Frau des römischen Consuls Servius Sulpicius Rufus (51 v. Chr.) war; als Symposiarchin soll sie zu hemmungslosem Trinken aufgefordert haben, und auch sonst war ihr Ruf wohl nicht ganz einwandfrei: sagt man ihr doch nach, sie sei die Geliebte Cäsars gewesen.[5] Mit „pater" ist mutmaßlich der altitalische Fruchtbarkeitsgott Liber pater gemeint, der später dem griechischen Dionysos gleichgesetzt wurde.[6] Da die Motette im Jahr 1568 gedruckt wurde – Theodor Gerlach datiert die von ihm unterschriebene Vorrede zu den *Selectissimae cantiones* auf das Fest des Heiligen Bartholomäus, den 24. August – könnte spekuliert werden, das Stück sei zur Hochzeit des bayerischen Thronfolgers Wilhelm mit Renata von Lothringen entstanden, die am 22. Februar, also im Fasching 1568 mit großem Aufwand gefeiert wurde.[7]

Lasso und die geistliche Parodie

Lassos Motette – wenn es denn eine solche ist – endet mit „Gaudeamus omnes", dem Beginn mehrerer Introitusgesänge in der Messe, der nicht nur als Text, sondern auch als Melodie zitiert wird. Bevor die Frage aufgeworfen wird, wie dieses Zitat im Kontext des *Nunc gaudere licet* zu verstehen ist, also ob Lasso den Introitusbeginn etwa in parodistischer oder gar blasphemischer Absicht verwendet, ist kurz auf die Frage des Umgangs mit Texten liturgischen Ursprungs im weltlichen Umfeld bei Lasso insgesamt einzugehen. Vorauszuschicken ist, dass die geistliche Parodie im Mittelalter wurzelt, diverse von Lasso aufgegriffene Texte haben sich über Jahrhunderte hinweg in unterschiedlichen Redaktionen bis ins 16. Jahrhundert gehalten. Dass der Komponist beim

---

[4] Schmid, „Lassos ‚Nunc gaudere licet'", 50.
[5] Schmid, „Lassos ‚Nunc gaudere licet'", 51.
[6] Schmid, „Lassos ‚Nunc gaudere licet'", 51.
[7] Zur Hochzeit vgl. Horst Leuchtmann, *Orlando di Lasso: Sein Leben. Versuch einer Bestandsaufnahme der biographischen Einzelheiten* (Wiesbaden, 1976), 50 und 146-50. – Ob das Stück tatsächlich für die Münchner Fürstenhochzeit von 1568 entstanden ist, hängt von folgendem Problem der Überlieferung ab: Der Druck von 1568 enthält eine hinsichtlich des Textes fehlerhafte Fassung; statt „ut lex Posthumiae iubet magistrae laetitiae" heißt es dort sinnfrei „ut lex post ut lex post iubet magistrae laetitiae". Diese „Lesart" kann nur deshalb zustande gekommen sein, weil man bei Gerlach in Nürnberg mit der „lex Posthumiae" nichts anzufangen wußte. Erst der zweite Druck unseres Stücks, der bei le Roy & Ballard herausgekommene *Vingtieme livre de chansons* (1569-20), enthält den richtigen Text. Somit sind zwei Möglichkeiten denkbar: 1) Gerlach erhielt von Lasso das Stück mit dem richtigen Text, den er nicht verstanden hat. Unser Druck wäre dann der Erstdruck, das Stück könnte tatsächlich zu den Hochzeitsfeierlichkeiten entstanden sein. 2) Dem *Vingtieme livre de chansons* von 1569 mit dem richtigen Text ging ein heute verlorener früherer, ebenfalls korrekt textierter Druck voraus, der wiederum Gerlach als Vorlage gedient haben könnte; in diesem Fall wäre die Möglichkeit, dass das *Nunc gaudere licet* zur Fürstenhochzeit entstanden ist, nur dann gegeben, wenn dieser hypothetische Druck ebenfalls 1568 erschienen wäre.

Parodieren geistlicher Texte (wie bei der Wahl seiner Texte generell[8]) nicht gerade zimperlich war, zeigt die Anzahl entsprechender Stücke ebenso wie der mitunter jedenfalls heute als blasphemisch aufgefasste Umgang mit den Vorlagen.[9] Im Folgenden sei ein kurzer Überblick gegeben.

Da haben wir zunächst Parodien auf präexistente Texte (Tabelle 1). In beiden Stücken greift die Umtextierung den Anfang unverändert (bzw. beim *Vinum bonum et suave* nur minimal abweichend) auf, so dass die Vorlage unmittelbar erkennbar ist; die Fortsetzung allerdings geschieht in freier Weise. Dass es sich jeweils um Parodien handelt, ergibt sich aus der wörtlichen Übernahme des Beginns der Vorlage. Beim Text des *Vinum bonum et suave* handelt es sich um einen ganzen Komplex von Strophen, die in immer wieder neuer Zusammensetzung unter Weglassung und Hinzufügung von Strophen im Mittelalter weit verbreitet waren. Selbst die formale Gestalt der Strophen kann abweichen: Lassos Komposition liegt eine Fassung zugrunde, deren Strophen aus drei statt vier Verszeilen bestehen; verbreitet sind indes auch textlich abweichende Versionen, die den Strophenbau der Vorlage aufgreifen.[10]

Tabelle 1. Lassos Parodien auf präexistente Texte

Parodie	Vorlage	Gesamtausgabe	Erstdruck, -beleg
Iam lucis orto sidere Statim oportet bibere, Ergo bene erimus Si bene potaverimus. …[a]	Iam lucis orto sidere, Deum precemur supplices, Ut in diurnis actibus, Nos servet a nocentibus. …	GA XXI[b], Nr. 508	1564-5
Vinum bonum et suave, Nunquam bibi vinum tale, Vinum cor laetificat. …	Verbum bonum et suave, Personemus, illud Ave, Per quod Christi fit conclave Virgo, mater, filia. …	GA XXI, Nr. 509	1570-6

[a] Eine abweichende Fassung bei Paul Lehmann, *Die Parodie im Mittelalter* (Stuttgart,² 1963), 128.
[b] Orlando di Lasso, *Sämtliche Werke*, Band 21: *Magnum opus musicum … Lateinische Gesänge für 2, 3, 4, 5, 6, 7, 8, 9, 10 u. 12 Stimmen. In Partitur gebracht von Carl Proske*, Teil XI: Für 8, 9, 10 und 12 Stimmen, redigiert von Adolf Sandberger (Leipzig, [1926]; Nachdruck: New York, 1973), 84-90 (im Folgenden zit. als GA XXI; die zweite, nach den Quellen revidierte Auflage liegt noch nicht vor).

[8] Der alternde, sehr fromm gewordene Komponist entschuldigt sich in der Vorrede seines *Libro de villanelle, moresche, et altre canzoni* (1581-6) mit den hinsichtlich ihrer Texte höchst zweifelhaften Moreschen und Villanellen: Freunde hätten ihn zur Publikation gedrängt. Und die dem Papst gewidmeten *Lagrime di San Pietro* (1595-1) habe Lasso in Anlehnung an das Vorbild des Textdichters Tansillo „als einen an die höchste kirchliche Instanz gerichteten, außergewöhnlichen Beweis persönlicher Bußbereitschaft geplant, … aus kirchlicher Sicht hatte er ja allen Grund, angesichts unzähliger, von ihm vertonter ‚schlüpfriger' Texte Reue zu empfinden." (Zitat aus Fritz Jenschs Einleitung zu Orlando di Lasso, *Sämtliche Werke. Neue Reihe* 20: *Lagrime di San Pietro*, hrsg. von Fritz Jensch [Kassel etc., 1989], VII.)
[9] Auch zeitgenössisch stießen Lassos Texte nicht durchgängig auf Zustimmung; vgl. David Crook, „A Sixteenth-Century Catalog of Prohibited Music", in *Journal of the American Musicological Society* 62 (2009), 1-78, der Katalog mit verbotenen Stücken (nicht nur von Lasso) ist abgedruckt 62-70; voraus geht eine Auflistung erlaubter oder empfohlener Sätze (58-62) sowie Instruktionen zum Umgang mit erbaulicher Musik bei den Jesuiten (55-68). Hingewiesen sei ferner auf Horst Leuchtmann, „Kritik an Lasso?", in *Musik in Bayern* 46 (1993), 55-61.
[10] Etwa „Vinum bonum et suave, / Bonis bonum, pravis prave, / Cunctis dulcis sapor, ave, / Mundana laetitia." Vgl. Lehmann, *Parodie*, 124 ff.; Martha Bayless, *Parody in the Middle Ages. The Latin Tradition* (Ann Arbor, Michigan, 1998), 109. Eine ganze Gruppe unterschiedlicher Fassungen ähnlich wie beim *Vinum bonum et suave* bildet außerdem das *Fertur in conviviis*; hierzu existiert allerdings keine Vorlage, es handelt sich um ein auf den Archipoeta zurückgehendes Trinklied; vgl. Bernhold Schmid, „Lasso's ‚Fertur in conviviis': On the History of its Text and Transmission" in *Orlando di Lasso Studies*, hrsg. von Peter Bergquist (Cambridge, 1999), 116-31, besonders 124-27. Zu diesem Stück vgl. auch im vorliegenden Text unten 107-9.

Im *Magnum opus Musicum* 1604-1, jener von Lassos Söhnen betreuten „Gesamtausgabe" der Motetten ihres Vaters, wird *Iam lucis orto sidere* kontrafaziert: die Parodie wird durch deren Vorlage ersetzt. In diesem Kontext zu erwähnen ist außerdem Lassos dem *Vinum bonum*-Komplex entstammendes *Ave color vini clari*,[11] das ebenso wie die obengenannten Parodien dem Typus des Trinklieds zuzurechnen ist. Hier wird zwar keine Textvorlage parodiert, dass man das *Ave color vini clari* aber zumindest in unmittelbarer Nähe der Parodie sah, zeigt ein Versuch, diesem Stück einen präexistenten Text in kontrafazierender Absicht zu unterlegen: Ein aus Kloster Neresheim stammendes, heute in der Thurn und Taxis-Bibliothek in Regensburg aufbewahrtes Exemplar des Drucks 1579-3 (einer Auflage der oben schon genannten *Selectissimae cantiones*) enthält handschriftlich eingetragen Passagen aus dem *Crinale Beatae Mariae Virginis* des Kartäusers Conrad von Haimburg († am 17. August 1360).[12] Nicht der vollständige Text des *Ave color vini clari* ist kontrafaziert, sondern nur die ersten sechs Verszeilen, der Kontrafakturversuch ist also wohl gescheitert.

Original:	**Kontrafaktur:**
Ave color vini clari,	Ave Virgo Sponsa nata,
Ave sapor sine pari,	Christi mater sublimata,
Tua nos inebriari	Ab aeterno ordinata,
Digneris potentia.	Dei placens oculis.
O quam felix creatura,	Aue, rosa, quae de Regum
Quam produxit vitis pura	Ramis es trans Caelos

Die Gegenüberstellung des ursprünglichen *Ave color vini clari* mit dem präexistenten kontrafazierenden Text macht den Vorgang hinlänglich klar: Man wollte offenbar einen den geistlichen Parodien zumindest eng verwandten Text, eben das *Ave color vini clari*, durch einen „Originaltext" ersetzen. Es liegt damit ein zum Kontrafakt auf *Iam lucis orto sidere* paralleles Verfahren vor, (ein zur Parodie eines Originaltexts umgekehrter Vorgang), nämlich die Rückgängigmachung einer Parodie; im Unterschied zu *Iam lucis orto sidere* geschieht dies aber gleichsam in fiktiver Weise, da ja Conrad von Haimburgs Text selbstverständlich nicht die Vorlage für das *Ave color vini clari* ist.

    Lasso dürfte für derartige Parodien nach geistlichen Texten bekannt gewesen sein. Es existiert nämlich in einem Druck aus dem Jahr 1609, dem *Musicalischen Zeitvertreiber* (gedruckt bei Paul Kauffmann in Nürnberg)[13] eine Lasso zugeschriebene Parodie auf einen Dialog zwischen dem Zelebranten und der Gemeinde mit dem Beginn (Vorsänger): „Vitrum nostrum gloriosum", (Gemeinde): „Eo gratissimum" (Beispiel 1).

---

[11] Lehmann, *Parodie*, 125; außerdem Bayless, *Parody*, 109-11.

[12] Vgl. *Conradus Gemnicensis. Konrads von Haimburg und seiner Nachahmer Reimgebete*, hrsg. von Guido Maria Dreves, Analecta Hymnica Medii Aevi 3 (Leipzig, 1888), 22-26. Der handschriftlich unterlegte Text Konrads weicht von dessen Original geringfügig ab, vgl. dazu den kritischen Bericht zum *Ave color vini clari* in Orlando di Lasso, *Sämtliche Werke. Zweite, nach den Quellen revidierte Auflage der Ausgabe von F. X. Haberl und A. Sandberger*, Band 11: *Motetten VI (Magnum opus musicum, Teil VI)*, neu hrsg. von Bernhold Schmid (Wiesbaden etc., 2012), LXXIV (im Folgenden zit. als GA² XI).

[13] RISM 1609[28].

Beispiel 1. *Vitrum nostrum gloriosum*, Anfang. Das Altus-Stimmbuch ist nicht erhalten

Der (bisher nicht identifizierte) Text gehört in den Umkreis der Saufmesse. Boetticher hält die Zuschreibung an Lasso für falsch,[14] das Stück dürfte in der Tat kaum authentisch sein. Bei Kauffmann stützte man sich wohl auf die Autorität Lassos als Verkaufsargument, dem man offenbar derartiges zutraute.

Im abzuhandelnden Kontext ist eine zweite Gruppe von Stücken vorzustellen, zu denen auch das *Nunc gaudere licet* gehört. Es handelt sich um Kompositionen, in denen wörtliche geistliche Zitate (Text und Musik) mit eventuell parodistischer Absicht in ein textlich und oft auch musikalisch komisches Umfeld gestellt werden (Tabelle 2).[15]

Tabelle 2. Geistliche Zitate in parodistischer Absicht bei Lasso

Textincipit	Zitat	Gesamtausgabe	Erstdruck, -beleg
Fertur in conviviis	Requiem aeternam	GA² III,[a] Nr. 141	1564-3,9 und 1564-13,29
Nunc gaudere licet	Gaudeamus omnes	GA XIX, Nr. 472	1568-3,36
Il estoit une religieuse	Ave Maria Pater noster	GA² XII,[b] 74-76	1565-10,1

[a] Orlando di Lasso, *Sämtliche Werke. Zweite, nach den Quellen revidierte Auflage ...*, Band 3: *Motetten II (Magnum opus musicum, Teil II)*, neu hrsg. von Bernhold Schmid (Wiesbaden etc., 2004). Im Folgenden zit. als. GA² III.
[b] Orlando di Lasso, *Sämtliche Werke. Zweite, nach den Quellen revidierte Auflage ...*, Band 12: *Kompositionen mit französischem Text I*, neu hrsg. von Horst Leuchtmann (Wiesbaden, 1982). Im Folgenden zit. als. GA² XII.

Fertur in conviviis endet mit „Requiem aeternam", wobei „Requiem" zunächst vom Bass solistisch in tiefer Lage vorgetragen wird, während „aeternam" in imitierenden, vom

---

[14] Wolfgang Boetticher, *Orlando di Lasso und seine Zeit 1532-1594. Repertoire-Untersuchungen zur Musik der Spätrenaissance*. Band I: *Monographie, Neuausgabe mit einem Fortsetzenden Literaturbericht 1958-1998, Verzeichnis der Kontrafakturen, Addenda und Emendata* (Wilhemshaven, 1999), 16.

[15] Vgl. hierzu auch die Auflistung bei Bernhard Meier, „Melodiezitate in der Musik des 16. Jahrhunderts", in *Tijdschrift van de Vereniging voor Nederlandse Muziekgeschiedenis* 20 (1964-65), 1-10, hier 3.

Sopran zum Bass absteigenden Einsätzen beginnt und anschließend vom Tenor als Cantus firmus vorgetragen wird (Beispiel 2a). Das Zitat ist textlich wie musikalisch deutlich hervorgehoben und vom Zuhörer als solches zweifelsohne zu erkennen (Beispiel 2b).

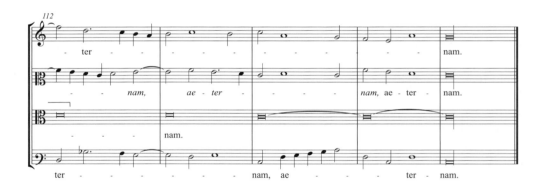

Beispiel 2a. *Fertur in conviviis*, T. 106-16

Beispiel 2b. Beginn des Introitus *Requiem aeternam* (nach *Graduale Triplex*, 669). Benutzt wurde die Ausgabe Solesmes, 1979

„Requiem aeternam" mag innerhalb des Texts auf den ersten Blick als frech parodistisch oder gar blasphemisch zu verstehen sein; allerdings kann man dem *Fertur in conviviis*, so deftig und lustig es zunächst zu sein scheint, das Wissen der im Lied sprechenden Person um den eigenen Zustand und vielleicht sogar die Tendenz zur Verzweiflung nicht absprechen, wenn man Textstellen wie „meum est propositum in taberna mori" („es ist mir aufgesetzt, im Wirtshaus zu sterben") oder „Deus sit propitius huic potatori" („Gott möge diesem Säufer gewogen sein") berücksichtigt. Die beiden letzten Verszeilen „donec sanctos angelos venientes cernam, | cantantes pro ebrijs: Requiem aeternam" („bis ich die Heiligen Engel kommen sehe, | die für die Betrunkenen Requiem aeternam singen") drücken den Wunsch nach Erlösung aus; die Hoffnung auf ewige Ruhe ist also keineswegs aufgegeben. So gesehen kann von Blasphemie nicht mehr die Rede sein. Auch im Kontrafakt *Tristis ut Euridicen*, eine reichlich boshafte, parodistische Totenklage auf Jacob Clemens non Papa, der offenbar als Säufer bekannt war,[16] ändert sich da nichts: „fas est nam | cantare pro mortuo: Requiem aeternam" („nun ist es recht, | für den Toten Requiem aeternam zu singen"), heißt es versöhnlich am Ende.[17] Anders sieht es bei der zweiten Kontrafaktur zum *Fertur in conviviis* aus, derjenigen im *Magnum opus Musicum* 1604-1. Dort verschiebt sich der Blickwinkel massiv, das „Requiem"-Zitat erhält eine völlig neue Bedeutung. Der Text warnt nachdrücklich vor dem Saufen. Alles, was im Original als quasi positiv dargestellt ist, wird ins Gegenteil verkehrt. So steht im Original „[vinum] loqui facit clericum optimum latinum" („[der Wein] bewirkt, dass ein Geistlicher bestes Latein spricht"); das Kontrafakt verändert zu „loqui facit homines pessimum latinum" („bewirkt, dass die Menschen schlechtestes Latein sprechen"); bemerkenswert ist auch die Änderung von speziell „clericum" zu allgemein „homines". Folgerichtig bringt das „Requiem" am Ende keine Wendung ins Positive, wenn es heißt: „donec malos angelos venientes cernant, | cantantes his non fore: Requiem aeternam" („bis sie die bösen Engel kommen sehen, | die für sie nicht Requiem aeternam singen werden"). Der Text bleibt auch beim „Requiem"-Zitat seiner Absicht treu, das Original ins Gegenteil zu verkehren. Hier ist an Parodie oder Blasphemie absolut nicht zu denken.[18]

Il estoit une religieuse[19] greift die Choralzitate mehrmals auf. Auch hier sind sie deutlich hervorgehoben.[20] Wie auch beim „Requiem aeternam" im *Fertur in conviviis* sorgen große Notenwerte und satztechnisch eigenständige Gestaltung für ihre herausragende Stellung im Satz: „Pater" (T. 5-8) ist als paarige Imitation über dem Cantus firmus gestaltet (Beispiel 3a), „Pater et l'Avé Maria" (T. 18-24) als Cantus firmus im Bass (Beispiel 3b), wobei die übrigen Stimmen wenigstens teilweise die langsame Gangart des Choralzitats aufgreifen (Beispiel 3c und 3d); ansonsten ist der Satz dem Typ der Pariser Chanson verpflichtet.

---

[16] Das Kontrafakt ist abgedruckt in GA² III, XCIII. Zu Clemens non Papa vgl. Henri Vanhulst, „Clemens non Papa ‚grant yvroigne et mal vivant' (1553)", in *Beyond Contemporary Fame. Reassessing the Art of Clemens non Papa and Thomas Crecquillon. Colloquium Proceedings Utrecht, April 24-26, 2003*, hrsg. von Eric Jas (Turnhout, 2005), 18-25, hier 21-23. – Sich über verstorbene Musiker lustig zu machen war offenbar durchaus häufiger der Fall, vgl. etwa Katelijne Schiltz, „Tod in Venedig. Adrian Willaert als Rezipient burlesker Lamenti", in *Tod in Musik und Kultur. Zum 500. Todestag Philipps des Schönen*, hrsg. von Stefan Gasch und Birgit Lodes, Wiener Forum für Ältere Musikgeschichte 2 (Tutzing, 2007), 359-76.

[17] Ein Parallelfall findet sich in von Lassos Text zum Teil weit abweichenden Überlieferungen des *Ad primum morsum* (GA XIX, Nr. 474). Der Text endet dort ebenfalls mit einer Bitte an Gott um [ewige] Ruhe: „Det Deus huic requiem, qui bibit ante diem. Amen." Vgl. Lehmann, *Parodie*, 133. Vgl. außerdem Folke Gernert, *Parodia y „Contrafacta" en la Literatura Románica Medieval y Renacentista. Historia, Teoría y Textos*, Bd. II: *Textos* (San Millán de la Cogolla, 2009), 154 Fußn. 18 (dort wohl irrtümlich „huie" statt „huic").

[18] Zum *Fertur in conviviis* und seinen Kontrafakta vgl. auch Bernhold Schmid, „Aspekte der Kontrafaktur im 15. und 16. Jahrhundert. Satz, Funktion, Gattung", in *Die Kunst des Übergangs. Musik aus Musik in der Renaissance*, hrsg. von Nicole Schwindt, Trossinger Jahrbuch für Renaissancemusik 7 Kassel etc., (2007), 39-62, hier 54-58.

[19] Zu dieser Chanson vgl. David J. Rothenberg, „,Le *Pater* et L'*Avé Maria* sont enfilés en une Patenostre': Lasso's *Il estoit une religieuse* and the Tradition of *Pater noster – Ave Maria* Settings", in *Musik in Bayern* 69 (2005), 53-70.

[20] Ausnahme sind die T. 3-4 des Stücks, wo nur der Text „l'Avé Maria", nicht aber die Melodie zitiert wird.

Beispiel 3a. *Il estoit une religieuse*, T. 5-8

Beispiel 3b. *Il estoit une religieuse*, T. 18-24

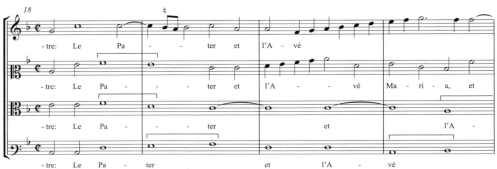

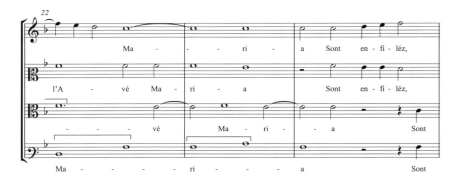

Beispiel 3c. Beginn des *Pater noster* (nach *Graduale Triplex*, 812)

Beispiel 3d. Beginn des *Ave Maria* (nach *Antiphonale Romanum*, 668; hier angeglichen an die „germanische" Lesart Lassos). Benutzt wurde die Ausgabe Paris etc., 1949)

Die Koppelung des *Pater noster* mit dem *Ave Maria* hat Tradition, wobei sich die Verbindung der Texte daraus ergibt, dass sie zusammen mit dem *Credo* die Stundengebete eröffnen."[21] Weithin bekannt wurde Josquins Komposition beider Texte in einer Motette. Das *Magnum opus Musicum*, jene Zusammenstellung von Lassos Motetten durch seine Söhne, enthält eine zweiteilige Motette *Pater noster*, II. pars *Ave Maria*. Es ist allerdings umstritten, ob beide Teile ursprünglich zusammengehören;[22] Lasso muss die Tradition der Verbindung des *Pater noster* mit dem *Ave Maria* jedoch gekannt haben, da Josquins Motette in Mus.ms. 12 der Bayerischen Staatsbibliothek, einem Codex der Hofkapelle aus dem dritten Jahrzehnt des 16. Jahrhunderts, enthalten ist.[23]

Mit den Choralzitaten im *Il estoit une religieuse* liegt (im Gegensatz zum „Requiem aeternam" im *Fertur in conviviis*) nun in der Tat eine freche, durchaus blasphemische Parodie im frivolen Kontext vor.[24] Zum Verständnis sei der Originaltext und eine Übersetzung gegeben:

Il estoit une religieuse	Es war eine Nonne vom Ave Maria-Orden, die
De l'ordre de l'Avé Maria,	so sehr in einen Pater [gemeint ist ein Mönch]
Qui d'un Pater estoit tant amoureuse,	verliebt war, dass sie ihren zarten Körper
Que son gent corps auec le sien lya.	mit seinem verband. Die Äbtissin kam und
L'Abesse vint demander qu'il y a,	fragte, was geschehen war. Beide antworteten:
Lors respondirent l'un & l'autre:	Das Pater [noster] und das Ave Maria sind
Le Pater & L'Avé Maria	verschlungen zu einem Rosenkranz.
Sont enfilés en une Patenostre.	

Es ist eindeutig, dass die Zitate nicht als einzelne parodiert werden, sondern zusammengehörig, also in der traditionellen Verbindung beider Texte. Dies ergibt sich schon daraus, dass eine Nonne vom Ave Maria-Orden sich der körperlichen Liebe mit einem Pater, einem zum Priester geweihten Mönch, hingibt, und noch mehr natürlich aus der Ausrede beider, sie seien zu einem Rosenkranz verbunden, in dessen Ablauf bekanntlich immer wieder das *Ave Maria* und das *Pater noster* gebetet werden.

---

[21] Vgl. Daniel E. Freeman, „On the Origins of the Pater noster-Ave Maria of Josquin Des Prez", in *Musica Disciplina* 45 (1991), 169-219, hier 187-88. Vgl. auch Rothenberg, „Le *Pater* et L'*Avé Maria*", 56-60 und Winfried Kirsch, „Das Bild des Beters im Zeitalter des Humanismus. Zu einigen *Pater noster-Ave Maria*-Vertonungen von Josquin Desprez bis Orlando di Lasso", in *Quellenstudium und musikalische Analyse. Festschrift Martin Just zum 70. Geburtstag*, hrsg. von Peter Niedermüller, Cristina Urchueguía und Oliver Wiener (Würzburg, 2001), 83-106. – Im Fall der *Missa Pater noster* von Ludwig Daser erklingen das *Pater noster* und das *Ave Maria* ab T. 16 des *Credo* gleichzeitig, zu Beginn des Satzes werden das *Pater noster* (Text und Melodie) sowie das gregorianische *Credo I* parallel geführt; hier haben wir also alle drei Texte und Melodien in einer Komposition zusammengefasst (vgl. dazu Bernhold Schmid, „Cantus firmus und Kanon: Anmerkungen zu Ludwig Dasers *Missa Pater noster*", in *Canons and Canonic Techniques, 14th-16th Centuries: Theory, Practice, and Reception History. Proceedings of the International Conference, Leuven, 4-6 October 2005*, hrsg. von Katelijne Schiltz und Bonnie J. Blackburn (Leuven, 2007), 283-302, hier 294 und 295-96, Beispiel 14.8.

[22] Orlando di Lasso, *Sämtliche Werke*, Band 13: *Magnum opus musicum …*, Teil VII: *Für 6 Stimmen* (Leipzig, [1901], Nachdruck: New York, 1973), Nr. 352. – Zur Diskussion, ob beide Sätze zusammengehören, vgl. Rothenberg, „Le *Pater* et L'*Avé Maria*", 64-65 und Bergquist in Orlando di Lasso, *The Complete Motets* 21: *Motets for Three to Twelve Voices from Magnum Opus Musicum (Munich, 1604)*, hrsg. von Peter Bergquist, Recent Researches in the Music of the Renaissance 148 (Middleton, 2006), xix. Eine ausführliche Diskussion enthält die zweite, nach den Quellen revidierte Auflage von Lasso, *Sämtliche Werke*, Band 13 (Wiesbaden, 2013), LXII-LXIII.

[23] Vgl. Martin Bente, Marie Louise Göllner, Helmut Hell und Bettina Wackernagel, *Bayerische Staatsbibliothek, Katalog der Musikhandschriften*, 1: *Chorbücher und Handschriften in chorbuchartiger Notierung*, Kataloge Bayerischer Musiksammlungen 5/1 (München, 1989) 74-75. Vgl. auch Rothenberg, „Le *Pater* et L'*Avé Maria*", 65-66. Die Auflistung von Drucken mit *Pater noster / Ave Maria*-Paaren bei Rothenberg 69-70 ist jedoch insofern irrelevant, als die Drucke aus der Hofbibliothek und nicht aus der der Hofkapelle stammen.

[24] Zum Folgenden vgl. Rothenberg, „Le *Pater* et L'*Avé Maria*", 53-54 und 57.

Auch im vorliegenden Fall kann sich die Bedeutung der Zitate im neuen Textumfeld einer Kontrafazierung komplett wandeln, wobei ein einigermaßen nachvollziehbarer Zusammenhang zwischen Text und Musik aber nicht durchgängig gewahrt bleibt. So in einem geistlichen Kontrafakt zu unserer Chanson, das in der bei Haultin in La Rochelle erschienenen *Mellange d'orlande de Lassus* (1575-6) enthalten ist: Die Verszeile „Le Pater & L'Avé Maria" wird dort zu „Seigneur Dieu, quelle joye il y a"[25] geändert. Das *Pater noster*-Zitat trifft durchaus sinnvoll auf „Seigneur Dieu",[26] hinsichtlich der musikalischen Textausdeutung her aber sinnfrei ist die Fortsetzung „quelle joye il y a", da schon die Hervorhebung dieser Passage durch den komplexen Satz in langsamen Notenwerten nicht einleuchten will und noch weniger das Melodiezitat des *Ave Maria*.

Das „Gaudeamus omnes"-Zitat in Lassos Motette

Beim dritten Stück der Gruppe mit wörtlichen Zitaten aus liturgischen Texten bzw. Melodien, dem *Nunc gaudere licet*, steht das „Gaudeamus omnes" zunächst ohne die dazugehörige Melodie (weitgehend blockhaft im Dreiermetrum deklamiert, ehe es – jetzt im Zweiermetrum – im Bass in Breven als Cantus firmus vorgetragen wird (Beispiel 4a und 4b). In den Oberstimmen stehen immer wieder aufsteigende Dreiklänge über den Cantus firmus-Tönen, so dass beinahe der Eindruck einer Reihung in sich bewegter Klänge entsteht.

Beispiel 4a. *Nunc gaudere licet*, T. 32-46

---

[25] Der vollständige Text des Kontrafakts in GA² XII, CIX.
[26] Zu Choralzitaten im ernsthaften Kontext vgl. Meier, „Melodiezitate", 2.

Beispiel 4a. Continued

Beispiel 4b. Begin des Introitus *Gaudeamus omnes* (nach *Graduale Triplex*, 405)

Im Folgenden haben wir uns den semantischen Verknüpfungen zu widmen, in denen „Gaudeamus omnes" (oft auch verkürzt als „Gaudeamus") auftreten kann, was nach einem Überblick über den Introitus *Gaudeamus omnes* – die kirchlichen Feste, an denen er zu singen ist, sowie seine Verbreitung und Beliebtheit – geschehen soll. Doch zuvor seien kurz einige Beispiele für Choralzitate in außerliturgischen musikalischen Zusammenhängen generell angeführt, um das Umfeld oder auch mögliche Wurzeln für Zitate in der Musik des 16. Jahrhunderts wenigstens anzudeuten. Diverse Melodien zu französischen Chansons sind mitunter Bearbeitungen gregorianischer Vorlagen, wie Henri Davenson gezeigt hat. Der Chanson *Le roi Renaud* liegt das *Ave maris stella*

zugrunde, *J'ai vu le loup, le Renard, le lièvre* basiert auf dem *Dies irae*, der Totensequenz.[27] Dorothy S. Packer diskutiert Trinklieder in der Form des Vaudeville basierend auf gregorianischen Chorälen.[28] Eine Parallele zum Aufgreifen des Chorals in der Chanson bietet das Theater. In seinem Buch *Music in the French Secular Theater, 1400-1550* widmet Howard Mayer Brown[29] ein Kapitel geistlichen Musikeinlagen. So findet sich als Ausgangspunkt für komische Situationen immer wieder der Beginn der Praefation „Per omnia saecula saeculorum. Amen". Brown nennt mehrere Beispiele.[30] Am Ende eines von einer Hochzeit handelnden Stücks wird als Refrain „Requiescant in pace" gesungen.[31] Selbstverständlich spielt die Parodie liturgischer Gesänge oder liturgischen Geschehens eine Rolle. Brown gibt Beispiele für scherzhafte Litaneien aus der Farce *Trois nouveaulx martirs*, mit denen die drei Helden sich und worunter sie leiden vorstellen (Beispiel 5).[32]

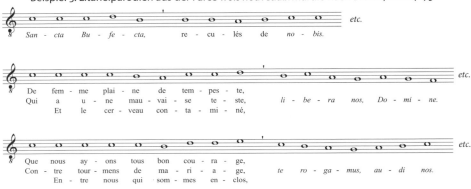

Beispiel 5. Litaneiparodien aus der Farce *Trois nouveaulx martirs* nach Brown, *Music*, 175

[27] Henri Davenson, *Le Livre des Chanson ou Introduction a la Chanson Populaire Francaise* (Neuchâtel, 1944), 120-24 und Nr. 60, 363 (*J'ai vu le loup*).
[28] Dorothy S. Packer, „François Rabelais, Vaudevilliste", in *The Musical Quarterly* 57 (1971), 107-28, hier 112 mit Fußn. 12, wobei sie sich hinsichtlich des Vorkommens gregorianischer Melodiezitate u.a. auf die oben zitierten Arbeiten von Brown und Davenson stützt. Im Zusammenhang mit Lassos *Nasenlied* und der „latent sexuelle[n] Bedeutung der Nase" weist Horst Leuchtmann auf Choralparodien bei Rabelais hin; er zitiert aus dessen *Gargantua und Pantagruel*: „Ad formam nasi cognoscitur ad te levavi." Vgl. Orlando di Lasso, *Sämtliche Werke. Zweite, nach den Quellen revidierte Auflage …, Band 18: Kompositionen mit deutschem Text I*, neu hrsg. von Horst Leuchtmann (Wiesbaden, 1970), LXX.
[29] Cambridge MA, 1963.
[30] Brown, *Music*, 172-73 mit Anmerkung 3.
[31] Brown, *Music*, 173.
[32] Brown, *Music*, 175; auch das folgende Notenbeispiel ist von dort übernommen. Komische Szenen unter Verwendung von Choralzitaten oder Nachahmung liturgischer Musik bzw. entsprechender Texte in parodistischer Absicht finden sich noch in der Oper des 19. und frühen 20. Jahrhunderts: So bringt Berlioz in der 5. Szene von *La damnation de Faust* (Auerbachs Keller) eine hölzern komponierte „Amen"-Fuge; und Branders Lied von der Ratte aus derselben Szene endet mit „Requiescat in pace. Amen"; das lateinische Zitat fehlt bei Goethe. – Busonis *Doktor Faust* enthält im zweiten Bild (Schenke in Wittenberg, eine Szene, deren Anfang zu Auerbachs Keller analog ist) eine Parodie: „Te, Deum, laudamus, / qui fecisti vinum, / Te, Dominum, glorificamus, / qui feminam creavisti. / Dum puellas adoramus, / te eisdem exultamus. / Circulate pocula / in saeculorum saecula." Dort kommt übrigens auch das unten noch zu erwähnende studentische *Gaudeamus igitur* vor. – Die letzte Szene von Verdis *Falstaff* (3. Akt, 2. Teil, Ziffer 43) enthält eingebunden in ein größeres Ensemble, aber dennoch dominant hervortretend eine Parodie auf alternatim vorgetragene Gebetsfloskeln nach Art der Litanei oder der Fürbitten: Alice, Meg und Quickly singen:

Auf dieselbe Floskel folgen die Texte: „Domine fallo guasto", „Fallo punito Domine" und „Fallo pentito Domine". Falstaff antwortet in der Mollvariante der Floskel jeweils mit den Worten:

Die Frechheit der Parodie besteht nun nicht nur darin, dass sie in den turbulenten Schluss einer Komödie eingebaut ist, sondern mindestens ebenso im Wortspiel „Domine" – „l'addomine", also eben darin, dass „Domine" (Herr) jeweils auch als Wortbestandteil von „addomine" (Unterleib) erklingt.

Ein letztes Beispiel: das Carissimi zugeschriebene *Requiem jocosum* für zwei Sopranstimmen über einem ebenfalls gesungenen Bass. Die beiden Oberstimmen sind mit *Quand mon mari vient de dehors* unterlegt – ein Text, den auch Lasso vertont hat.[33] Der Bass trägt als Cantus firmus in langen Notenwerten *Requiem aeternam* vor.[34]

Zum *Gaudeamus omnes*: Wir haben es mit einem denkbar weit verbreiteten Gesang zu tun. Ursprünglich handelt es sich um den Beginn einer ganzen Anzahl von Introitusgesängen zu diversen Heiligenfesten. Im *Graduale Triplex*[35] trifft es auf die Feste der Hl. Agathe, des Hl. Benedikt, auf Marienfeste allgemein (*Ad libitum, pro solemnitates et festis B. M. V.*), speziell auf Mariae Himmelfahrt (dieses Fest wird im Introitustext erwähnt, während im Rahmen des *Commune Beatae Mariae Virginis* nur von „de cuius solemnitate" oder „festivitate", die Rede ist) und schließlich auf den 1. November, Allerheiligen. Die Texte unterscheiden sich nur gering: genannt wird das jeweilige Fest und der jeweilige Heilige, bei Agathe fällt als Martyrerin der Alleluia-Ruf weg. Meist wird als Psalmvers „Eructavit cor meum …" verwendet, am Fest des Hl. Benedikt wird „Magnus Dominus et laudabilis nimis …", an Allerheiligen „Exsultate iusti in Domino …" gesungen. Im 16. Jahrhundert traf das *Gaudeamus omnes* offensichtlich für eine größere Anzahl an Festen zu; das 1511 bei Johannes Winterburger in Wien erschienene *Graduale Pataviense*[36] enthält es unter der Rubrik „De Virginibus Int[roitus]" (fol. 162r/v). Anstelle des Namens der entsprechenden Jungfrau steht „N.", gefolgt von „virgine". Rubriziert ist das *Gaudeamus omnes* dort außerdem mit „Visitacionis Beate Marie", „Assumptionis M.[arie]", „De vno Marti[re]" und mit „De Pluribus sanctis". (Außerdem finden zusätzlich zu den oben genannten weitere Psalmverse Verwendung.) In diesem Zusammenhang sei noch darauf hingewiesen, dass Josquin eine Messe über die *Gaudeamus omnes*-Melodie komponiert hat; aus dem Choral werden Soggetti gewonnen, teilweise wird er auch als Cantus firmus verwendet.[37] Und Cristobal de Morales' Motette *Jubilate Deo* verwendet den Beginn des *Gaudeamus omnes* als Ostinato; Tomás Luis de Victoria hat eine *Missa Gaudeamus* über Morales' Motette geschrieben.[38]

Die immense Beliebtheit des *Gaudeamus omnes* unterstreicht ein die Messe und ihre Bestandteile erläuternder deutscher Text aus der Zeit um 1480, der als die älteste deutschsprachige Messauslegung gilt. Dort wird zu Beginn des Abschnitts über die einzelnen Teile der Messe über den Introitus gehandelt;[39] zitiert wird derjenige zum Fest der Visitatio der Jungfrau Maria: „Gaudeamus omnes in Domino diem festum celebran-

---

[33] GA² XII, 23-24.
[34] Vgl. Robert Haas, *Die Musik des Barock*, Handbuch der Musikwissenschaft 3 (Wildpark-Potsdam, 1928), 131.
[35] Ausgabe Solesmes, 1979.
[36] *Graduale Pataviense (Wien 1511)*, Faksimile, hrsg. von Christian Väterlein, Das Erbe deutscher Musik 87 (Kassel etc., 1982).
[37] Erstgedruckt bei Ottaviano Petrucci, *Misse Josquin* (Venedig, 1502). Edition: Josquin des Prez, *New Edition of the Collected Works*, hrsg. von Willem Elders u.a. (Utrecht, 1988-), Band 4.2.
[38] Editionen: Cristóbal de Morales, *Opera Omnia 2, Motetes I-XXV*, hrsg. von Higinio Anglès, Monumentos de la música española 13 (Rom, 1953), 184 ff.. Tomás Luis de Victoria, *Opera Omnia 1, Missarum liber primus*, hrsg. von Higinio Anglès, Monumentos de la música española 25 (Rom, 1965), 99 ff..
[39] Die folgenden wörtlichen Zitate nach *Die älteste Gesamtauslegung der Messe (Erstausgabe ca. 1480)*, hrsg. von Franz Rudolf Reichert, Corpus Catholicorum. Werke katholischer Schriftsteller im Zeitalter der Glaubensspaltung 29 (Münster, 1967), 49-52 (die genauen Fundstellen, denen die Zitate entnommen sind, werden im Haupttext in Klammern angegeben). Die Messauslegung (Erstausgabe bei Friedrich Creussner in Nürnberg, nicht nach 1482; vgl. die genannte Edition von Reichert, Einleitung, XIX) wurde mehrfach gedruckt und auch abgeschrieben, wie Reichert in der Einleitung, XIX-LVI, feststellt. Schließlich erfuhr der Text eine Neubearbeitung durch Adam Walasser (erstgedruckt bei Johann Mayer 1572 in Dillingen), die ebenfalls mehrere Auflagen erlebte (vgl. Reichert, Einleitung, L-LIII).

tes in honore Marie virginis de cuius visitatione gaudent angeli et collaudent Filium Dei." (49, Zeile 12 ff.) Und kurz danach die deutsche Übersetzung: „Frewen wir uns all in dem Herren des hochzeytlichen tages, den wir feyernn in ere der allerseligsten junckfrawen Marie, durch der heymsuchung sich frewent die engel und mitloben den Sun Gottes." (49, Zeile 25 ff.) Ein mit „Gaudeamus omnes" beginnender Introitus wird also zum Beispiel für Introitusgesänge insgesamt herangezogen. Die unmittelbar sowohl nach dem lateinischen Text als auch nach der deutschen Übersetzung stehenden Kommentare „Das heyst und ist der Introit" (49, Zeile 15) bzw. „Das sind die wort des Introits;" (50, Zeile 1) lassen fast den Schluss zu, dass das *Gaudeamus omnes* gar als der Introitus schlechthin gesehen wurde. Dieser Eindruck verstärkt sich, wenn an späterer Stelle zu lesen ist: „Und darnach spricht der priester den Introit widerumb *Gaudeamus omnes* etc.," (51, Zeile 13 f.); noch deutlicher in diese Richtung geht die Formulierung „das *Gaudeamus* oder der Introit" (51, Zeile 18 f.). Dennoch ist sich der Autor darüber im Klaren, dass es auch andere Introiten gibt, da er kurz nach dem lateinischen Zitat des Introitus In Visitatione BMV schreibt: „Doch so seyn die Introit ungeleych nach der zeyt oder den heiligen oder von den selen; und gewoenlich all suntag ein ander Introit." (49, Zeile 21 ff.). Trotzdem ist festzuhalten, dass das *Gaudeamus omnes* stellvertretend für den Introitus insgesamt herangezogen wird; es hat sicherlich eine herausgehobene Stellung, da es ja als Beginn zahlreicher Introiten verwendet wird, wie auch unsere Messauslegung feststellt: „Nun allwegen so da ein fest der muter Gotes, Marie der junckfrawen, oder sust ein ander groß fest ist, dar an man singt den Introit *Gaudeamus*," (50, Zeile 14 ff.). Da es sich um große Feste handelt, ist Freude angesagt, wie unser Text mehrmals betont: „Nun sollen wir uns frewen des hochzeytlichen festes oder tages der heymsuchung Marie" (50, Zeile 10 ff., hier wieder auf die Visitatio BMV bezogen), oder an anderer Stelle, unmittelbar nach der deutschen Übersetzung des lateinischen *Gaudeamus*: „Das sind die wort des Introits; und ist der meynung, das wir uns alle frewen sollen in dem Herren." (50, Zeile 1 f.); der Text liefert als Begründung dazu den Satz 4, 4 aus dem Brief des Apostels Paulus an die Philipper.[40]

Die Beliebtheit des *Gaudeamus omnes*, seine große Verbreitung und nicht zuletzt der Inhalt des Textes, also der Ausdruck der Freude, mag als Ursache für die Übernahme des Textincipits in andere, außerliturgische Bereiche gelten, wo sich offenkundig ganze Assozisationsketten mit diesem Text verbinden. Die oben schon herangezogene deutschsprachige Messauslegung aus der Zeit um 1480 verweist im Zusammenhang mit dem *Gaudeamus omnes* auch auf die weltliche Freude: „Wann keyn frewd – weder geystlich noch weltlich – gantz seyn mag denn die frewd, die da gesucht wirt in dem Herren."[41]

---

[40] Wie sehr der Gesang geschätzt wurde, zeigt schließlich auch die Rolle, die er bei der franziskanischen Mission in Kalifornien gespielt hat. Craig H. Russell, *From Serra to Sancho. Music and Pageantry in the Californian Missions* (Oxford, 2009) beschäftigt sich ausführlich damit; hier sei nur das Chorbuch des Franziskaners Narciso Durán aus dem Jahr 1813 erwähnt, das dieser für die Neubekehrten der Missionsstation San Jose benutzte (vgl. die Angaben im Internet zu Russell, *From Serra to Sancho* unter <http://www.oup.com/us/companion.websites/9780195343274/appendix/appendices/pdfs/A2-5_Bancroft.pdf>, zuletzt aufgerufen am 19. Juli 2012). Das Repertoire an Propriumsmelodien ist dort massiv reduziert, bezogen auf die Introiten schreibt Russell: „Durán hammers *all* the Introits into the same melodic mold of the *Gaudeamus omnes*" (vgl. Russell, *From Serra to Sancho*, 33-34). Hier wird die *Gaudeamus omnes*-Melodie also tatsächlich zum Introitus schlechthin. (Ähnlich verfuhr er übrigens mit *Alleluia* und *Communio*.) Sein Vorgehen begründet Durán mit der Notwendigkeit, den bekehrten Indianern das Singen der Melodien zu erleichtern (vgl. Russell, *From Serra to Sancho*, 64 Fußn. 43: spanischer Originaltext, 35: Übersetzung ins Englische).

[41] *Gesamtauslegung der Messe*, hrsg. von Reichert, 50, Zeile 2 ff..

Grimms Wörterbuch, Stichwort *Gaudieren, gaudium*,[42] erläutert die „einführung in die alltagsrede": Diese „geschah nicht blosz durch das latein der schule, sondern mehr noch durch das der kirche, wo man von *gaudere, coelorum gaudia* u. ähnl. genug hörte...". Der Ruf „gaudeamus" wird auf sein Vorkommen in Liedern zum Martinsfest zurückgeführt; parodistische Absicht wird nicht gesehen: „und diesz anknüpfen der festlust an kirchliche gewohnheiten ist von haus aus nicht verspottung, es kam aus dem drange, auch für die weltliche lust den tiefsten grund zu gewinnen." Das „gaudeamus" im weltlichen Bereich ist Grimm zufolge also zunächst ganz einfach als Ausdruck der Freude zu sehen, ohne jegliche doppeldeutige Absicht. Auch Trinklieder – „bibelworte in zechermunde; das studentische *gaudeamus* ruht ja auf kirchlichem hintergrunde" – sind Grimm zufolge so zu sehen. „Gaudeamus omnes" kommt bei Grimm nicht vor, sicherlich ist „gaudeamus" aber davon abzuleiten.

Tatsächlich findet sich in Martinsliedern das Wort „gaudeamus" („gaudeamus omnes" war hier auch nicht auffindbar); erwähnt sei hier nur das verschiedentlich von lateinischen Passagen durchsetzte Lied Nr. 7 aus dem zweiten Teil von Forsters Liederbuch, dessen Text folgendermaßen lautet:[43]

> Presulem sanctissimum veneremus gaudeamus/
> wöllen wir nach graß gan/ höllereyd/
> so singen vns die vögelein/ hollerey/
> in hoc solemni festo.
> Zir zir passer
> der gurz gauch frey/ sein melodey
> hellt über berg vnd tieffe dal/
> Der Müller in der ober mül
> der hat ein feyste ganß/ ganß/ ganß/ ganß/
> Die hat ein faisten dicken langen waidelichen kragen kragen/
> die wöllen wir mit vns tragen.
> Drußla drußla drußla drußla drußla gickgack gickgack/
> Dulci resonemus in gloria.

Auch wenn Martin nicht unmittelbar genannt wird, ist das Lied unter die Martinslieder zu zählen, da es bei Forster in einer Reihe von Martinsliedern steht (mit „Presulem sanctissimum" dürfte der Heilige gemeint sein), da schließlich die im Kontext mit diesem Heiligen stehende „Ganß" erwähnt wird.[44]

Von hier aus ist der Weg hin zum Parodistischen nicht weit, vor allem dann nicht, wenn das Trinken ins Spiel kommt. So druckt Hoffmann von Fallersleben ein Martinslied ab, bei dem Parodie auf liturgische Lesungen zumindest angedeutet wird, wie zumindest

---

[42] Vgl. Jacob und Wilhelm Grimm, *Deutsches Wörterbuch* (Leipzig, 1854-1961), Bd. 4 (1878), Sp. 1539.
[43] J. Petreius, *Der ander Theil, kurtzweiliger guter frischer teutscher Liedlein, zu singen vast iustig* (Nürnberg, 1540); RISM 1540²¹. Die Textabschrift erfolgte nach dem Discantus-Stimmbuch des Exemplars der Bayerischen Staatsbibliothek München 4 Mus.pr. 167, Beibd. 1. Der Text ist ediert bei August Heinrich Hoffmann von Fallersleben, *Die deutschen Gesellschaftslieder des 16 und 17. Jahrhunderts* (Leipzig, 1844), 179.
[44] Der Text hat auffallende Parallelen zu Lassos *Audite nova*; vgl. Orlando di Lasso, *Sämtliche Werke. Zweite, nach den Quellen revidierte Auflage ...*, Band 20: *Kompositionen mit deutschem Text II*, neu hrsg. von Horst Leuchtmann (Wiesbaden, 1971), XLVI. Hingewiesen sei noch auf das dem zitierten bei Forster vorausgehende Martinslied *Den besten Vogel den ich waiß* (Nr. 6); das mit „so singen wir benedicamus domino" endet (abgedruckt bei Hoffmann von Fallersleben, *Gesellschaftslieder*, 178). Auch hier haben wir es mit einem liturgischen Zitat in einem weltlichen Lied wohl ohne parodistische Absicht zu tun.

dem Anfang „In illo tempore" zu entnehmen ist; und auch hier wird wieder „gaudeamus" gerufen:[45]

> In illo tempore sedebat Dominus Martinus, o ho!
> Bonus ille Martinus inter anseres im Stroh,
> Und sie waren alle froh,
> […]
> Drum sind wir da
> Und halten Martinalia.[46]
> Herbei, herbei zur Märtensgans!
> Herr Burkhart mit den Bretzeln, Iubilemus!
> Bruder Urban mit der Flaschen, Cantemus!
> Sanct Bandel mit den Würsten, Gaudeamus!
> Sind alles starke Patronen
> Zur feisten Märtensgans,
> […]
> Bruder Urban, gebt uns Vinum!
> […]
> So leben wir in glimper gloria
> Und singen unsers Herren Märtens gaudia,
> Eia, wären wir da!
> Per omnia tempora.

Im Zusammenhang mit dem Trinken finden sich bekanntlich zahlreiche Parodien, selbstverständlich auch ohne, dass „gaudeamus omnes" oder „gaudeamus" vorkommt. Belege dafür sind Lassos schon erwähnte Sätze *Iam lucis orto sidere* und *Vinum bonum et suave*. Säufer- oder auch Spielermessen, die hier nicht weiter diskutiert werden sollen, gibt es zuhauf.

Doch zurück zum *Gaudeamus omnes*: Der Introitus wurde nämlich selbst schon zum Objekt für Parodie. In einer mit „Confitemini Dolio quoniam bonum. Quoniam in taberna misericordia eius" beginnenden Saufmesse aus dem 16. Jahrhundert lautet der Introitus: „Lugeamus omnes in Dolio, diem maestum ululantes sub honore quadrato Decii, de cuius potatione gaudent miseri."[47] Analog zu den für die verschiedenen Feste unterschiedlichen Fassungen des originalen *Gaudeamus omnes* tritt auch die Parodie in mehreren Versionen auf. Neben der oben zitierten ist mir eine weitere, diesmal aus einer Spielermesse, bekannt: „Lugeamus omnes in Decio diem festum deplorantes pro dolore omnium lusorum, de quorum nuditate gaudent Decii et collaudant filium Bachi."[48]

Es liegt auf der Hand, dass allzu weltliche Festlichkeiten heftiger Kritik unterzogen werden können; gerade das *Gaudeamus omnes* wird dazu herangezogen, auf die Freude im „richtigen" Sinn hinzuweisen und Auswüchse zu kritisieren. Schon die mehr-

---

[45] Hoffmann von Fallersleben, *Gesellschaftslieder*, 181-82.
[46] „Martinalia" erinnert an Ausdrücke wie „Saturnalia" oder „Bacchanalia" (vgl. „Bacchanalia" in Lassos *Nunc gaudere licet*), ist wohl in Analogie zu diesen Termini entstanden und zu verstehen.
[47] Vgl. Bayless, *Parody*, Zitate aus 100 und 103. Vorlage für das „Confitemini" sind die Psalmverse 105, 1 und 135, 1: „Confitemini Domino quoniam bonus. Quoniam in aeternum misericordia eius.", wie Bayless, *Parody*, 100 feststellt.
[48] Der Text stammt aus der Spielermesse der *Carmina Burana* (München, Bayerische Staatsbibliothek, Clm 4660, 93v-94v); zit. nach Lehmann, *Parodie*, 247.

fach zitierte Messauslegung von ca. 1480 weist ja im Zusammenhang mit unserem Introitus darauf hin, dass auch die weltliche Freude im Herren sein muss: „Wann keyn frewd – weder geystlich noch weltlich – gantz seyn mag denn die frewd, die da gesucht wirt in dem Herren."[49] Erasmus von Rotterdam wird deutlicher, wenn er in seiner Schrift *Ecclesiastae sive de ratione concionandi* ebenfalls mit Bezug auf *Gaudeamus omnes* formuliert: „Nimirum hoc sentit propheta, cum (Ps. CXIX.17) ait: *haec dies, quam fecit dominus, exultemus et laetemur in ea*, quodque canit ecclesia sancta: gaudeamus omnes in domino. Convenit enim, ut in die, quam fecit dominus, exultemus et epulemur, sed in domino. Nec decet, ut ex die, quam fecit dominus, faciamus diem Satanae."[50] (Unmittelbar vor der zitierten Stelle spricht Erasmus von der den Christen würdigen „vera hilaritas" und ihrem Wesen.)

Kritik mit freilich anderen Mitteln als den in theologischen Abhandlungen angewandten liegt dann vor, wenn die Parodie zur Satire kippt, wenn also das *Gaudeamus omnes*-Singen im weltlichen Kontext – sei es als naiver Ausdruck der Freude, sei es parodistisch gemeint – im negativen Sinne eines wenig erstrebenswerten Lebenswandels gesehen und angeprangert wird: Moralisieren und Vorschläge lehrhaften Charakters zur „Besserung" prägen so manchen Text. Als Beispiel sei ausschnittsweise Hans Sachs' Gedicht *Der Gesang der vollen Brüde* gegeben, der gleich zweimal „gaudeamus" zitiert[51]; der Anfang lautet:

> Wer hier vorbei geht, schau' geschwind
> Auf uns, die vollen Brüder wir sind
> Und all' das *Gaudeamus* singen,
> Fortunas Lob die Becher klingen,
> Den Bacchus haben wir erwählt,
> Zu unserm Abgott aufgestellt.

Und später:

> Fröhlich das *Gaudeamus* singen
> Mit allen kurzweiligen Dingen.

Ausführlich wird ein liederlicher Lebenswandel beschrieben. Wohin das führt, erfährt der Leser am Schluss:

> Wenn es dann an das Alter geht,
> Erst unsre Sach' baufällig steht.
> So leer und öd' steht unser Haus,
> Der beste Hausrath ist heraus,
> Alles Silbergeschirr, Kupfer und Zinn
> Ist mit der Schlemmerei dahin,
> Dergleichen Kleider und Bettgewand
> Steht bei den Juden aus als Pfand,
> Und ist nichts da als Angst und Noth,
> Da uns erst gute Hilf' thät' Noth.

---

[49] *Gesamtauslegung der Messe*, hrsg. von Reichert, 50, Zeile 2 ff..
[50] Zit. nach *Desiderii Erasmi Roterdami Ecclesiastae sive De Ratione Concionandi libri quatuor*, hrsg. von Friedrich August Klein (Leipzig, 1820), 231. Nachweis des Psalmzitats vom Hrsg. Klein.
[51] Zit. nach <http://gutenberg.spiegel.de/buch/5219/71> (zuletzt aufgerufen am 23. August 2012). Der online-Version liegt folgende Ausgabe zugrunde: *Hans Sachs' ausgewählte poetische Werke*, hrsg. von Karl Pannier (Leipzig, 1884).

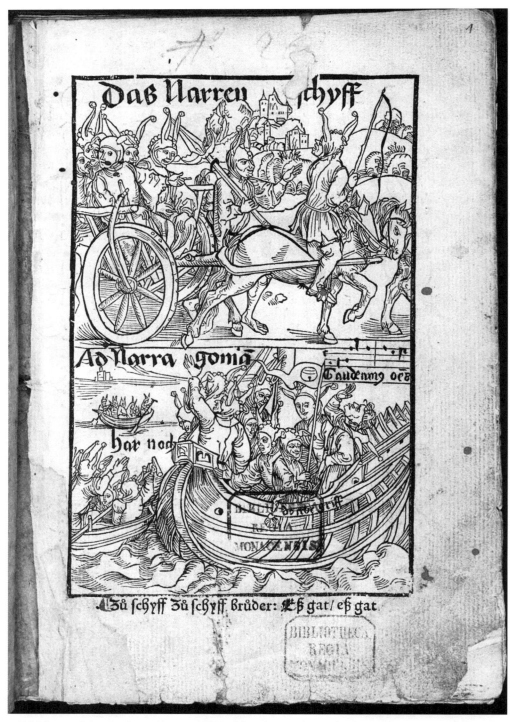

Abbildung 1. Sebastian Brant, *Narrenschiff*, Titelblatt des Drucks Basel: Johann Bergmann, 1494, Albrecht Dürer zugeschriebener Holzschnitt. (Bayerische Staatsbibliothek München, Rar. 121, mit freundlicher Genehmigung)

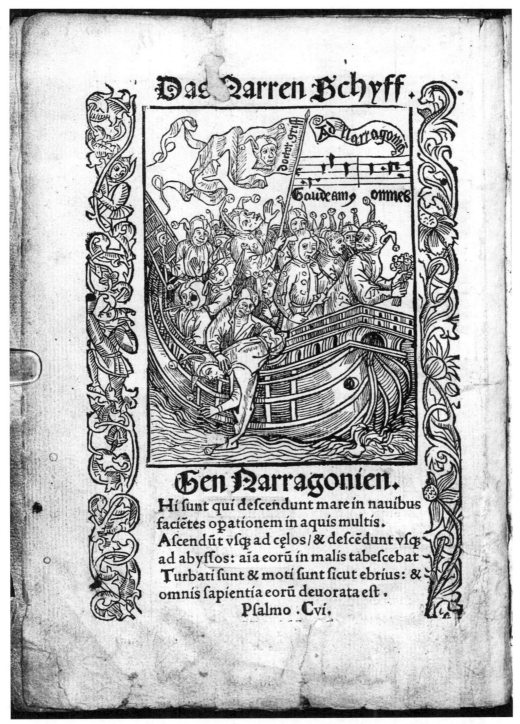

Abbildung 2. Sebastian Brant, *Narrenschiff*, Illustration fol. a.i^v, identisch auf t.iiij^r aus dem Druck Basel: Johann Bergmann, 1494, Albrecht Dürer zugeschriebener Holzschnitt. (Bayerische Staatsbibliothek München, Rar. 121; mit freundlicher Genehmigung)

> So wir sind alt, kraftlos und krank,
> Vergehet uns der frohe Sang,
> Wir singen dann nur ‚weh mir, weh!'
> Bis die arme Seele von uns geh'.

Die mahnende oder warnende Absicht liegt auf der Hand. Eine daraus abzuleitende lehrhafte Empfehlung für eine bessere Lebensführung findet sich im „Beschluß":

> Drum nehm' ein Mann an uns sich Lehre
> Und in dem Hause mäßig zehre,
> Wie es trägt Handel und Gewerbe,
> Damit er Nahrung sich erwerbe,
> Daß er im Alter habe Zehrung
> Sammt Weib und Kindern mit Verehrung,
> Bis ihn Gott nimmt aus diesem Leben,
> Darfür das ew'ge ihm zu geben,
> Wo End' wird alles Ungemachs –
> Das wünschet allen uns Hans Sachs.

Der Text ist der sogenannten Narrenliteratur zuzurechnen, die – im späten 15. Jahrhundert beginnnend – jeweils Beispiele für menschliche Torheit oder Fehlverhalten vorführt,[52] wozu Saufen und Völlerei zählen. Ein Hauptwerk und Ausgangspunkt für weitere Texte dieses Genres liegt mit Sebastian Brants 1494 bei Johann Bergmann in Basel erschienenem *Narrenschiff* vor, in dem der Autor „das Fehlverhalten des einzelnen" auf satirische Weise kritisiert und „den Zusammenhang zwischen ‚Unordnung' des einzelnen und der ‚Unordnung' des Ganzen" aufzeigt. „Das Werk ist als Weisheitsspiegel angelegt, Erziehungsziel ist der vir bonus …".[53] Wie sehr das auch in Sachs' Gedicht vorkommende „Gaudeamus"-Singen mit Narren zu tun hat, zeigen zwei Albrecht Dürer zugeschriebene Illustrationen zum *Narrenschiff* (Abbildung 1 und 2).

Rechts oberhalb des mit Narren beladenen Schiffs ist jeweils der Beginn des *Gaudeamus omnes* abgebildet, ein *C*-Schlüssel auf der dritten Linie zeigt eine Quinttransposition nach oben an,[54] gesungen wird außerdem im sogenannten „germanischen" Choraldialekt, wie der Terzsprung e'-g' bei „(gaude)-a-(mus)" klar macht. Günter Hess erläutert die Aufnahme des auch an *Allerheiligen* zu singenden *Gaudeamus omnes* in die Illustration auf fol. a.iv^v/fol. t.iiij^r und verweist auf den parodistischen Zusammenhang, wenn er schreibt: Damit „ist zweifellos eine Umkehr des liturgischen Zitats intendiert, das die Formel heiliger Festesfreude auf der Ebene der *risus stultorum* zum paraliturgischen Gesang am Hochfest *Aller Narren* verfremdet. Nicht zuletzt spricht eine Wendung des Impressum für diese Interpretation: *Gedruckt zů Basel vff die Vasenaht*

---

[52] Klaus Bitterling, „Narrenliteratur", in *Lexikon des Mittelalters* (München etc., 1980-99), Bd. VI (1993), Sp. 1027-29, hier Sp. 1027.

[53] Dieter Wuttke„Brant, Sebastian", in *Lexikon des Mittelalters*, Bd. II (1983), Sp. 574-76, Zitat Sp. 575. — In Hans Sachs' *Narrenschneiden*, einem Fastnachtspiel satirisch-moralisierenden Inhalts, schneidet ein Arzt einem Patienten eine Anzahl von Narren aus dem Leib, die für diverse negative Verhaltensweisen stehen. Wieder steht am Ende eine lehrhafte Moral. In den Versen 312-14 wird Sebastian Brants *Narrenschiff* erwähnt; vgl. Hans Sachs, *Meisterlieder, Spruchgedichte, Fastnachtspiele*, hrsg. von Hartmut Kugler (Stuttgart, 2003), 131.

[54] Das *Gaudeamus omnes* ist auch sonst in Quinttransposition überliefert: So enthält das Graduale aus dem Zisterzienserinnenkloster Seligenthal bei Landshut (1270/1277; London, British Library, Ms. Add. 16950) auf fol. 21r den Introitus zum Fest der Hl. Agathe ebenfalls auf *g* beginnend.

/ *die man der narren kirchwich nēnet.*"[55] Berücksichtigt man jedoch die Absicht von Brants Dichtung, auf satirische Weise Kritik zu üben, dann ist das Notenzitat des *Gaudeamus omnes* sicherlich ebenfalls als Parodie im satirisch-kritischen Sinn zu sehen. Im Kapitel 108: *Das schluraffen schiff*, zu dem die von Hess herangezogene Illustration (fol. t.iiij[r]) gehört, wird schließlich der Introitus-Beginn erwähnt, womit sich seine Verwendung im Sinn der kritischen Satire bestätigt. Das Kapitel endet mit einer moralisierenden Belehrung. Zunächst wird gesagt, dass der Kluge, „der selber wol Weiß / was man důn vnd lossen sol", „kumbt zůo land mit fůg". Dann ist von den Narren die Rede:

> Wer aber der keyns über al
> Kan / der ist jnn der narren zal
> Ob der diß schiffs sich hat versumbt
> So wart er biß eyn anders kumbt
> Er würt gselschafft fynden geryng
> Mit den er Gaudeamus sing
> Oder das lied jm narren don
> Wir hant vil brueder dussen gelon
> Das schiff ouch würt zů boden gon[56]

Wer keine Weisheit hat, gehört zu den Narren. Wenn er das eine Narrenschiff nicht erreicht, dann trifft er bald auf ein zweites, auf dem er „Gaudeamus" und „das lied jm narren don" singen kann. Damit ist möglicherweise ein „Sauoffizium" gemeint, eine Parodie auf die mönchischen Stundengebete, die im Kapitel 72: *Von groben narren*, dargestellt wird; es ist offenkundig, dass Brant auf Säufer- und Spielermessen anspielt:

> So hebt die suw die metten an
> Die prymzyt / ist jm esel thon
> Die tertz ist von sant Grobian /
> Hůtmacher knecht / syngen die sext
> Von groben fyltzen ist der text /
> Die wuest rott sytzet jnn der non
> Schlemmer vnd demmer dar zů gon /
> Dar noch die suw zůr vesper klingt
> Vnflot / vnd schamperyon / dann syngt
> Dann würt sich machen die complet
> Wann man / all vol / gesungen hett[57]

---

[55] Günter Hess, *Deutsch-lateinische Narrenzunft. Studien zum Verhältnis von Volkssprache und Latinität in der satirischen Literatur des 16. Jahrhunderts*, Münchener Texte und Untersuchungen zur deutschen Literatur des Mittelalters 41 (München, 1971), 248, Illustration bei Hess 249.

[56] Zitate nach folgender Ausgabe: Sebastian Brant, *Das Narrenschiff. Studienausgabe. Mit allen 114 Holzschnitten des Drucks Basel 1494*, hrsg. von Joachim Knape (Stuttgart, 2005), 496-97, Verse 143, 140 und 148-56. Knape merkt an, dass „geryng" soviel wie „mit Leichtigkeit" bedeutet. Die folgende Übersetzung von H. A. Junghans in modernes Deutsch nach <http://gutenberg.spiegel.de/buch/2985/109/> (zuletzt aufgerufen am 20. Juli 2012). Der online-Version liegt folgende Ausgabe zugrunde: Sebastian Brant, *Das Narrenschiff*, hrsg. von Hans-Joachim Mähl (Stuttgart, 1964): „Wer aber davon allzumal | Nichts weiß, gehört zur Narrenzahl. | Ward er nicht in dies Schiff genommen, | So wird gar bald ein andres kommen, | Wo er Gesellschaft viel trifft an | Und *Gaudeamus* singen kann | Oder das *Lied im Narrenton* | Viel Brüder müssen noch draußen stehn, | Auch *das* Schiff wird zu Grunde gehen."

[57] Zitiert nach Brant, *Narrenschiff*, hrsg. von Knape, 352-53, Verse 47-57. Junghans (vgl. Brant, *Narrenschiff*, hrsg. von Mähl, online unter <http://gutenberg.spiegel.de/buch/2985/73/>) übersetzt: „Dann hebt die Sau die *Mette* an: | Die *Prim'* erschallt im Eselston, | Die *Terz* ist von Sankt Grobian, | Hutmacherknechte singen die *Sext*, | Von groben Filzen ist der Text; | Die wüste Rott sitzt in der *Non'*, | Die schlemmt und demmt aus vollem Ton, | Darnach die Sau zur *Vesper* klingt, | Unflat und Schamperjan dann singt, | Bis die *Complet* den Anfang nimmt, | In der man »All sind voll!«"

* * *

Mit dem *Gaudeamus omnes* verbindet sich also ein breites Spektrum an Konnotationen, das vom zunächst harmlosen Ausdruck der Freude über Parodie bis hin zur moralisierenden Satire reicht. Wo steht nun Lassos *Nunc gaudere licet*? Betrachten wir zunächst das dazugehörige Kontrafakt aus dem *Magnum opus Musicum*:

> Nunc gaudere licet, dolor hinc et curae! Gaudendum est, ut res postulat et jubet magister laetitiae, quia, o pueri, rediere vacationis tempora! Gaudeamus omnes.

> Jetzt darf man sich freuen. Fort mit Schmerz und Sorgen! Man soll sich freuen, wie es die Sache fordert und wie es der Herr der Freude befiehlt, weil, ihr Knaben, die Ferienzeiten wiedergekehrt sind. Lasst uns alle froh sein.

Sicherlich ist hier das Choralzitat ganz naiv als Ausdruck der Freude der Schüler über den Ferienbeginn zu verstehen. Die Freude kommt zudem durch die Änderung von „Bibendum est" zu „Gaudendum est" noch stärker zur Geltung als im Originaltext, da im Text insgesamt dreimal von „gaudere" die Rede ist statt nur zweimal, wie in der Vorlage. Und vielleicht lässt sich „magister laetitiae" („Herr der Freude") ja als eine Bezeichnung für Gott deuten.

Doch wo steht der Originaltext des *Nunc gaudere licet*? Zunächst ist festzuhalten, dass sich in Lassos Trinkliedern mehrfach „gaudium" oder „gaudere" in unterschiedlichen Wortformen findet: So lautet die zweite Verszeile der Motette *Ad primum morsum*[58] „Gaudia sunt nobis maxima, dum bibo bis". Es handelt sich um eine die Freuden und Gründe des Trinkens rühmende Aufzählung mit wohl mäßig parodistischer Absicht, die in gewisser Weise an ein anderes Trinklied, das *Si bene perpendi, quinque causae sunt bibendi*[59] erinnert, wiewohl dort „gaudere" oder dergleichen nicht vorkommt. Mit „et in potatione gaudeamus" schließt das schon erwähnte *Iam lucis orto sidere*; hier tritt die parodistische Absicht offen zu Tage: das einem Hymnus entnommene Textincipit manifestiert dies hinlänglich. Beim *Nunc gaudere licet* hingegen fällt zunächst der offenbar gelehrte Hintergrund des Stücks auf, da Catull zitiert wird, da schließlich mit den „bacchanalia" antike Festlichkeiten erwähnt werden. Spätmittelalterliche Faschingsbräuche gehen auf die antiken Saturnalien, Bacchanalien etc. zurück, allerdings nicht als ungebrochene Traditionen, sondern aufgrund von Rückgriffen auf antikes Brauchtum.[60] Der Fasching wurde von den Theologen kritisiert, als eine wichtige Brauchtumsgestalt galt der Narr.[61] Von daher dürfte klar sein, dass das *Gaudeamus omnes* im Originaltext von Lassos Motette wohl kaum als Ausdruck naiver Freude (wie im Kontrafakt) gedacht ist. Stattdessen stellt sich die Frage, ob Lassos Text insgesamt der satirisch-kritischen Narrenliteratur zuzurechnen ist oder doch eher als deftiger Festgesang verstanden werden kann, somit also den teilweise auch vom Trinken handelnden Martinsliedern

---

anstimmt." Von Hans-Joachim Mähl stammt auch die Idee, „das lied jm narren don" beziehe sich auf das Sauoffizium, da er in einer Fußnote zu dieser Textstelle auf das Sauoffizium verweist.
[58] GA XIX, Nr. 474.
[59] GA² XI, Nr. 299.
[60] Kühnel, „Fastnacht", Sp. 313.
[61] Werner Mezger, „Narr, V. Brauchtum", in *Lexikon des Mittelalters*, Bd. VI (1993), Sp. 1023-26, hier Sp. 1026.

nahesteht. Vielleicht sind die Grenzen ja auch fließend. In Lassos Stück (so scheint mir jedenfalls) überwiegt der zweite Aspekt, da keinerlei lehrhaftes Moralisieren oder kritische Satire erkennbar ist. Folgende Deutung sei deshalb vorgeschlagen: Lassos Stück ist Ausdruck der Freude über eine willkommene Festlichkeit (und steht damit in Analogie zu den Martinsliedern), hat aber zugleich humanistischen Hintergrund, wie die Rückgriffe auf antikes Gedankengut zeigen. Folgt man dieser Interpretation, kann das *Gaudeamus omnes*-Zitat als Andeutung liturgischer Parodie gesehen werden, freilich ohne dass die parodistische Absicht im Zentrum des Textes steht.

Abstract

Orlando di Lasso's motet *Nunc gaudere licet*, which possibly began life as a drinking song during the Munich ducal wedding of 1568, ends with a musical and textual quotation of the start of the well-known introit *Gaudeamus omnes*. In the 16th century there was a tradition of quoting the sacred *Gaudeamus omnes* in secular contexts (whether as an expression of joy or with parodistic or blasphemous intentions). The introit is quoted in folly literature, which exhibits human errors satirically with moralising purposes. In Sebastian Brant's *Ship of Fools*, *Gaudeamus* is quoted and appears on two of the illustrations (attributed to Albrecht Dürer) that were included in the first edition (Basel, 1494). This article attempts to interpret the *Gaudeamus omnes* quotation in Lasso's motet against this background.

Research and Performance Practice Forum

Re-constructing Jesuit Thea*tre* for the Modern Stage: *Daphnis, Pastorale,* an Eighteenth-Century Jesuit College Music-Drama

■

Elizabeth Dyer

Creating a historically informed re-construction of a Jesuit drama on a modern stage is not simply a matter of primary research and scholarly understanding of the theatrical history of the Society of Jesus.[1] Rather, it is an interrelated process among primary research, academic study, and informed experimentation. The small but significant media collection of modern re-creations of Jesuit college music-dramas provides visual results of this process. Four genres within the Jesuit college music-drama oeuvre—a Passion, an oratorio, a pastorale, and an opera—have been revived in performance during the past few years.[2] A detailed inquiry into performance issues for all four productions would be an immense task. Therefore, this essay examines a discreet selection of the practical processes involved in the modern production of a single work, *Daphnis, Pastorale*.[3]

The recent production of *Daphnis, Pastorale* at the University of York is the result of a historically informed creative process and does not purport to duplicate the original performance by the Jesuit college of Namur on May 19, 1728, which was presented in honour of Thomas John Francis Strickland (c. 1682-1740), an English Dominican priest, three days following his first celebration of mass as the Bishop of Namur in the Saint-

---

[1] For an index of published literature concerning Jesuit college theatre, see Nigel Griffin, *Jesuit School Drama: A Checklist of Critical Literature*, rev. ed. (London, 1986). Major recent studies include Jean Marie Valentin's studies of Austrian and German Jesuit theatre, *Les Jésuites et le théâtre (1554-1680): Contribution à l'histoire culturelle du monde catholique dans le Saint-Empire romain germanique* (Paris, 2001) and *Theatrum Catholicum: Les jésuites et la scène en Allemagne au XVIe et au XVIIe siecles* (Nancy, 1990); Judith Rock, *Terpsichore at Louis-le-Grand: Baroque Dance on a Jesuit Stage in Paris* (St. Louis, 1996); Giovanna Zanlonghi's investigation of Jesuit theatre in Milan, *Teatri di Formazione: Actio, parola e immagine nella scena gesuitica del Sei-Settecento a Milano* (Milan, 2002); a collection of essays on Spanish Jesuit theatre edited by Ignacio Arellano, *Paraninfos, segundones y epígonos de la comedia del Siglo de Oro* (Barcelona, 2004); and John W. O'Malley (ed.), *The Jesuits: Cultures, Sciences, and the Arts, 1540-1773*, 3 vols. (Toronto, 1999-2012).
[2] Recent re-staged Jesuit college music-dramas include Marc-Antoine Charpentier's *David et Jonathas*, performed in 2009 at Georgetown University, Georgetown, Washington, D.C.; an anonymous work, *Daphnis, Pastorale*, performed at the University of York, York, U. K., in 2008; a second work by Marc-Antoine Charpentier, *Mors Saülis et Jonathae*, performed at the University of Missouri-Columbia, Columbia, Missouri in 2003; and Johann Bernhard Staudt's *Patientis Christi memoria*, performed in 2002 at Boston College, Boston, MA. Regarding this last, see also T. Frank Kennedy's essay, 'Jesuit Opera in Seventeenth-Century Vienna: *Patientis Christi memoria* by Johann Bernhard Staudt (1654-1712)', in O'Malley (ed.), *The Jesuits,* vol. 2.
[3] University of Liège, Manuscrits et Fonds anciens, Bibliothéque générale des Philosophie et Lettres, Ms. 357.c. This manuscript appears as Ms. 667 in Carlos Sommervogel, S. J. (rev. ed.), *Bibliothèque de la Compagnie de Jésus*, 10 vols. (Paris, 1890-99), s. vv. 'Namur, Collége de', No. 89, note (vol. 5, 1561; references to this entry hereafter abbreviated to 'Sommervogel'). The anonymous music manuscript, laid out in full score and written in a single clear hand, is a fair-hand copy with no deletions. The 2008 performance was made possible through the Arthur Ramsden Award from the Society of Theatre Research, London.

Aubain Cathedral.[4] Its contemporary representation necessitates new approaches to the design, especially the stage and action, as well as contemporary solutions for the casting and linguistic content. Moreover, the absence of practical production information in Ms. 357.c and the disappearance during the World Wars of the only known printed programme from the original performance left certain essential performance factors unknown, such as the type and number of dramatic insertions.

Therefore, to reconstruct a plausible rendition of the 1728 *Daphnis, Pastorale*, programmes from eighteenth-century *Daphnis* plays staged by the Namur, Ypres (Ieper), and Bruges (Brugge) Jesuit colleges were consulted for performance information not present in the manuscript.[5] This collection of plays featuring the character of *Daphnis* share several characteristics that indicate that the writers of the late eighteenth-century presentations were familiar with the earlier productions. First, the characters are allegorical, and represent one or more towns, the Jesuit college and/or prominent nobles and second, the arrival of the character of *Daphnis* is central to the story and occurs at the end of the performance. In those areas in which these programmes yielded multiple options, the 1741 *Daphnis* performance by the Namur Jesuit college was usually preferred as a source above the other programmes. This choice of preference is not only due to the fact that the 1741 programme is nearest in date to the 1728 performance, but also because both the 1728 and 1741 productions were staged by the Jesuit college of Namur. These primary sources are supplemented by recent scholarly literature investigating pastoral ballets and dances in Jesuit and court theatres in Paris; at the time of writing, a study of Jesuit college theatrical productions from the francophone regions of modern-day France and Belgium has yet to be published.[6] The following recreates the conditions encountered and resolutions ventured in the modern performance of *Daphnis*, which took place on November 27, 2008.

The Jesuit College of Namur, and University of Liège, Ms. 357.c

The Jesuit college of Namur was located in Wallonia, the francophone region of modern-day Belgium. The Namur Jesuit college was founded in 1610, the eleventh Jesuit college established in the Gallo-Belgian Jesuit Province. Those colleges which preceded Namur in the province were Tournai (1553), Luxembourg (1555), Cambrai (1563), Valenciennes (1565), Saint-Omer (1567), Douai (1568), Aire (1576), Liège (1582), Mons (1583), and Lille (1606). The sovereignty of Namur passed through many hands before modern-day Belgium, including Namur, was recognized as an independent nation in 1830. During

---

[4] Sommervogel, 'Daphnis pastorale presentée à Monseigneur Monseigneur Thomas Jean Franç. Strickland de Sizerge eveque de Namur Abbé Seculier de la Collégiale de Nôtre Dame, et de St. Pierre de Preaux en Normandie, etc. Par le College de la Compagnie de Jesus de la méme Ville. Représentée par les Escolliers dudit College la (19) May 1728. A Namur, Chez Oger Lahaye, 1728,' vol. 5, 1561, no.89.

[5] *Daphnis* (Bruges: Francisci Beernaerts, 1754), Stonyhurst College Library F.137, no. 3. *Daphnis, Pastorale* (Namur: Jean François La Fontaine, 1741), Stonyhurst College Library F.149, No. 1. Referenced in Sommervogel, vol. 5, 1562, No. 96. *Galateae Daphnidis* (Ypres: Jacobum Franciscum Moerman, 1762), Stonyhurst College Library, F.137, no. 2. *Tityrus* (Ypres: Jacobum Franciscum Moerman, n. d.), Stonyhurst College Library, F.137, No. 1.

[6] For a study of Benedictine, Augustinian, and Jesuit college dramatic activity in the Gallo-Belgian Jesuit Province, see Elizabeth Dyer, 'The Emergence of the Independent Prologue and Chorus in Jesuit School Theatre c. 1550-c. 1700, Derived from a Comparative Analysis of Benedictine, Augustinian and Jesuit School Theatre, Lay Youth Confraternity Theatre and the Oratorio Vespertina of the Congregation of the Oratory' (Ph.D. diss., University of York, 2011).

the 1640s, Namur was part of the Spanish Netherlands until France re-took the region in 1692. The English and Dutch flag flew jointly over Namur from 1695 to 1713 following the invasion of William III of Orange. The 1713 Treaty of Utrecht awarded Namur and the surrounding region to the Austrian Habsburgs until 1794, when the area was recaptured by France. The 1728 performance of *Daphnis, Pastorale*, therefore, occurred during the period of Habsburg rule.

There are several possibilities for the original purpose of the gilded and parchment-bound Ms. 357.c. It might have been a gift to Bishop Strickland's English compatriots at the English Jesuit college of Saint-Omer and later transported to Liège following the closure of the Saint-Omer college in 1773.[7] Alternately, the college of Namur might have sent this manuscript to the English Jesuit college in Liège. This latter scenario appears the most probable in light of a handwritten inscription of unknown date, 'Coll. Soc. Jesu Leodii in insula,' which appears in the upper right-hand corner of the manuscript frontispiece. 'Leodii' is the Latinized form of Liège and the phrase 'in insula,' meaning 'from the island,' was commonly used among Jesuits to specify English Jesuits. After the suppression of the Jesuits and closure of the Liège and Saint-Omer Jesuit colleges in 1773, the assets of these two English Jesuit colleges were combined by Prince-Bishop Velbruck into a new educational institution in Liège, the Grand Collège en Ile, which was directed by secular clergy and not by the Jesuits. Here the noun 'en Ile,' that is, 'the island' primarily refers to the physical location of the school.[8] The 'Coll. Soc. Jesu' portion of the inscription indicates that the manuscript was specifically identified as the property of the English Jesuit college in Liège, and not that of its post-suppression successor, the Grand Collège en Ile. To complete this brief history, the revolutionary war forced the closure of the Grand Collège en Ile in 1794, but in 1817 King Willem I of the Netherlands established the newly founded University of Liège in the old Grand Collège en Ile buildings.[9]

Solo Ensemble

Although Ms. 357.c does not contain a cast list, the manuscript identifies each role as they enter. Five solo roles appear in the original manuscript: La Nymphe de la Sambre, Aminth, Damon, La Déesse des Flores, and les Echos.[10] Except for Aminth, an *haute-contre*, the roles are written for the *dessus* (soprano) voice. No evidence has been found to suggest that *castrati* took part in the Namur Jesuit college theatrical productions.[11] Similarly, there is no indication that the Namur students performed dramatic roles in falsetto, although there is evidence of falsettists in contemporary performances at

---

[7] William H. McCabe, S. J., *An Introduction to the Jesuit Theatre* (St. Louis, 1983), 71.
[8] Sommervogel, vol. 4, 1810.
[9] John Edwin Sandys, *A History of Classical Scholarship* (New York, 1908), vol. 3, 292.
[10] The 2008 costumes for the soloists: the Nymph wore a long-sleeved A-line blue velvet gown, sleeveless gold velvet over-robe with a train, blue glass jewellery, and white stockings. The Déesse wore the same blue gown and white stockings as the Nymph, to which were added a green taffeta sash, wreaths of flowering vines, and a necklace of carved green leaves. Echoes also wore the same dress but with a red taffeta sash and white stockings. Aminth wore a red peasant blouse, blue waistcoat, blue knee-breeches, black stockings, and black shoes. Damon was dressed in a blue blouse, an embroidered waistcoat, black knee-breeches, black stockings, and black shoes.
[11] Elizabeth Dyer, 'Voices in the Jesuit Theatre, c. 1660-c. 1730' (paper delivered at the *International Early Music Association Conference*, University of York, July 2009).

Parisian courts and theatres.[12] The soprano roles in the 1728 *Daphnis* were therefore most likely sung by students with unchanged voices.[13]

The *Daphnis* manuscript does not specify the allegorical symbolism attached to the main characters, elements crucial to the performance of these roles. However, the allegorical symbolism of the Nymph, the Déesse, and the Echoes is evident from their names. The Nymph represents the Sambre River, the smaller of the two rivers bordering the city of Namur; La Déesse des Flores and the Echoes require no explanation. For Aminth and Damon, more information than provided in the manuscript is needed. Damon could be either the celebrated Athenian musician who taught Pericles or the legendary friend of Phintias who assumed Phintias's punishment in order that his friend might right his affairs before his death sentence was carried out.[14] Similarly, Aminth could represent Aminth, an Etruscan winged genius similar in appearance to Cupid, or be an alternate spelling of Amyntas, the musician-shepherd and lover of the shepherdess Phyllis; both characters are present in contemporary Jesuit theatrical productions.[15] An examination of the cast lists from the 1741 Namur and the 1762 Ypres *Daphnis* plays reveals a shepherd named Damon and both Damon and Aminth as shepherds, respectively (Figure 1). Based upon the information from these programmes, the 2008 production presented Aminth as a shepherd symbolizing music and Damon also as a shepherd, symbolizing friendship, trust, and loyalty.

The musical hierarchy of the solo characters was a factor in assigning the roles for the 2008 performance. Although there are five named roles in the 1728 *Daphnis* manuscript, only four have a significant amount of music to perform. Aminth, Damon, and the Nymph are onstage throughout the work. However, the Déesse and the Echoes appear only in the second half. In fact, the Echoes add aural spectacle to only a single *air de cour* by Damon, 'Qu'on entende, Bergers le son de vos musettes' ('Shepherds, let us hear the sound of your pipes').[16]

Table 1 presents the total number of measures of music sung by the four major soloists in each formal division. As her central role in the dramatic action and the data in Table 1 shows, the Nymph is the starring role of the pastorale. The Nymph not only has the greatest amount of music to perform, but she is also entrusted with the two *da capo* Italianate arias in the work, one in each partition. Aminth, whose dramatic role is chiefly one of dialogue with the Nymph or Damon, bears the second greatest musical responsibility. Damon is the equal of Aminth in the first half, but becomes the least prominent of the four in both dramatic action and solo time in part two. Déesse and Damon's performance time in the second partition are roughly equal in terms of the amount of music sung, but dramatically Déesse is more central to the dramatic action of the second half than Damon.

---

[12] Martha Elliott, *Singing in Style: A Guide to Vocal Performance Practice* (New Haven CT, 2007), 42-43. James Stark, *Bel canto: A History of Vocal Pedagogy* (Toronto, 1999), 206-12.

[13] It is a generally accepted practice in modern performances to cast women in roles originally sung by boys when boys are not obtainable. This practice was extended to the casting decisions for the 2008 performance.

[14] Christopher Riedweg, *Pythagorus: His Life, Teaching and Influence*, trans. Steven Rendall (Munich, 2002), 40-41. Phintias is also written as Pythias.

[15] Guiliano Bonfante and Larissa Bonfante, *The Etruscan Language: An Introduction*. (rev. ed., Manchester, 2002), 78.

[16] *Daphnis, Pastorale* (Ms. 357.c), 53-56. Dyer, 'The Emergence', Appendix III, bb. 734-82. Unless otherwise noted, all translations mine, edited by Dr. Paulene Aspel and Robin Bier. Hereafter, libretto and score citations are given in page number(s) for Ms. 357.c and bar numbers for the modern edition, referred to as 'Dyer'.

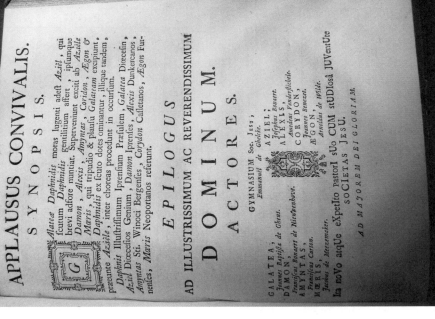

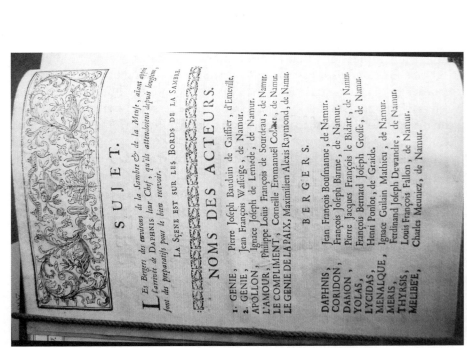

Figure 1. Examples of cast lists from two *Daphnis* plays

a. *Daphnis, Pastorale*, Jesuit College of Namur, 10 April 1741, Stonyhurst College Library F.149, No. 1, p. 2

b. *Galateae Daphnidis*, Jesuit College of Ypres, 1762, Stonyhurst College Library F.137, No. 2, p. 8

Table 1. The four major roles in *Daphnis, Pastorale* (1728) with number of bars for each role

Role	Part I	Part II
Nymphe	130	162
Aminth	119	86
Damon	119	33
Déesse	–	48

The instrumental ensemble of the 1728 production is not specified in Ms. 357.c and few details about the instrumental forces used in college theatrical performances in the Gallo-Belgian Jesuit Province have come to light.[17] What is known chiefly concerns the performances of *histoires sacrées* by Marc-Antoine Charpentier at the Louis-le-Grand/ Collège de Clermont Jesuit college in Paris during the 1680s. Jean Duron writes in his preface to Charpentier's *Mors Saülis* and Catherine Cessar writes in her notes to the critical edition of Charpentier's *Sacrificium Abrahae* that Charpentier might have used only flutes in performance, or may have doubled the treble lines with flutes and violins.[18]

Similar to Charpentier's *histoires sacrées*, the instrumental forces for the 1728 *Daphnis* consists of two unspecified *dessus* parts, an alto instrument, and continuo with figured bass. In the 2008 performance, the instrumental parts were realized by a conservative ensemble of two violins, viola, bass viol, and chamber organ.[19] Just as flutes might have been used in Charpentier's works, it is possible that the two *dessus* parts in *Daphnis* might have been performed by a pair of oboes, perhaps doubled by violins. There are two major indications that oboes, rather than flutes, would be the most appropriate choice for *Daphnis*. First, the melodic range as written exceeds that of the flute and recorder but is characteristic of the oboe.[20] Second, the libretto of *Daphnis* frequently refers to the sound of the oboe: for example, 'Ne cessons point d'unis nos voix / Au doux son des hautbois.' ('We shall never cease to unite our voices / To the soft sound of the oboes.')[21]

The decision to select the bass viol rather than the cello for the continuo part was similarly based upon Charpentier's compositions for Louis-le-Grand/Collège de Clermont.[22] The use of chamber organ or harpsichord or both instruments are all equally represented within known Jesuit theatre performance practice.[23] Judging from pictorial

[17] John Spitzer and Neal Zaslaw, *The Birth of the Orchestra: History of an Institution, 1650-1815* (New York, 2004), 205-6.
[18] Marc-Antoine Charpentier, *Mors Saülis et Jonathae*, ed. Jean Duron, trans. Mary Creswick (Versailles, 1992), ix-xi. Ibid., *Sacrificium Abrahae*, ed. Catherine Cessac, trans. Mary Criswick (Versailles, 1995), xvii-xxvii.
[19] Period instruments and bows were used. The pitch selected for the production was a'=415. The pitch was chosen for the practical reason that the strings maintained their tuning best at this pitch. The instrumental ensemble was in costume for the 2008 production: neutral peasant blouses, neutral knee-breeches, black stockings and black shoes, and matching dark red waistcoats.
[20] A pair of oboists not being available for the 2008 performance, a pair of flutes was used in the concluding choruses, imitating bird-song in response to the text 'Que tout l'intéresse; que tout l'empresse. / Venez petits oiseaux / Sous ce tendre feüillage, / Mêlez votre ramage / Au bruit de ces eaux.' ('May everything interest him; may everything impress him. / Come, little birds / Under this tender foliage, / Join your song / To the noise of these waters.'), Ms. 357.c, 58-66; Dyer, 781-866. The flutes were hidden backstage, one on each side, for their role as birds and their part in the transformation scenes, discussed below.
[21] Ms. 357.c, 75-87; Dyer, 979-1138.
[22] Charpentier, *Mors Saülis et Jonathae*, xvii-xxvii.
[23] Jan Dismas Zelenka, *Sub Olea Pacis*, ed. Vratislav Bĕlský (Prague, 1987), vol. 2, 12. Johann Bernard Staudt, *Ferdinandus Quintus*, ed. Walter Pass and Karl Plepelits Denkmäler der Tonkunst in Österreich 132 (Graz, 1981). *Theophilus* (Anon.,

Figure 2. Cast lists from two mid eighteenth-century *Daphnis* plays showing no evidence of a choral ensemble

a. *Daphnis*, Jesuit College of Bruges, 1754. F.137 No. 3, p. 2

b. *Tityrus*, Jesuit College of Ypres, n. d., probably after 1762, F.137 No. 1, p.14. 'Caecus' Library, Stonyhurst College, U. K.

evidence beginning as early as the mid-sixteenth century, the chamber organ appears to have been the preferred keyboard instrument for open-air performances.[24] The original performance of *Daphnis* might have taken place in the garden of the Bishop's palace or on a stage erected in the college courtyard; it is not known whether the Namur Jesuit college had its own indoor theatre by 1728. Therefore, the 2008 performance sought to simulate the ensemble for an outdoor performance, and chamber organ was chosen to complete the continuo section.[25]

Chorus

The vocal forces required by the *Daphnis* manuscript include a choral ensemble in addition to the five solo roles. The nine choruses found within the pastorale are scored for a four-part choir, soprano, haute-contre, tenor, and bass. The manuscript does not indicate the size of the choral ensemble or whether the soloists were also members of the chorus. An examination of the printed programmes from four mid-eighteenth century *Daphnis* performances provides the names of the characters (Figures 1 and 2, above), but there is no indication of a separate choral ensemble in any of these programmes. If the six soloists (at least two singers sang the role of the Echoes) formed the chorus without additional personnel, two of the soprano roles would have to have been sung by falsettists who reverted to their changed voices for the choruses.[26] As mentioned above, there is no evidence of the use of falsettists in eighteenth-century Jesuit school theatrical productions in the Gallo-Belgian Province, and if falsettists sang both soprano roles and the lower voices of the chorus in the 1728 performance, the *Daphnis* manuscript offers no clues.[27]

However, the absence of a choral ensemble in these four programmes does not necessarily mean that such an ensemble was not present in performance. A study of contemporary Jesuit theatre programmes for music-dramas reveals it was common practice not to include chorus members in the printed cast lists even when synopses of choruses appear in the programme.[28] Those that did print the names of the chorus reveal

---

Munich, 1647), in Elida Maria Szarota, *Das Jesuitendrama im deutschen Sprachgebiet: e. Periochen-Edition: Texte und Kommentare*, 3 vols. (Munich: Fink), vol. 1/1, 689-704. *Philothea* (Anon., Munich, 1643) in Elida Maria Szarota, *Das Jesuitendrama im deutschen Sprachgebiet: Eine Periochen-Edition: Texte und Kommentare*, 3 vols. (Munich, 1979), vol. 1/1, 649-52. Hereafter referred to as Szarota.

[24] Jan Bloemendal, *Spiegel van het dagelijks leven?: Latijnse school en toneel in de noordelijke Nederlanden in de zestiende en de zeventiende eeuw* (Hilversum, 2003), 40. For example, see Pieter Brueghel the Elder (c. 1525-1569), *De Matigheid* (*Temperance*), after 1559. A complete digital copy of Brueghel's sketch is available at <http://www.chrisdenengelsman.nl/Kunstkolom/Breughel Pieter/Breughel Pieter tekeningen.htm>.

[25] The 2008 decision to place the instruments on a raised platform was governed primarily by the need for the musicians to follow the action onstage, a necessary arrangement as this performance was not conducted. The platform also allowed the orchestra to participate in the transformation scenes in the second partition.

[26] There is no evidence found in the recovered primary documents for Belgian Jesuit theatre to support the proposition that falsettists performed in both voices within a single production. However, in order to investigate whether such a performance scenario was even feasible for *Daphnis*, an experiment was conducted in which a tenor and a bass falsettist sang the role of La Déesse des Flores and Damon, respectively, and their corresponding changed voice parts the chorus. (As the Echoes are off-stage for the duration of part two, the Déesse and Damon became the logical choices if falsettists were used in this manner.) Upon trial, this performance practice proved awkward for both singers, especially for choruses immediately following their solos.

[27] Elliott, *Singing in Style*, 42-43. Stark, *Bel canto*, 206-12.

[28] Dyer, 'Voices in the Jesuit Theatre'.

the wide variation in ensemble size at this time (Table 2). As seen in the table, the size of the chorus generally falls between ten and thirty singers, although productions with choruses of over one hundred singers were occasionally staged.[29] The information in Table 2 provides general parameters for the number of musicians who might have sung the choruses in the 1728 production of *Daphnis*, and therefore similarly informs any modern reconstruction of the pastorale.

Table 2. Choral ensemble size in eight select contemporary Jesuit theatre productions

Year	Title (key words)	Chorus	School	Sources[a]
1727	Innocentia Victrix	30	Mindelheim	Szarota 3/2, 1665–1672
1727	Thomae Mori	12	Olmutz	BL T.1857, 6
1728	Dolus Bonus	31	Ratisbon	BL 840.e.5, 13
1728	Volubilis Fortunae	11	Olmutz	BL T.1857, 7
1729	Ludovicus XII	29	Fribourg	Szarota 3/2, 863-70
1729	Chanté à le fête	10+	Dijon	ULg 43.921.1, 42:1
1730	Aaron a Moyse	14	Munich	BL 840.e.5, 17
1730	Cyrus	24	Amberg	Szarota 1/1, 335-42

[a] BL = British Library; ULg = University of Liège.

There are numerous allusions in the text of *Daphnis* indicating that pastoral characters were present on the stage and sang in the choruses. The Nymph, for example, calls together an ensemble of nymphs, gods, and shepherds, singing:

> Naiades, Dieux des bois, Bergers, que tout l'assemble.
> Qu'on prépare des chants après tant des soupirs,
> Daphnis rameine ensemble la joie et les plaisirs.[30]

> Naiads, Gods of the woods, Shepherds, let all come together.
> Let us prepare songs after so many sighs,
> Let Daphnis bring together joy and pleasures.

The other soloists similarly interact with pastoral characters not specified in the music manuscript. For example, Damon commands the shepherds to make music: 'Qu'on entende, Bergers le son de vos musettes' ('Shepherds, let us hear the sound of your pipes').[31] The Déesse directs a troupe of shepherds to dance. The text of the Déesse's *air*

---

[29] Zelenka, *Sub Olea Pacis*, 2/12. Performed by the Jesuit college in Prague in 1723, 142 singers formed the chorus for *Sub Olea Pacis*. The work also requires eight solo roles and an instrumental ensemble of at least twenty.
[30] Ms. 357.c, 49; Dyer, 634-39.
[31] Ms. 357.c, 54-56; Dyer, 741-59.

de cour also intimates that shepherds sang the choruses: 'A vos tendres concerts, Bergers, mêlez la danse' ('In your gentle choruses, Shepherds, lead the dance').[32] The presence of shepherdesses as well as shepherds in the cast is suggested by the Nymph in her final recitative:

> Heureux Bergers, trop heureuses Bergéres
> Chantez cens es cens fois,
> Assis sur la tendre fougère,
> 'Le généreux Daphnis, Élève de Pallas,
> Le gracieux Daphnis l'honneur de nos prélats'.[33]

> Happy Shepherds, overjoyed Shepherdesses,
> Sing hundreds and hundreds times
> Seated upon the tender fern,
> 'Generous Daphnis, pupil of Pallas,
> Gracious Daphnis, the honour of our Prelates'.

Thus, although Ms. 357.c and the programmes of other *Daphnis* plays do not include choral singers, an examination of the 1728 libretto reveals the possibility that several types of pastoral characters were included in the production together with the soloists. The text of the pastorale also implies that at least one sub-group of these characters, the shepherds, functioned as a choral ensemble.

Based upon this textual and programmatic evidence, four additional singers in the guise of shepherds were added to the 2008 production cast.[34] Also, the Déesse and the Echoes, who otherwise appear only in second half, were double-cast as shepherds in part one of the pastorale.[35] The soloists joined in singing the choral numbers with the ensemble of shepherds. The choral forces for the 2008 production thus totalled ten singers, a conservative decision placing the production among the smallest of those presented in Table 2, yet large enough to address the vocal imbalance issues previously discussed.[36]

Reconstructing Additional Characters

Having established the validity of adding choral singers by means of historical Jesuit theatre practice and references in the source libretto, a comparison of the 1728 music manuscript and the programmes from the four *Daphnis* productions reveals that the

---

[32] Ms. 357.c, 69; Dyer, 905-8.
[33] Ms. 357.c, 76; Dyer, 1011-27.
[34] The small performance space did not allow for a large cast, and so the nymphs, wood-gods, and shepherdesses referenced in the libretto were not included in the 2008 production. The choral ensemble were costumed as shepherds in cream-colored peasant blouses, matching yellow waistcoats, blue, brown, or black knee-breeches, black stockings, and black shoes. The shepherds were arranged in four dancing pairs, and these were indicated by the colour of their breeches and their arm-ribbons. Partners were assigned by the actors' heights, with the shortest performers at the front of the stage in order for all the actors to be clearly visible to the audience.
[35] Szarota, 1/1, 649-52. Double-casting was not uncommon in Jesuit theatre music-dramas. For example, seminary student George Pröll sang the role of David in the second music-drama and Orcus, the god of the underworld, in the third music-drama inserted in the tragedy *Philothea*, performed in Munich in 1643.
[36] Ten singers with the entrance of Daphnis in the second half. The total vocal forces in the 2008 production were four sopranos, two haute-contres, two tenors, and two basses.

Table 3. Comparison of the casts in five eighteenth-century *Daphnis* Jesuit programs

Daphnis, Pastorale (Namur, Anon., 1728), MS 357.c	*Daphnis, Pastorale* (Namur: Jean François La Fontaine, 1741), Stonyhurst College Library F.149, No. 1	*Daphnis* (Brugis: Francisci Beernaerts, 1754), Stonyhurst College Library, F.137, No. 3	*Galateae Daphnidis* (Ipris: Jacobum Franciscum Moerman, 1762), Stonyhurst College Library, F.137, No. 2	*Tityrus* (Ipris: Jacobum Franciscum Moerman, n.d.), Stonyhurst College Library, F.137, No. 1
La Nymphe de la Sambre	Génie (2)	Genius Brugensis	Daphnis	Daphnis
La Déesse des Flores	Apollon	Faunus (Pan)	Gymnasium Soc. Jesu	Fauns (5)
Echos	L'Amour	Daphnis	Galatea	Lycidas
Aminth	Le Compliment	Thyrsis	Damon	Tityrus
Damon	Le Génie de la Paix	Tityrus	Amyntas	Alphesiboeus
Choeur	Daphnis	Meliboeus	Moeris	Meliboeus
	Coridon	Alexis	Aziel	Menalcus
	Damon	Alphesiboeus	Alexis	
	Yolas	Lycidas	Corydon	
	Lycidas	Coridon	Aegon	
	Menalque			
	Meris			
	Thyrsis			
	Melabée			
	Ballet:			
	La Renommée			
	L'Amour			
	Le Zele			
	Le Mérite			
	La Religion			
	La Force			
	La Temperance			
	La Prudence			
	La Paix			
	Apollon			
	Les Bergers			

1728 production might have had a significantly larger cast than found in Ms. 357.c (Table 3). Compared to the five solo roles identified in the 1728 *Daphnis* score, the number of roles listed in the four programmes range from twenty-four (1741, Namur) to ten (1762, Ypres). Immediately noticeable in the cast lists are a number of additional shepherd roles.[37] Principal among these is the title role of Daphnis, who is not accorded a role in the 1728 music manuscript. Also absent in Ms. 357.c are mythological characters such as Apollo, who appears in the 1741 performance, and Pan, present in the Bruges and most likely also in the undated Ypres programmes. A ballet of nine religious genii, Apollo, and shepherds concludes the 1741 Namur production, a dramatic insertion not present in Ms. 357.c. Several of the programme cast lists likewise include a 'spirit' character, such as the 'Genius Brugensis' of the 1754 Bruges play and 'Gymnasium Soc. Jesu' of the 1762 Ypres play; 'Gymnasium Soc. Jesu' may be translated as College of the Society of Jesus. This type of character might be viewed as equivalent to the 'Nymphe de la Sambre' role in the 1728 production in the same way that the role of 'La Déesse des Flores' is similar to 'Le Génie de la Paix' in the Namur *Daphnis* pastorale of 1741.

The eight character roles added to the ensemble of 2008 were selected for inclusion based upon the information in the cast lists of these programmes, with preference given to the 1741 programme, as well as textual clues in the libretto. As an example of the latter, the goddess Minerva, symbolizing wisdom and learning, is referenced three times in part one alone in the 1728 *Daphnis* text, such as in this exchange between Aminth and Damon:

> *Aminth*
> Ausi pays eloignéz ainsi qu'au Pays-Bas
> Daphnis en sa tendre jeunesse
> Donna des preuves de sagesse
> Sous les auspices de Pallas.
>
> *Damon*
> Oui, Minerve la savante
> Par les doctes sentiers de la main,
> L'a conduit et pour répondre à notre attente
> Des lors fit voir en lui ce que devait
> Namur en espérer d'appui.[38]
>
> *Aminth*
> In the remote country as in the Low Countries
> Daphnis in his tender youth
> Gave proof of wisdom
> Under the auspices of Pallas.
>
> *Damon*
> Yes, Minerva the wise

---

[37] In the 2008 production, the six additional chorus members assumed the names of the shepherds found in the 1741 Namur performance: Coridon, Menalque, Meris, Thyrsis, Lycidas, and Yolas.

[38] Ms. 357.c, 28-29; Dyer, 309-17. The curious fact that Minerva/Pallas Athena is called by both her Greek and Roman names in the libretto appears to be only a matter of poetic meter.

> Led him by the hand along learned paths,
> And in response to our expectations
> Caused it to be seen in him that for which
> Namur could hope for support.

The name of the goddess also appears in conjunction with Daphnis in the pastorale's final choral paean of praise:

> Le généreux Daphnis, Élève de Pallas,
> Le gracieux Daphnis l'honneur de nos prélats.[39]

> Generous Daphnis, pupil of Pallas,
> Gracious Daphnis, the honour of our Prelates.

Minerva does not appear among the characters listed in Table 3, but Apollo, representing music is not only in the 1741 play but also takes part in the concluding ballet. Apollo is not, however, mentioned in the 1728 libretto, although he and Minerva (as Pallas Athena) are often paired in classical Greek tragedies.[40] On the strength of her presence in the libretto, Minerva was added to the 2008 cast, and Apollo, as Minerva's dance partner, became part of the production based upon his presence in the 1741 performance at the Jesuit college of Namur.[41]

The Greco-Roman god Pan was another character added to the 2008 cast.[42] In the same manner as Minerva, he, too, is invoked in the text of Ms. 357.c. The Déesse sings in an *air de cour* towards the end of the pastorale:

> A vos tendres concerts, Bergers, mêlez la danse;
> Le Dieu Pan vous invite à l'ombre des ormeaux.
> Il s'engage lui même à marquer la cadence
> Par les doux sons de ses pipeaux.[43]

> In your gentle choruses, Shepherds, lead the dance;
> The God Pan calls you to the shade of the elms.
> He himself promises to keep the time
> With the soft sounds of his pipes.

In this scene, the Déesse suggests that Pan plays an important role in the stage action, performing as onstage musician for the dancing shepherds. Not only does the character of Pan appear in the 1728 libretto, but he also figures in the cast of the Bruges

---

[39] Ms. 357.c, 82-87. Dyer, 1092-1138.
[40] Euripides, *Ion*, ed. and trans. Robin Waterfield (New York, 2001). Aeschylus, *Eumenides*, ed. and trans. Anthony J. Podlecki (Warminster, 1989).
[41] The actors portraying Minerva and Apollo, in order to show their divine nature, were the tallest, 6'2" and 6'5", respectively. In order to create the illusion of Apollo and Minerva possessing even greater height, their two attendants were the smallest members of the ensemble. Minerva's costume was a gold-edged white tunic, a twisted red cord sash, a sword, and a crown of laurels. Apollo's costume consisted of a sleeveless cream tunic with an embroidered hem, a long-sleeve gold lamé undershirt, gold cloth drape, and a twisted red cord sash.
[42] Pan's costume, created and donated by Grace Smith and Mark Burghagen, was a sleeveless faux deer-skin jacket hung with strands of ivy and ribbons of cloth on the sleeves and body of the jacket, contoured knee-breeches of a black furry material, leggings with painted hooves, and pan-pipes.
[43] Ms. 357.c, 69-70; Dyer, 905-27.

production of 1754 (Figure 2a) under an alternate name, Faunus, making his inclusion plausible in a reconstruction of *Daphnis, Pastorale*.[44]

The Character of Daphnis

The absence of the character of Daphnis in the 1728 musical score together with his implied importance as the title role of the play presents one of the greatest challenges in constructing a modern performance of *Daphnis, Pastorale*. His arrival is the goal of the dramatic action of the pastorale, as shown in this dialogue between the Nymph and the Déesse in the opening scene of part two:

> *Nymphe*
> Quelle Divinité se présente ici bas
> Que sa voix est douce et charmante!
> Mais, pour me rendre plus contente
> Dismoi Daphnis ne viens il pas?[45]
>
> *La Déesse des Flores*
> Nymphe, consolez vous, je devance ses pas.[46]
>
> *Nymph*
> What Divinity presents herself here?
> How sweet and charming is her voice!
> But, to make me even more content,
> Tell me, is not Daphnis coming?
>
> *Spirit of Spring*
> Nymph, take comfort, for I precede him.

In fact, Daphnis' arrival is the awaited conclusion for all of the *Daphnis* plays examined here. He appears in all of the programmes in Figures 1 and 2, but only among the cast members in the 1741 production at the Namur Jesuit college. In the Bruges and Ypres programmes his name is, however, found in both the synopses and the brief explanations of the allegorical significance of the dramatic characters. In the 1754 play, Daphnis signifies the most illustrious of 'our people', presumably the bishop and/or the local nobles.[47] Similarly, the statement in the 1762 Ypres programme shows that the character of Daphnis represents the most excellent bishop of Ypres.[48] For the undated production in Ypres, Daphnis symbolizes joy and rejoicing.[49] Only the programme for the 1741 Namur play does not specify the allegorical significance of the character of Daphnis in the production.

---

[44] Antoine Furetière, *Dictionaire universel* (The Hague and Rotterdam: Arnout et Reinier Leers, 1691), cited in Rock, *Terpsichore at Louis-le-Grand*, 195.
[45] Ms. 357.c, 41. Dyer, 556-60.
[46] Ms. 357.c, 41. Dyer, 560-61.
[47] *Daphnis* (1754), 44: 'Daphnis Illustrissimum nostrum'.
[48] *Galateae Daphnidis* (1762), 8: 'Daphnis Illustrissimum Iprensium Praesulem.'
[49] *Tityrus* (n. d.), 14: 'Daphnis illustrissimum jubilantem.'

The similarities among the Namur, Ypres, and Bruges *Daphnis* plays suggest that the later performances are revisions of the 1728 Namur *Daphnis*—almost certainly in the case of the 1741 Namur *Daphnis* play. This observation is not necessarily a forgone conclusion, as the surviving documentation does not include the texts and is limited to the four theatrical programmes and one music manuscript presented here. Although not identifying the Daphnis character with a person, virtue, or emotion as in the Ypres and Bruges plays, the synopsis for the 1741 programme indicates that Daphnis enters at the conclusion of the action: 'Les Bergers des environs de la Sambre & de la Meuse, aïant appres l'arrivée de Daphnis leur Chef, qu'ils attendoient depuis longtem, font des praparatifs pour le bien recevoir' ('The shepherds from the banks of the Sambre and Meuse rivers gather to await the arrival Daphnis, their chief, who had been a long time away, and make preparations for the celebration of his return').[50] The 1728 pastorale appears to have employed the same dramatic structure; the absence of the title character in the play itself implies that Daphnis enters after the conclusion of the music drama. Daphnis' arrival is eminent at the end of Ms. 357.c, for the Déesse, pretending to espy Daphnis from afar, says to the Nymph:

> Hatez vous, quittez votre rive,
> Venez aimable Nymphe au devant de Daphnis
> Le voici, je le vois, sur vos bords; il arrive
> Suivi des Graces et des ris.[51]

> Haste, leave your bank,
> Come, gentle Nymph, before Daphnis.
> There he is, I see him at your border; he arrives
> Followed by Graces and laughter.

This correlates with the synopses found in the Bruges and Ypres plays (Figure 1b and Figures 2a and b), in which Daphnis likewise enters at the conclusion of the pastorale.

The observed dramatic structure of the Ypres, Bruges, and 1741 Namur *Daphnis* plays explains why the title character might not be found within the 1728 score. A further examination of these and other theatrical programmes from the Gallo-Belgian Jesuit Province colleges, interpreted in light of research conducted by William H. McCabe and Judith Rock, reveals that Daphnis' arrival onstage most probably occurred either via a ballet or a symbolic pageant. In his chapter 'Substitutions for the Chorus,' McCabe demonstrates how ballet in some cases replaced the inserted choruses in Jesuit theatrical productions.[52] Although McCabe mentions a single instance of this practice in Spanish, Portuguese, German, and Italian Jesuit colleges, his focus centres upon the tradition of ballet in the English Jesuit college of St. Omer as well as a brief introduction to the ballets by Gabriel François Le Jay for the Jesuit Collège Louis-le-Grand/Collège de Clermont in Paris. Rock's study of the ballets performed by the Collège Louis-le-Grand/Collège

---

[50] *Daphnis, Pastorale* (1741), 2. My translation.
[51] Ms. 357.c, 48-49. Dyer, 626-31.
[52] McCabe, S. J., *An Introduction to the Jesuit Theatre*, 203-13.

de Clermont from 1660 to 1762 builds upon previous research conducted by scholars Régine Astier, Ernest Boysse, and Robert Lowe.[53]

The work by these scholars and an examination of the theatrical productions by the Namur, Ypres, and Bruges Jesuit college productions during the seventeenth and eighteenth centuries reveals that a ballet usually concluded pastorales such as *Daphnis*. Typically, these ballets enacted an allegory and employed mythological and pastoral characters.[54] The presence of a ballet with a cast of allegorical characters in the 1741 Namur programme supports the findings of Rock, Astier, and others, and is strong evidence that a similar ballet concluded the 1728 *Daphnis* production. While the cast lists for the Bruges and Ypres productions do not specify a ballet, the synopses relate a celebration of Daphnis' arrival with a striking similarity of phrase, further supporting the proposition that these productions are revisions of the 1728 Namur production.[55]

With sufficient evidence from both primary and secondary sources, it is not unreasonable to suggest that a ballet featuring or led by Daphnis concluded the 1728 production by the Namur Jesuit college. Featured in the cast of the ballet were probably Agaia, Euphrosyne, and Thalia, the Graces mentioned by the Déesse in the quote above as the companions of Daphnis. The ballet probably also included the characters from the pastorale, as occurred in the 1741 Namur ballet. With no other information in the libretto or manuscript, a reconstruction of the ballet presented in 1728 would be chiefly a matter of conjecture or an adoption of the ballet cast from the 1741 Namur performance.

The absence of music in Ms. 357.c for a ballet presents less of a difficulty for a modern construction of 1728 performance. A suite of dances could quite easily be constructed from extant collections of early eighteenth-century French dance music. It would also be possible to build a suite using excerpts from the original score or to adapt a ballet from another Jesuit college, such as Louis-le-Grand, to suit the *Daphnis* pastorale. The absence of ballet music in the manuscript suggests that not only was the concluding ballet of a pastorale less of a formal construct than the pastorale drama itself but also assumes that the performance practice was so familiar to the manuscript recipients as to require no additional music.

Metaphor and Spiritual Allegory in *Daphnis*

Ballet is not the sole form used to conclude Gallo-Belgian Jesuit college theatrical productions, for, though considerably more rare than ballet, some plays conclude with a symbolic pageant or series of tableaux. For example, the production of *Bacqveville delivré de prison & de mort par S. Ivlien* by the Jesuit college at Ath concludes with

---

[53] Rock, *Terpsichore at Louis-le-Grand*, Régine Astier, 'Pierre Beauchamps and the Ballets de Collège', in *Dance Chronicle* 6 (1983), 139-63. Ernest Boysse, *Le théâtre de jésuites* (Paris, 1880), 31-58. Robert Lowe, *Marc Antoine Charpentier et l'opéra de collège* (Paris, 1966), 175-95.

[54] Lowe, *Marc Antoine Charpentier*, 187. Three examples of ballets performed at Louis-le-Grand contemporary to the performance of Ms. 357.c were *L'Ambition* (1727), *Les Voeux de la France* (1728), and *Les Aventures d'Ulysses ou la Génie vainquer des obstacles* (1729).

[55] *Daphnis* (1754), 44: '...ac Daphni festivas inter choreas procedunt obviàm.' *Galateae Daphnidis*, (1762), 8: '...Daphnidis ex scuto dotes ominantur, illique tandem, præeunte *Azièle*, inter choreas procedunt in occursum.' *Tityrus* (n. d.), 14: '...atque unà cum *Faunis* ad *Daphnida* jubilem ipsi gratulaturi festivas inter choreas festinant.'

students enacting anagrams of St. Julian's name.[56] The absence of evidence of a ballet in the 1728 score together with a lack of dancers experienced in Baroque dance forms rendered it not possible to conclude the 2008 production with a ballet, and therefore an alternate form of conclusion was needed that expressed the dramatic climax of *Daphnis* in a manner consistent with historical precedence in Gallo-Belgian Jesuit Province college productions. The solution ventured for this production was a ceremonial pageant in which the arrival of Daphnis was developed into a spectacle summarizing, in mimed action and with simplified dances, the multiple symbolic metaphors represented by the character of Daphnis in the 1728 libretto.[57]

Central to the creation of this pageant was the determination of who or what Daphnis represented in the 1728 pastorale. A detailed study of Ms. 357.c reveals not one but three metaphors for Daphnis within the pastorale.[58] One of these is the representation by Daphnis of the newly elected bishop of Namur, a metaphor similar to that found in the 1762 Ypres production. This proposed allegorical symbolism is consistent with the information known about the circumstances of the 1728 performance; the frontispiece of Ms. 357.c states that the 1728 pastorale was presented in honour of Thomas John Francis Strickland (c. 1682-1740) (Figure 3).[59]

Figure 3. *Daphnis, Pastorale*, Jesuit College of Namur, 1728, Frontispiece. University of Liège, Ms. 357.c, p.1

---

[56] *Bacqveville delivré de prison & de mort par S. Ivlien* (Ath, 26 August, 1630). Harvard University, Houghton Library, Item *66-200. 'Quelques Enfans poursuivent ceste action de grace, faisant sur le Nom de S. Iulien plusiers Anagrammes.'
[57] Daphnis' costume consisted of a peasant blouse, neutral-colored breeches, and period greatcoat decorated with ribbons.
[58] Elizabeth Dyer, 'Practicing What You Preach: Portraying the Ideal in Jesuit College Stage Productions, 1551-1773' (paper presented at *Image, Music, Identity: Constructing and Experiencing Identities through Music within Visual Culture*, University of Nottingham, 6 June 2009).
[59] John Callow, 'Strickland, Thomas John Francis (c.1682–1740)' in *Oxford Dictionary of National Biography*, ed. Lawrence Goldman, <http://www.oxforddnb.com>, accessed June 2013.

The symbol of Daphnis for Bishop Strickland is first presented in an *air de cour* in part one sung by Aminth. In this passage, the bishop is portrayed as a good priest who discharges his religious duties seriously and because of this is well-known by and popular with the people of the region:

> Maint hameux, connoissant son zèle,
> Demande Daphnis comme nous.
> S'il nous préfère à tous,
> Nous allons vivre heureux sous ce guide fidèle.[60]

> Many villages, knowing his zeal,
> Call for Daphnis as we do.
> Should he prefer us above the others,
> We shall live happily under this faithful guide.

The profession of the love of Namur for the bishop continues in an exchange between Damon and Aminth:

> *Damon*
> Ha! que le ciel nous est propice et secourable
> Perise ce hameau plutôt que ce Pasteur aimable
> Ne soit aimé de son troupeau.

> *Aminth*
> Ah! que n'est la voix des guerrières trompettes
> Pour faire retentir nos hameaux et nos bois
> Du bruit de ses sacrés exploits![61]

> *Damon*
> Ha! How heaven is good and favourable to us!
> This village would perish sooner than this kind Shepherd
> Be not loved by his flock.

> *Aminth*
> Ah! That we had the voice of those war trumpets
> To make our villages and our woods ring
> With the clamor of his sacred exploits!

The image of the Shepherd in the above passage is an example of a symbolic linkage that appears throughout the work. The pastoral figure of Daphnis simultaneously signifies Christ the Good Shepherd and, as a representative of Christ in the Church, the bishop. The image of the bishop as a servant to the Roman Catholic Church through the metaphor of Daphnis forms the main thrust of the Nymph's first *da capo* aria:

---

[60] Ms. 357.c, 24; Dyer, 272-76.
[61] Ms. 357.c, 73-74; Dyer, 949-62.

Prince, l'amour de tes sujets
Heureux fait partir mon Daphnis.
J'aurai toute ma joie
Si ta bonté veut que je voie
Daphnis servir l'Eglissée et l'Etat en ces lieux.[62]

Prince, the love of your happy subjects
Causes my Daphnis to leave.
I will have all my joy
If your goodness desires that I see
Daphnis serve the Church and State in these places.

The bishop is expected to serve the Church not only well but with fervour. His 'sacred exploits' are mentioned in the previous passage while an earlier excerpt praised 'his zeal.' Thus, Bishop Strickland's dedication to the Roman Catholic Church is emphasized in the pastorale as much as Namur's joy in securing him as their bishop.

Daphnis is also drawn in the text to represent the local ruling noble, the 'State' mentioned in the Nymph's aria above. By itself, this single intimation would be insufficient evidence to propose an additional symbolic layer to Daphnis, and indeed, the symbolic link between Daphnis and the count of Namur is not as strong as that of Daphnis and the bishop. However, the count is reminded multiple times within the pastorale of his duty to protect and secure the region of Namur. As demonstrated below by two separate examples from the libretto, the count's duty is consistently announced via the same shepherd metaphor of Daphnis-as-Christ similar to those passages alluding to the bishop:

> *Aminth*
> C'est un sage Pasteur dont l'amour vis et tendre
> Pour l'intérêt de son troupeau
> Fera la sureté du Bourg et du hameau.[63]
>
> *Aminth*
> It is a wise Shepherd whose strong and tender love
> For the well-being of his flock
> Will ensure the security of the town and village.
>
> *Aminth*
> A l'abri des frimats, à couvert de l'orage,
> Sans plus craindre des loups la fureur ni la ragé;
> Paissez, troupeaux, Daphnis veille pour vous.[64]
>
> *Aminth*
> Sheltered from frost, protected from storm,
> No longer fearing the fury and rage of the wolves;

---

[62] Ms. 357.c, 31-33; Dyer, 370-465.
[63] Ms. 357.c, 29-30; Dyer, 322-47.
[64] Ms. 357.c, 52; Dyer, 730-33.

> Graze, flock, for Daphnis watches over you.

There are other allusions to this ruler in the text, of which the most notable is the concluding chorus of part one. Although the performance of 1728 honoured a Catholic bishop, the chorus sings:

> Ainsi parmi les biens qu'ici le ciel t'en voie
> Puisse tu pour l'appui de l'auguste maisson
> Avant les jours de le viellesse
> Parmi la joie et l'allégresse
> Te voir naitre bientôt un noble rejetton.[65]

> Thus amidst the goods that heaven sends to you
> May you, for the sake of the august house
> Before the days of old age
> Amidst joy and felicity
> Soon see the birth of a noble offspring.

It seems much more probable that these wishes of fecundity were offered to an important noble than to the celibate Bishop Strickland.

Thus, the final choruses of each half of the pastorale were addressed to two different influential persons; the count of Namur in the first half and the bishop in the second half.[66] To realize this in performance, the characters of the count and contessa of Namur were created and seated in a private box at one side of the stage in the 2008 performance.[67] The function of these noble characters was not merely one of stage-dressing, for they played an important role in the inserted pageant as well as providing an active recipient for the praises, admonitions, and good wishes directed to them by the onstage ensemble. The presence of the count and the contessa in the production became all the more important to the pageant because the means available were insufficient to allow the Bishop Strickland to be similarly portrayed in this performance.[68]

A study of the plot as a whole reveals an over-arching spiritual allegory that centres upon the third and final significance of the character of Daphnis in *Daphnis, Pastorale*. In this possible interpretation of the plot, Daphnis is a metaphor for Christ, a concept briefly introduced above.[69] The allegorical symbolism between Daphnis and Christ is, however, more elaborately crafted than those passages that merely employ the

---

[65] Ms. 357.c, 34-38; Dyer, 466-515.
[66] Ms. 357.c, 77-87; Dyer, 1060-1138. Final chorus, part two: 'Ne cessons point d'unis nos voix / Au doux son des hautbois.' See text at note 33 above.
[67] At the opening of the performance, the count and contessa were formally announced and escorted to their seats accompanied by the opening section of the purely instrumental *Musette* number from the manuscripts.
[68] Although the character of Bishop Strickland was in the original design for the 2008 performance, the prohibitive costume hire resulted in the character being cut from the production. The donation of costumes and actors for the count and contessa by the Lords of Misrule of York is hereby gratefully acknowledged. The count's costume consisted of an embroidered blouse, breeches, a crimson coat trimmed with fur, black stockings, black shoes, and rings. The contessa wore an A-line embroidered white gown with white stockings and white shoes. Their heads were bare in preparation for their role in the pageant.
[69] Elizabeth Dyer, 'Christ, Minerva, and la Noblesse Oblige in a Unique Eighteenth-Century Franco-Belgian Jesuit Music Drama' (paper presented at *Music and Morality*, The Institute of Musical Research & Institute of Philosophy, London, 17 June 2009).

extended metaphor to the bishop and the nobleman. As well as the character of Daphnis, the Nymph and the Déesse are central to this proposed spiritual allegory.

The secular plot of the pastoral is a vehicle for the metaphorical symbolism of the spiritual allegory. On the surface of all of the *Daphnis* plays examined in this essay, the plot concerns a group of mythological characters awaiting the arrival of Daphnis, the son of Hermes and a Sicilian nymph. This basic plot is refined in the 1728 *Daphnis* to be specific to Namur. The plot of Ms. 357.c provides a mythological explanation for and spring celebration of the annual breaking up of the river-ice and the subsequent return of prosperity to Namur, a city that depended upon the river traffic for its economy. In part one of *Daphnis*, the Nymph laments that Namur remains under the spell of winter, leaving her river frozen and still:

> Mon onde en ce moment mécontente et es plaintive,
> Vient de s'arrêter sur sa rive,
> Et voiant de l'Etê différer les beaux jours,
> Refuse sans Daphnis de reprendre son cours.[70]

> My flowing waves, now unhappy and lamenting,
> Halt upon their bank,
> And seeing how Summer delays its beautiful days,
> Refuse without Daphnis to resume their course.

Only Daphnis has the power to bring summer to Namur, and he has delayed his customary appearance. After the Déesse announces the imminent of arrival of Daphnis, the Nymph joyfully heralds the arrival of spring at the end of part two:

> En faveur de Daphnis la feconde
> Nature se pare de mille agréments.
> J'entens l'onde qui coule avec un doux murmure;
> Les prés semes de fleurs et couverts de verdure.[71]

> To favour Daphnis, fertile
> Nature adorns herself with a thousand decorations.
> I hear the waters which flow with a soft murmur;
> The meadows are sewn with flowers and covered with green.

The remainder of the pastorale celebrates pastoral activities and games in preparation for Daphnis' entrance following the conclusion of the pastorale.

The single brief statements found at the beginning of each formal division, the only non-musical information provided in the manuscript, outline the spiritual allegory: 'Prémiere entrée la Nymphe de la Sambre soupire après l'arrivée de Daphnis' ('First entrance The Nymph of the Sambre [River] sighs for the arrival of Daphnis'), and 'La Déesse de Flores Vient Annoncer l'arrivée de Daphnis' ('The Spirit of Spring comes to announce the arrival of Daphnis'), respectively.[72] The Nymph's character and actions

---

[70] Ms. 357.c, 12; Dyer, 152-60.
[71] Ms. 357.c, 66-67; Dyer, 867-79.
[72] Ms. 357.c, 5; Dyer, 1; and Ms. 357.c, 39; Dyer, 516 (my translation).

throughout part one consistently project the metaphor of the Soul lamenting its sinful state and anxiously awaiting the arrival of the prophesied Christ, as shown in this excerpt from the opening scene:

> *Nymphe*
> Serai je toujours languissante,
> Dans une triste et longue attente?
> Daphnis enfin ne paroîtra t'il pas?
>
> *Aminth*
> Dis-nous, Nymphe, dis nous le sujet de ta peine
> Ne pouroit-on la soulager.
>
> *Nymphe*
> Non, non, le seul Daphnis pouroit me dégager
> Des mille affreux soucis que son absence entraine.[73]
>
>
> *Nymph*
> Shall I be always listless,
> Forever waiting sadly?
> Will Daphnis ever appear?
>
> *Aminth*
> Tell us, Nymphe, tell us the cause of your sorrow
> That we might soothe your pain.
>
> *Nymph*
> No, no, only Daphnis could release me from
> The thousand horrible fears brought on by his absence.

Here, the 'thousand horrible fears' could be interpreted as the unforgiven sins burdening the Soul. The Nymph continues in the character of her moral metaphor in part two in a state of increasing anticipation of Daphnis' arrival. Once the Déesse convinces her that Daphnis is indeed coming and that he is expected very soon, the Nymph rejoices:

> L'agréable nouvelle
> Que tu viens porter en ces lieux!
> Et puissent aujourd'hui mes yeux
> Être témoins de ton récit fidèle.[74]
>
> What pleasant news
> You bring to these places!
> And may it be that today my eyes
> Will bear witness to your faithful tale.

---

[73] Ms. 357.c, 6-8; Dyer, 26-49.
[74] Ms. 357.c, 42-43; Dyer, 578-82.

In this *récit*, the Nymph's reaction to the good news brought by the Déesse is expressed in a turn of phrase that is reminiscent of Simeon at Christ's presentation at the temple in Jerusalem. In his blessing of the Christ-child, Simeon says, 'For mine eyes have seen thy salvation', a phrase to which the Nymph's final two lines in this passage might refer.[75]

La Déesse des Flores appears to symbolize John the Baptist within the spiritual allegory of Ms. 357.c. The metaphor of the Déesse as John the Baptist is introduced in the very first exchange of dialogue in part two of the pastorale:

La Déesse des Flores
Nymphe, faites cesser vos mortelles alarmes;
Reprenez vos appas; le ciel enfinse rend
À l'excés de vos larmes.

Nymphe
Dismoi Daphnis ne viens il pas?

La Déesse des Flores
Nymphe, consolez vous, je devance ses pas.

Nymphe
Le verrai je bientôt? Puis je'espérer? hélas!

La Déesse des Flores
Faites cesser votre cruelle peine,
Reprenez vos appas dés aujourd'hui.
Je vous l'amené pour ce doux objet de vos voeux.
Ne songer plus qu'à préparer des jeux.[76]

Spirit of Spring
Nymph, make an end to your mortal fears,
Reclaim your charms; the heavens at last give way
To the excess of your tears.

Nymph
Tell me, is not Daphnis coming?

Spirit of Sprong
Nymph, take comfort, for I precede him.

Nymph
Shall I see him soon? Can I hope? Alas!

Spirit of Spring
Put an end to your cruel pain,
Reclaim your beauty today.

---

[75] Luke 2:30.
[76] Ms. 357.c, 40-41; Dyer, 552-61.

> I bring him to you, a sweet sight for your eyes.
> Now think of nothing but the preparation of games.

La Déesse des Flores's part in the above dialogue is notably similar to the sacred mission of John the Baptist, described in these two verses from the gospel of Luke:

> And [John] shall go before [Christ]…to make ready a people prepared for the Lord. (Luke 1:17)

> And thou, child [John], shalt be called the prophet of the Highest, for thou shalt go before the face of the Lord to prepare his ways: to give knowledge of salvation unto his people by the remission of their sins through the tender mercy of our God. (Luke 1:76-77)[77]

Just as John the Baptist preceded Christ, so does the Déesse precede Daphnis, whose symbolic association with Christ has previously been established. The Déesse des Flores proclaims the coming of Daphnis, similar to John, 'the prophet of the Highest.' The Déesse – John the Baptist and Daphnis – Christ association was further illustrated by means of an aural association between the Déesse and Daphnis *in the 2008 production*. This aural association was created by using the instrumental symphony that appears in Ms. 357.c immediately before the Déesse announces Daphnis' imminent arrival as the musical accompaniment for the pageant celebrating the arrival of Daphnis at the conclusion of the pastorale.

John the Baptist is charged to prepare the people for the coming of the Christ, and the Déesse calls for the 'preparation of games' by the Nymph and shepherds to receive Daphnis. The description of Daphnis as a 'sweet sight for your eyes' by the Déesse might be interpreted as the Nymph/Soul's salvation through the remission of sins, if eyes may be considered the window of the soul. The 'mortal fears' the Déesse speaks of above refer to an earlier moment in the pastorale when the Nymph/Soul cries out in anguish:

> Que me sent-il, hélas! d'être immortelle?
> Si je ne vois Daphnis, j'aime autans le trépas.[78]

> What is the use for me to be immortal?
> If I do not see Daphnis, I wish for my own demise.

The nature of the Nymph is thus portrayed in the pastorale as both mortal and immortal, indicative of the dual symbolism attached to the character. Most nymphs in classical mythology are immortal, and thus the mortal aspects of the Nymph, such as her fear and sadness, might be interpreted to belong to those moments in the pastorale when she represents the Soul.[79] Within this metaphor, the Nymph's 'excess of tears' that caused the heavens 'to at last give way' might represent the Christian perception of the damned

---

[77] See also Isaiah 40:3, 'The voice of him that crieth in the wilderness, Prepare ye the way of the Lord, make straight in the desert a highway for our God.'
[78] Ms. 357.c, 7-8; Dyer, 41-43.
[79] William F. Hansen, *Classical Mythology: A Guide to the Mythical World of the Greeks and Romans* (New York, 2005), 40-42. Hansen writes that not all nymphs are immortal: some live only 'ten times as long as a phoenix'.

condition of human Soul from the time after the fall of Adam to Christ's crucifixion and resurrection.

The pageant inserted into the 2008 production in lieu of a concluding ballet was designed to simultaneously illustrate Daphnis as a triple metaphor for the bishop, the count, and Christ, as well as to fulfil the dramatic purpose of the pastoral and spiritual plots. The pageant involved the entire vocal and instrumental cast, including the onstage audience of the count and the contessa. Not only was the entire ensemble involved in the spectacle, but the set also underwent a seasonal change in preparation for Daphnis' arrival in the pageant.

During the course of the pastorale, and in response to specific cues in the text, the stage was transformed by the ensemble from winter to spring. The concert hall for the 2008 performance was without a scenic apparatus, and therefore the stage layout, sets, and set changes were designed as if the play were performed on an outdoor stage without curtains. The set changes were kept as simple as possible, as these were carried out by the cast in full view of the audience. All of the properties necessary to complete the transformation were therefore concealed on the stage to allow the cast members to effect the changes in the smallest amount of time.

The Transformation Scenes

The stage design for the 2008 performance was based upon the description printed in the 1741 *Daphnis* programme from Namur: 'La sçene est sur le jonction de la Sambre & de la Meuse.' ('The scene is set on the banks at the meeting of the Sambre and the Meuse').[80] The libretto indicates that the scenic background included deciduous trees as the Nymph calls for the trees to put forth their leaves in part two:

> Sombres forêts, riants bocages
> Couvrez ces lieux de vos ombrages.[81]

> Solemn forests, laughing groves
> Cover these places with your shades.

There is additional evidence in the libretto to indicate that part one of the pastorale is set in winter-time:

> *Damon*
> De nos bois le triste feüillage
> N'offre plus de charmant ombrage.

> *Aminth*
> Dans nos vastes prairies

---

[80] *Daphnis, Pastorale* (Namur: Jean François La Fontaine, 1741), F.149/12. The representations of the Sambre and Meuse Rivers, each thirty-five feet long and three feet wide, were of blue satin with an overlayer of dark blue gauze. To add more spectacle to the performance as well as signal the beginning of each act, Minerva and Apollo laid down a river on the stage during the instrumental overture of each partition, the Sambre in part one and the Meuse in part two.
[81] Ms. 357.c, 51-52; Dyer, 640-709.

Autre fois si fleuries,
L'on ne voit plus bon, dir les innocents troupeaux
Au son des chalumeaux.

Damon
Et cette onde autre fois si pure
Refuse au doux sommeil l'agréable murmure,
Qui nos tenoit lieu de pavots.[82]

Damon
The saddened foliage of our wood
Offers no more its charming shade.

Aminth
In our vast meadows
Once so full of flowers,
One can no longer see the innocent flocks leaping
To the sound of the shepherd's pipe.

Damon
And this flowing water, once so pure,
Denies to our sweet sleep its pleasant murmur,
Which lulled us in lieu of poppies.

In this passage, Damon calls attention to the bare branches of the trees and the frozen rivers, while Aminth mourns the barren fields and meadows. Based upon this evidence from the libretto and the programme from the 1741 Namur performance, the stage for part one and the first half of part two was set in winter at the meeting of the Meuse and Sambre rivers (see Figure 4).

For the 2008 production, the impression of winter was created by banks of snow arranged about the stage area; these snowbanks were constructed of white cloths overlaid with white and sparkling tulle. The transformation of the stage from winter to spring during the second half of part in preparation for the pageant was effected in three incremental stages; these stages were integrated into the dramatic action in response to specific cues in the text.

The first stage of the transformation was the melting of the snow and river-ice in response to the Nymph's *da capo* aria 'Sombres forêts, riants bocages,' the first passage in the libretto to signal a change of season. The simple but effective visual of the snow melting was created by attaching a string, invisible to the audience, to a corner of each snowbank. The organist and two hidden flautists were given the other end of the strings to pull on cue. At a signal given by the Déesse during the ritornello of the Nymph's aria, the flautists and organist pulled their respective hidden strings, causing the 'snow' to appear to melt and run as the cloth snowbanks were pulled off the stage. This revealed the bare ground, i.e., the natural wood floor of the stage.

---

[82] Ms. 357.c, 12-15; Dyer, 160-210.

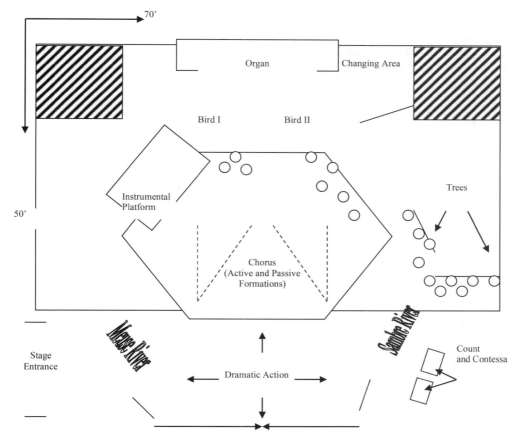

Figure 4. Stage design for November 27, 2008 performance of *Daphnis, Pastorale*, Sir Jack Lyons Concert Hall, University of York

Aminth's air following the Nymph's aria indicates what changes to the stage have taken place:

> Venez petits oiseaux
> Sous ce tendre feüillage,
> Mêlez votre ramage
> Au bruit de ces eaux.[83]

> Come, little birds
> Under this tender foliage,
> Join your song
> To the noise of these waters.

Although the evergreen trees used in the production could not produce the 'tender foliage' to which Aminth refers, the 'noise of these waters' reveals to the audience

---

[83] Ms. 357.c, 59-60; Dyer, 800-30.

that the river-ice has melted at last. The last vestiges of winter having been removed from the stage, the second stage of the transformation begins the process of re-dressing of the stage for the pageant in obedience to the Nymph's instructions:

> Zéphirs qui régnez dans nos plaines
> Ranimez les souples roseaux
> Qui bordent nos paisibles eaux
> Et par vos plus douces haleines
> Faites en pour Daphnis autant de chalumeaux.[84]

> Zephyrs, which reign in our plains,
> Revive the supple reeds
> Which skirt our peaceful waters,
> And with your gentlest breaths
> Make them for Daphnis into many flutes.

In response to the Nymph's air, grassy banks appear and flutes and recorders are added to the ensemble.[85] The third and last part of the set transformation takes place shortly before the beginning of the pageant. Once again, it is the Nymph who reveals the changes occurring in the scenery:

> En faveur de Daphnis la feconde
> Nature se pare de mille agréments…
> Les prés semes de fleurs et couvents de verdure.[86]

> To favour Daphnis, fertile
> Nature adorns herself with a thousand decorations…
> The meadows are sewn with flowers and covered with green.

Based upon this imagery in the Nymph's récit, a multi-coloured profusion of flowers and flowering vines blossom in the grassy areas.[87]

The Arrival of Daphnis

With the transformation from winter to spring complete, the stage is set to welcome Daphnis. The intention to create the pageant as a visual depiction of this production's interpretation of the layers of symbolism within Ms. 357.c also required a decision regarding the placement of the pageant in the production. The placement of the pageant was important, for it needed to fulfil the dramatic purpose of the play while appearing to arise naturally in the same manner as the missing ballet. The obvious solution was to

---

[84] Ms. 357.c, 56-57; Dyer, 756-80.
[85] In the 2008 production, the shepherds with their recorders represented the Zephyrs. The flutes were the 'little birds' backstage.
[86] Ms. 357.c, 66-67; Dyer, 867-78.
[87] The flowers and vines were hidden from audience view under burlap sacking covering banks of floral foam. The cast members reached under the burlap, pulled out the pre-arranged bunches of flowers and pushed them through the burlap into the underlying foam, creating clumps of flowers.

have the pageant immediately follow the concluding chorus of the Ms. 357.c score, thus replicating historical practices. When the pageant was tried in this position, however, the result proved to be unsatisfactory. The relatively brief pageant seemed anticlimactic after an hour's building of anticipation for Daphnis' arrival.[88]

Expanding the pageant was not an option for the 2008 production, and therefore a place was sought within the existing score that would fulfil the dramatic purpose of the pastorale while not interfering with the plot.[89] After trials in several other locations, the final decision was to divide the pastorale's final chorus into two sections and place the pageant between the two sections, as shown here:

[Section A]
Ne cessons point d'unis nos voix
Au doux son des hautbois.

[Pageant]

[Section B]
Heureux Berger, trop heureuses Bergéres
Chantez cens et cens fois,
Assis sur la tendre fougère.
'Le généreux Daphnis, Élève de Pallas,
Le gracieux Daphnis l'honneur de nos prélats.'[90]

[Section A]
We shall never cease to unite our voices
To the soft sound of the oboes.

[Pageant]

[Section B]
Happy Shepherd, overjoyed Shepherdesses,
Sing hundreds and hundreds of times
Seated upon the tender ferns
'Generous Daphnis, pupil of Pallas,
Gracious Daphnis, the honour of our prelates'.

---

[88] In the 2008 production, the duration of the pageant was approximately seven minutes. This was time enough for the accompanying allemande to be played three times through without pause. The description in this essay highlights only the four main points of arrival within the spectacle.

[89] The chief factor preventing an expansion of the pageant was the unavailability of dancers for this production. Although the pageant was entirely danced in the performance, as were all the instrumental passages in the pastorale, the singers' inexperience in eighteenth-century French dances required that all the dances be greatly simplified. The dances, not labelled in the manuscript, were identified by referring to Betty Band Mather, *Dance Rhythms of the French Baroque: A Handbook for Performance* (Bloomington, 1987). The dances were modified and taught to the ensemble by a member of the cast with extensive experience in Baroque dance. Rebecca Harris-Warrick, 'Magnificence in Motion: Stage Musicians in Lully's Ballets and Operas', in *Cambridge Opera Journal* 6 (1994), 189-203, and Françoise Carter, 'Number Symbolism and Renaissance Choreography', in *Dance Research: The Journal of the Society for Dance Research* 10 (1992), 21-39 were two important resources in designing a choreography consistent with contemporary practices.

[90] Ms. 357.c, 75-87; Dyer, 979-1138.

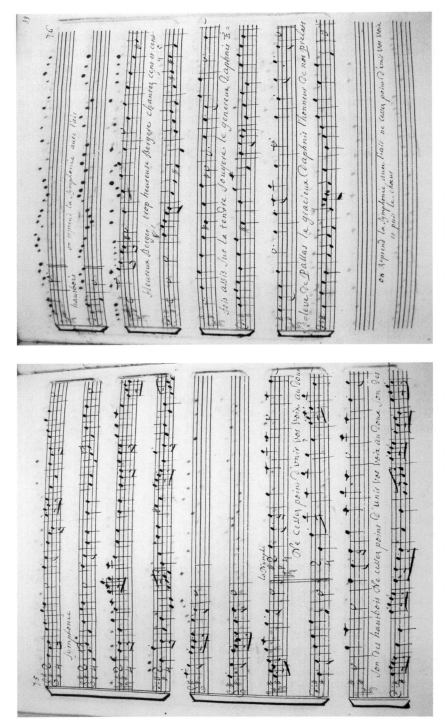

Figure 5. The point of insertion for the newly constructed pageant, University of Liège, Ms. 357-c, 81-82

The pageant is inserted in the chorus after the final cadence of 'Ne cessons point d'unis nos voix' and before 'Heureux Berger' (Figure 5).[91] This decision allows the 'Le généreux Daphnis' chorus to fulfil its original function as the concluding number of the pastorale, and, as the dramatic action of the plot is complete by this point in the piece, the insertion of the pageant before the second half of the chorus does not impede the unfolding of the dramatic narrative. The bi-partite structure of the final chorus renders it ideal for this purpose, as both sections of music are self-contained and composed in contrasting musical styles. 'Ne cessons,' for example, is an instrumental gavotte punctuated by periods of solo and choral singing, while the second section is a homophonic chorus in the meter and style of a pavane enlivened by fanfare-like arpeggios in the instrument parts.[92] When placed between these two significant sections of music, 112 and 47 measures, respectively, it was found in performance that the pageant was sufficiently near to the end to make the timing of Daphnis' arrival onstage appear genuine. The brevity of the pageant was also mitigated by following the symbolic pantomime with a choral anthem in praise of Daphnis.

The pageant of Daphnis' arrival is a sequence of four events, actions that express all of the metaphors attached to his character and to the pastorale. In the first event, Minerva and Apollo crown Daphnis with a wreath of laurels to represent the new bishop's prominence among his peers in eloquence and learning, as Damon stated in part one:

> Dés ses plus tendres ans l'on vit briller Daphnis
> Dans la lîce des beaux esprits;
> Et quand de ses lauriers la Déesse savante
> Couronnoit ses plus favoris,
> Daphnis sur la troupe éloquente
> En remportoit le prix.[93]

> From his tender years, we saw Daphnis shine
> In the ranks of beautiful spirits;
> And when with her beautiful laurels the learned Goddess
> Crowned her most favoured ones,
> Daphnis, amidst all of the eloquent ones,
> Won the prize.

This passage could be interpreted to apply to the count of Namur in the same manner; the count is raised in excellence above his peers. Also, in having the gods crown Daphnis, the divine origin of the count's right to rule Namur is illustrated. Daphnis' laurel wreath also symbolizes Christ's crown of thorns and Christ's assumption of the sins of humanity. By accepting the wreath from the gods, Daphnis/Christ signifies his acceptance of his death by crucifixion in order bring salvation.[94] For Daphnis as the chief of the shepherds, the coronation is merely a re-enactment of Minerva's past esteem for him.

---

[91] The first downbeat of the second section is required to complete the final cadence of 'We shall never cease.' The downbeat is repeated when the second section of the chorus begins.
[92] The opening entrée of Ms. 357.c is also a pavane.
[93] Ms. 357.c, 25; Dyer, 277-95.
[94] Matthew 36:39, Mark 14:36, Luke 22:42.

Once crowned, Daphnis then raises the kneeling Nymph, and in his turn crowns her with a wreath of a triple ring of pure white flowers.[95] In choosing to crown the Nymph among the other characters on the stage, Daphnis demonstrates that the Nymph is his chosen partner, his other half, in the pastorale.[96] In the metaphor of the bishop, Daphnis' action symbolizes his dedication to the Roman Catholic Church; the crowned Nymph now represents the Church crowned with the three-tiered papal tiara. The Nymph and her white wreath symbolize the contessa's purity and dedication to the Church, a metaphor that is made more apparent in action of the next event of the pageant. In the spiritual allegory, Daphnis' raising of the Nymph/Soul portrays Christ's forgiveness of sins as well as the promise of resurrection. Her coronation by Daphnis not only represents the establishment of Christ's church (the triple crown) but also symbolizes the place of the Soul in the kingdom of heaven.

In the third event, the coronation of the count and contessa by Daphnis and the Nymph, the metaphors attached to the characters of Daphnis and the Nymph are transferred to the count and contessa (and the bishop *in absentia*), completing the symbolic journey of the pastorale drama. Daphnis and the Nymph, accompanied by the entire ensemble, approach the box of the count and contessa. After the party kneels in homage, Daphnis offers his laurel wreath to the count, thus establishing, as suggested throughout the drama, that the character of Daphnis is a metaphor for the count and bishop. This offering also establishes a link among the count, bishop, and Christ, a link supported by evidence from the libretto. At the same time, the Nymph offers her crown of flowers to the contessa, thus transferring to her a symbol of purity and dedication to the Roman Catholic church. Her flowers, as a promise of future fruit, also represent the wish that the count and contessa will 'soon see the birth of a noble offspring' ('Te voir naitre bientôt un noble rejetton')[97] expressed in the final chorus of part one.

In return for his wreath and Daphnis' homage, the count gifts Daphnis with a flute, the traditional instrument of shepherds that the rest of the ensemble onstage possess except Daphnis, thus completing Daphnis' pastoral character. Within the spiritual allegory, the gift of the flute represents the gift of salvation from God for Christ to share with all humanity. Such a gift from the bishop to Daphnis as a representation of the count symbolizes the bishop's support of the count; similarly, a gift from the count to Daphnis as a representation of the bishop signifies the count's fealty to the Roman Catholic Church and a sign of support for the bishop. The presentation of the flute is followed by a second acknowledgement of the count and contessa by the assembled cast. An ensemble bow concludes the pageant.

Reconciling the *Ratio Studiorum* and *Daphnis*

The rules regulating Jesuit school theatres were published in 1599 in the *Ratio atque Institutio Studiorum Societatis Iesu*, commonly abbreviated *Ratio Studiorum*. The *Ratio*

---

[95] While Daphnis approaches the Nymph, Minerva and Apollo move to take up positions at either side of the back of the performing area.
[96] All of the other characters were arranged in pairs for the dances within the pastorale, but the Nymph danced alone until the arrival of Daphnis.
[97] Ms. 357.c, 37-38; Dyer, 507-151.

Studiorum was the official book of rules and regulations for Jesuit colleges and seminaries.[98] The thirteenth rule in the Rules for the Rector section concerns collegiate dramatic productions:

> Tragoediarum et comoediarum, quas non nisi latinus ac rarissimas esse oportet, argumentum sacrum sit ac pium; neque quicquam actibus interponatur, quod non latinum sit et decorum, nec persona ulla muliebris vel habitus introducator.[99]

> The subject matter of the tragedies and comedies, which ought to be only in Latin and extremely rare, should be holy and devotional. And nothing that is not in Latin and proper should be inserted into the action, nor should any female character or clothing be introduced.

Although it is possible to argue that the play is 'holy and devotional' through the presence of a spiritual allegory within the drama, *Daphnis, Pastorale* breaks the remaining three strictures of the rule. The language of the libretto, rather than the Latin required by the *Ratio*, is a compound of both early and eighteenth-century French with local dialectic variants.[100] Regarding the prohibition of female characters, not only does the cast include multiple female characters (presumably in female costume), but it also features a Nymph as the central character.[101] The rule 'nothing that is not in Latin and proper should be inserted into the action' was also probably broken in the 1728 performance and certainly in the 1741 performance by the insertion of a ballet at the conclusion of the drama.

On the surface, therefore, *Daphnis* appears to contravene the official rules. However, in 1600, the year after the formal publication of the *Ratio Studiorum*, Jesuit colleges in francophone regions requested and received a special dispensation from Claudius Aquaviva, the General of the Society, similar to one granted earlier to Jesuit colleges in the German Jesuit Provinces.[102] Rome permitted the Gallo-Belgian and German Jesuit Province colleges to include female characters as long as the practice was limited and the character were of solemn and modest bearing.[103] Therefore, in francophone Jesuit school theatre productions such as *Daphnis*, the presence of female characters was not an infraction of the *Ratio Studiorum*, but rather a practice specially permitted by the Society of Jesus.

---

[98] *Ratio atque Institutio Studiorum Societatis Iesu* (Rome: Tarquinius Longus, 1599).
[99] Claude Pavur, S. J. (trans. and ed.), *The Ratio Studiorum: The Official Plan for Jesuit Education* (St. Louis, 2005), 35.
[100] Elizabeth Dyer, 'A Unique Eighteenth-Century Walloonian Music-Drama Re-discovered', paper presented at *The Harvard Dialogues/The Lyrica Society for Word-Music Relations and American Comparative Literature Association Annual Conference*, Harvard University, 26 March 2009. In order to better communicate with the audience, the original linguistic mixture in the libretto was translated into and performed in modern French for the 2008 production. For similar reasons, the libretto excerpts presented in this essay are excerpted from the modern French version of the libretto created by the author for the 2008 production.
[101] James R. Farr, 'The Pure and Disciplined Body: Hierarchy, Morality, and Symbolism in France during the Catholic Reformation', in *Journal of Interdisciplinary History* 21 (1991), 391-414. In the 2008 production, the hair of the female characters was closely plaited and pinned to reflect the contemporary association of women's loose hair with political and social disorder.
[102] Henri Fouqueray, S. J., *Histoire de la Compagnie de Jésus en France des origines à la suppression (1528-1762)* (Paris, 1913), vol. 2, 717. Also cited in McCabe, *An Introduction to the Jesuit Theatre*, 180.
[103] George Michael Pachtler, S. J., *Ratio studiorum et Institutiones scholasticae Societatis Jesu per Germaniam olim vigents*, in Monumenta Germaniae Paedagogica, ed. Karl Kehrbach (1886; repr. Osnabrück, 1986), vol. 2, 488: '…dummodo id rarius et parcius fiat, gravesque et modestae sint personae quae producentur.' See also the chapter on female roles in Jesuit theatre in McCabe, *An Introduction to the Jesuit Theatre*, 178-97.

The Society's caution concerning the type of female character appears to have been honoured by all colleges, but the Society's limitation on the use of female characters seems to have been generally ignored. By the end of the seventeenth century, Jesuit colleges were performing plays with leading female characters more and more frequently. For example, a large number of tragedies about the martyrdom of Mary Stuart were performed from the end of the seventeenth century until well into the eighteenth century by Jesuit colleges in the Gallo-Belgian Jesuit Province; there is even a late sixteenth-century example of a Mary Stuart tragedy from the Braidense Jesuit college in Milan.[104] This common use of female characters in Jesuit theatre is in keeping with Judith Rock's findings in the Parisian Jesuit college. Rock reports that after 1699 female characters were included in nearly all of the comedies and tragedies performed by the college of Louis-le-Grand. Similarly, female roles appear in the *intermedia* and ballets at the college's theatrical productions beginning in the 1650s, the same period in which the use of the vernacular for these inserted forms became commonplace.[105] The 1728 *Daphnis*, with its leading female roles and its use of the vernacular, is thus consistent with its historical precedents, while the characters of the Nymph and the Déesse, as 'grave' and 'modest' roles, are in compliance with the spirit of the special license granted to Jesuit colleges in French-speaking areas.

Conclusion

The 2008 reconstructed production utilised the entire musical ensemble specified in the Ms. 357.c manuscript. Additional cast members for the 2008 production were created based upon the libretto of Ms.357.c and the 1741 Namur programme. The incorporation into the 2008 production of mute characters referenced in the libretto and the addition of a chorus of shepherds based upon the 1741 programme resulted in an ensemble comparable in size to the casts of the Namur, Bruges, and Ypres productions (Table 4).

The characters in the 1728 and 1741 productions, such as the 'Le Génie de la Paix' ('Spirit of Peace') in the 1741 *Daphnis*, illustrate the basic allegorical nature of the pastoral dramatic genre. If a ballet was part of the 19 May 1728, performance of Ms. 357.c, the details are not known. The cast of the ballet concluding the 1741 production has survived, however, and from this information it is possible to determine the function and purpose of the ballet in the 1741 Namur pastorale. In the 2008 production, a pageant, whose design was informed by a study of the libretto and an understanding of the history of ballet, pageant, and tableau in Gallo-Belgian Jesuit Province school theatre, substituted for the traditional ballet. Although only a substitute form, the newly created pageant fulfilled the same allegorical and dramatic purpose in the modern performance as did the ballet in the 1741 performance.

---

[104] *Maria Stuarta, Tragoedia* (New York, The Morgan Library and Museum, Ms. MA 0022, 1589). Three examples of late seventeenth-century/early eighteenth-century Mary Stuart plays: *Maria Stuarta*, Aalst, 1694 (Sommervogel, vol. 1, 200, No. 9); *Maria Stuarta Koninginne van Schotland*, Alost, 1699 (Sommervogel, vol. 1, 201, No. 15); and *Maria Stuarta Scotiae Regina, Tragoedia*, Eichstadt, 1709 (Eichstadt: Francisco Strauss, 1709). For a recent study of cross-dressing and cross-casting in the theatre productions of the college of Louis-le-Grand/Collége de Clermont, see Julia Prest, *Theatre under Louis XIV: Cross-Casting and the Performance of Gender in Drama, Ballet, and Opera* (New York, 2006), 43-55.

[105] Rock, *Terpsichore at Louis-le-Grand*, 12.

Table 4. Casts in *Daphnis* productions

1728 (Namur)	1741 (Namur)	2008 (York)
La Nymphe de la Sambre	Genie (2)	La Nymphe de la Sambre
La Déesse des Flores	Apollon	La Déesse des La Flores
Les Echos	L'Amour	Echos
	Le Compliment	Minerve/Pallas Athena
Shepherds	Le Genie de la Paix	Apollon
Damon		Pan
Aminth	*Shepherds*	Comte de Namur
Choeur	Daphnis	Comtesse de Namur
	Coridon	
Instruments	Damon	*Shepherds*
Instrument I	Yolas	Daphnis
Instrument II	Lycidas	Damon
Alto instrument	Menalque	Aminth
Basso continuo	Meris	Coridon
	Thyrsis	Yolas
Ballet	Melabée	Lycidas
Unknown		Menalque
	Instruments	Meris
	Unknown	Thyrsis
	Ballet	*Instruments*
	La Renommée	Violin I
	L'Amour	Violin II
	Le Zele	Viola
	Le Merite	Bass Viol
	La Religion	Chamber organ
	La Force	Flute I (Bird I)
	La Temperance	Flute II (Bird II)
	La Prudence	
	La Paix	*Ballet*
	Apollo	Replaced by pageant
	Les Bergers	

This essay has examined in detail a selection of the processes involved in the 2008 reconstruction of the 1728 Jesuit pastorale, *Daphnis*. This modern production was not designed with the purpose of recreating a precise copy of the original 1728 performance, but rather to present a historically informed modern re-staging. This included assembling the musical ensemble, formulating an interpretation of the metaphors and symbols within the libretto, and creating a dramatic insertion resembling contemporary practices as closely as circumstances allowed. Thus the 2008 performance incorporated data from the manuscript, programmes of *Daphnis* plays from Gallo-Belgian Jesuit Province colleges, and the research of Jesuit theatre scholars in order to generate innovative yet historically plausible solutions to the issues inherent in re-enacting a Jesuit college drama on the modern stage.

Abstract

This essay examines the practical processes involved in the 2008 recreation of *Daphnis, Pastorale*, a drama first performed by the students of the Jesuit College of Namur in 1728. The recreation necessitated new approaches to stage design and action, as well as contemporary solutionsor the casting and linguistic content. *Daphnis, Pastorale* is a form of Jesuit college music-drama characteristic of the francophone regions of Europe, and is the only known surviving example of its kind from Belgium. This work is all the more rare in that it uses French sprinkled with loan-words, rather than the neo-Latin typical of Jesuit drama. The process of constructing a historically informed performance of this unique member of the Jesuit music-drama repertoire reveals a reciprocal three-way relationship among knowledge gained through primary research, academic study, and informed experimentation.

Contributors to this Issue

∎

Alison Altstatt is Assistant Professor of musicology at the University of Northern Iowa. Her publications on the medieval sequence have appeared in *The Sequences of Nidaros: a Nordic Repertory and its European Context* (2006) and in *Cantus Planus: Papers Read at the 13th Meeting of the IMS Study Group, Niederaltaich, Germany, 2006* (2009). She is currently writing a monograph on the music and liturgy of Kloster Preetz and preparing an edition of Anne von Buchwald's *Initien Bok*.

Elizabeth Dyer is the head of the music department and director of choral activities at Our Lady of the Lake University in San Antonio, Texas. She completed her Ph.D. in musicology with John Potter at the University of York, U.K., where her dissertation investigated relationships among Benedictine, Augustinian, and Jesuit school dramas and their influence upon the development of the seventeenth-century oratorio in Italy. Among her recent awards are a Fulbright Scholarship to investigate Jesuit school theatre in Ireland 1551-1773, the Arthur Ramsden Award for Theatre Research for the live production of *Daphnis Pastorale*, an early eighteenth-century Jesuit college music-drama, the Sarofim Prize for Music Composition, and an ORSAS award for doctoral research in music.

Kate Helsen currently teaches music history at the University of Western Ontario, and is a researcher with the CANTUS Database. She is also an editor for the second volume of the *Inventories of Antiphoners in Flemish Collections* research project (Alamire Foundation), a contributor to the *Portuguese Early Music Database*, and is currently collaborating on a two-volume publication concerning the Office of Thomas Becket.

Lori Kruckenberg is Associate Professor of music at the University of Oregon, where she teaches courses in medieval and Renaissance music. Her scholarship focuses on Latin monophonic song in the Middle Ages—sequences, tropes, *nova cantica*—as well as the traditions of the cantrix in German-speaking lands, c. 950-1400. She has twice held fellowships from the Fulbright Commission and received the Noah Greenberg Award in 2012.

Pieter Mannaerts is lecturer in the history and theory of early music at the Fontys Conservatory in Tilburg. His research interests include chant in the Low Countries, *historiae*, the nineteenth-century rediscovery of chant, and music in the early decades of the twentieth century.

Bernhold Schmid studied musicology at the University of Munich, submitting his dissertation there in 1985 on the Gloria trope *Spiritus et alme* (published in 1988). Since 1985 he has been a researcher affiliated with the Music-Historical Commission of the Bavarian Academy of Sciences. Since 1996 he has worked on the edition of the collected works of Orlando di Lasso. He has published on music of the middle ages, the Renaissance, and the early twentieth century.